Critical Reading Across the Curriculum

Critical Reading Across the Curriculum

Volume 1: Humanities

Edited by Robert DiYanni and Anton Borst

Registered Offices
John Wiley & Sons, Inc., 111 River Street, Hoboken, NJ 07030, USA

Editorial Office
350 Main Street, Malden, MA 02148-5020, USA

For details of our global editorial offices, customer services, and more information about Wiley products visit us at www.wiley.com.

Wiley also publishes its books in a variety of electronic formats and by print-on-demand. Some content that appears in standard print versions of this book may not be available in other formats.

Library of Congress Cataloging-in-Publication Data is available for this book.

ISBN 9781119154860 (hardback)
ISBN 9781119154877 (paperback)

Cover image: dzima1/Gettyimages

Set in 10.5/12.5pt WarnockPro by Aptara Inc., New Delhi, India
Printed and bound in Malaysia by Vivar Printing Sdn Bhd

10 9 8 7 6 5 4 3 2 1

Contents

Notes on Contributors

Adrian Barlow is a senior member of Wolfson College, Cambridge, and president of the English Association. Formerly director of public programmes at the University of Cambridge Institute of Continuing Education, he has taught, lectured, and written widely on teaching literature and the relationship between pedagogy and assessment. He has edited the Cambridge Contexts in Literature series, and his publications include *World and Time: Teaching Literature in Context* and *Extramural: Literature and Lifelong Learning*.

Anton Borst is an instructional consultant at New York University's Center for the Advancement of Teaching. As a specialist in writing across the curriculum and digital pedagogy, he previously worked in faculty development at Hunter College and Macaulay Honors College. He received a PhD in English from the Graduate Center of the City University of New York, and has taught literature and writing at Hunter College, Baruch College, and Pace University.

Pamela Burger earned a PhD in English at the Graduate Center of the City University of New York, and she received an MFA in creative writing from New York University. She has taught literature and writing at Hunter College, Queens College, and Wesleyan University.

William V. Costanzo is a State University of New York distinguished teaching professor of English and film. He has taught courses in writing, literature, and film studies at Westchester Community College since 1970. Dr. Costanzo is active in the Society for Cinema and Media Studies and has published six books on writing and film, including *Double Exposure: Composing Through Writing and Film*, *Great Films and How to Teach Them*, and, most recently, *World Cinema Through Global Genres* (Wiley-Blackwell).

Robert DiYanni is a professor of humanities at New York University and an instructional consultant in the NYU Center for the Advancement of Teaching. He has written extensively on the teaching of literature and writing, interdisciplinary humanities, and critical and creative thinking. Among his books are *Connections, Literature, Modern American Poets, Arts and Culture, The Pearson Guide to Critical and Creative Thinking*, and, most recently, *Critical and Creative Thinking: A Brief Guide for Teachers* (Wiley-Blackwell).

Amy K. Hamlin holds a PhD in art history from New York University's Institute of Fine Arts. She has presented and published on the art of Paul Cézanne, Max Beckmann, William H. Johnson, Jasper Johns, and Kara Walker. An Associate Professor of Art History at St. Catherine University, she teaches across the art history curriculum and practices experimental pedagogies and socially engaged art history.

Michael Hogan is the author of twenty-two books, including a best-selling history, *The Irish Soldiers of Mexico*. His essays and articles have appeared in many anthologies and textbooks. For two decades he was head of the Humanities Department at the American School of Guadalajara and Professor of International Relations at the Autonomous University of Guadalajara. A member of the Organization of American Historians, he was awarded the gold medal of the Mexican Geographical Society.

Pat C. Hoy II has taught at the US Military Academy, Harvard, New York University, and Hendrix College. Author of numerous textbooks on composition, his essays and reviews have appeared in a spectrum of prestigious journals. Awards include the 2003 Cecil Woods, Jr. Prize for Nonfiction from the Fellowship of Southern Writers, the Spears Prize for best essay in *Sewanee Review* (2014), and two Golden Dozen Awards for distinguished teaching at NYU.

Thomas M. Kitts, PhD, is professor of English at St. John's University, NY. He is the author of *John Fogerty: An American Son, Ray Davies: Not Like Everybody Else, The Theatrical Life of George Henry Baker*, and many articles and reviews. With Gary Burns of Northern Illinois University, he edits *Popular Music and Society* and *Rock Music Studies*. He is the area chair of music for the Popular Culture Association/American Culture Association.

Thomas Petriano is professor and chair of religious studies at St. Joseph's College in Patchogue, NY. He received his doctorate in systematic theology from Fordham University in 1997. He teaches courses on belief and unbelief in the modern world, religions of Abraham, world religions, and liberation theology. He also participates in a global service-learning program that involves working with an indigenous community in Nicaragua.

Lawrence Scanlon is co-author of four books on teaching, literature, and rhetoric: *Teaching Nonfiction in *AP English*, *The Language of Composition*, *Literature and Composition*, and *Conversations in American Literature*. A high school teacher for more than thirty years, he was awarded the Dean's Award for Excellence in Education from the State University of New York. He teaches at Iona College and conducts workshops and institutes for teachers in the United States, Canada, Europe, Asia, and South America.

Louis Scheeder is founder and director of The Classical Studio and associate dean of faculty at the New York University Tisch School of the Arts. He has served as producer of the Folger Theatre Group, worked at the Royal Shakespeare Company and was associated with the Manitoba Theatre Centre. Co-author of *All The Words on Stage*, he has conducted acting workshops worldwide, and is a member of The Factory UK, an experimental theatre company dedicated to exploring spontaneity and argument in their myriad theatrical forms.

Matt Statler is clinical associate professor of management and organizations and director of business ethics and social impact programming at the NYU Stern School of Business. He has published on ethics, leadership, and strategy, and is co-editor of the *Encyclopedia of Disaster Relief*, the *Encyclopedia of Crisis Management*, and *Learning from the Global Financial Crisis*. He holds a PhD in philosophy from Vanderbilt University and was a Fulbright Scholar at the University of Heidelberg.

Preface

Critical reading is a term frequently invoked throughout academia; much less often is it explained. What are the steps and procedures that constitute this complex process? How can those steps and procedures be articulated to help teachers in the upper secondary and introductory college classroom explain them to, and practice them with, their students? Critical reading skills are not something we can assume our students – at any level – possess, and however effective we may be as critical readers ourselves, *teaching* the skills of critical reading is another matter entirely. Veteran teachers may rely on their experience and expertise in showing students how to read critically in their fields, but even the best teachers sometimes face challenges in translating their internalized practices into explicit strategies for their students.

To address this problem, we invited scholar-teachers from across the humanities to describe what they do as critical readers themselves. We asked them to demonstrate and apply the strategies and frameworks they typically use, and to explain what they do to help their students develop critical reading skills. *Critical Reading Across the Curriculum* is the result of their responses to that invitation.

The book's thirteen essays weave together various thematic threads, perhaps the most important of which is the connection between critical reading and writing. A number of contributors suggest that to teach critical reading effectively students need to write regularly in response to their reading. This writing can take the form of short reflections, annotations and marginalia, and analyses and arguments that range in length from a few sentences to full-term research papers.

In the title of his essay, "Reciprocal Acts: Reading and Writing," Pat Hoy identifies the close and necessary relationship between reading and writing, deftly mingling them himself while laying out in careful detail how to teach these intertwined processes. Like Pat Hoy, other contributors offer assignments linking reading and writing, such as Thomas Kitts,

Anton Borst, and Amy Hamlin, whose essays concern reading pop songs, digital reading practices, and creating and editing art history content on Wikipedia, respectively.

A second common theme is connecting critical reading skills with the world outside the classroom. In his essay on reading religious texts, Thomas Petriano emphasizes the transformative value of critical reading, whatever his students' status as religious believers. Lawrence Scanlon shows how rhetoric lies at the heart of his students' everyday interactions in school, at home, and online. And in her essay on using gender studies as a model for critical reading, Pamela Burger challenges students to read gender construction through increasingly complex texts, including the photographs of contemporary feminist artists Melanie Pullen and Cindy Sherman.

A third shared theme among our contributors is the importance of context in critical reading, especially of making contextual connections. Robert DiYanni raises issues of context in his consideration of E. B. White's *New Yorker* piece about the 1969 moon landing, and additionally in a set of exercises on Lincoln's Gettysburg Address. In his essay on teaching history, Michael Hogan argues for the centrality of understanding historical documents in terms of the social and political conditions that produced them. Adrian Barlow demonstrates the importance of invoking multiple contexts – literary, historical, social, cultural, and political – for analyzing and interpreting literature. And Anton Borst reflects on how to help students navigate – and critically engage – the digital context through which much of their reading is now mediated.

Pervading the book's essays is an emphasis on strategies for helping students attend and focus, techniques essential for getting students to re-read and reflect, to re-think and re-consider. Focusing their attention in these ways enables students to analyze and interpret texts – it allows them to begin thinking critically about what they read. Our authors explain how to make valid inferences from texts based on careful noticing of words and phrases, of details and images, of claims and supporting evidence. They provide guidance in comparing and contrasting texts in order to produce effective critical analysis.

In attending to each of these aspects of critical reading, contributors consistently emphasize the importance of questions in critical reading and critical reasoning. In his piece on reading film, William Costanzo links analytical questions to various theoretical approaches to film, including formal, cultural, and genre analysis. In his approach to the critical reading of philosophical texts, Matt Statler demonstrates Socratic questioning through a critical reading of Plato's *Meno*. Adrian Barlow develops a series of increasingly complex interpretive questions based on close reading, contextual reading, and comparative analysis of related texts. And in his essay on digital reading, Anton Borst questions the idea of the digital native in order to critically engage technology's impact on student reading practices.

Reading as dialogue, debate, and engaged conversation permeates the work gathered here. In his essay on theater, Louis Scheeder argues for the importance of argument in drama, highlighting the ways dialogue and debate dramatize a play's conflicts and concepts, and how William Shakespeare's iambic pentameter verse line provides essential keys to understanding the "thinking" of his characters. Adrian Barlow demonstrates how critical conversations between texts can produce effective readings of literature, a method also applied to the reading of images in the essays of Pat Hoy, Amy Hamlin, Pamela Burger, and William Costanzo. Thomas Petriano describes the reading of religious texts as a fundamentally dialogic act. And Robert DiYanni explains how critical reading requires both listening to and talking back to texts, engaging with them through reflection and dialogue.

Related to our contributors' emphasis on critical reading as conversation with texts and authors is a repeated emphasis on collaboration. Michael Hogan's essay on teaching history and Pat Hoy's on the reciprocity of reading and writing illustrate powerfully the ways students can work together to develop a critical understanding of texts. Other contributors also indicate ways for students to collaborate productively. Lawrence Scanlon's exercises – requiring students to do rhetorical analysis of paired texts of verse, prose, and speech – lend themselves well to collaborative engagement, as do the detailed exercises in William Costanzo's essay on the critical reading of films, Pamela Burger's essay on reading gender, and Amy Hamlin's piece on reading art history.

An overarching concern expressed throughout these essays is with the meaning of the term "critical reading." Our contributors uncover layers of implication in the term and demonstrate stunning variations in its application. All of them, however, understand the necessity for regular and sustained practice in developing critical reading skills. And so the essays in this book offer an abundance of inventive exercises and imaginative activities through which students may practice the various skills, techniques, and strategies of critical reading. These exercises, moreover, can be adapted and applied to a wide range of disciplines across the curriculum.

Teachers ourselves, our pedagogy has been greatly enriched through exploring the pedagogical perspectives of colleagues in humanities disciplines other than our own. The essays of the dedicated practitioners collected here reveal a careful attention to the craft of teaching critical reading. We hope you too may benefit from their experience, their insights, and their pedagogical expertise.

Robert DiYanni
Anton Borst

Acknowledgments

We want to thank our contributors for their willingness to share their experience and passion for teaching, and for all the hard work they devoted to the fine essays collected here. We are grateful to our sponsoring editor Jayne Fargnoli, who gave us generous encouragement and supported the project from the start. We also thank Liz Wingett, who managed the production of the book with grace and professionalism.

Others at Wiley who had a hand in bringing this book to press were Mary Hall, Katie DiFolco, Madeline Koufogazos, Haze Humbert, and Katherine Wong. We would also like to thank the freelancers who contributed their expertise – project manager and copy-editor Janet Moth, and indexer Sue Dugen.

Part I

Frameworks and Approaches

1

Reading Responsively, Reading Responsibly

An Approach to Critical Reading

Robert DiYanni

Critical reading, like critical thinking, is a term much bandied about by educators from elementary education through university study. Like critical thinking, critical reading means different things to different people. What critical reading is and why it matters are genuine educational concerns because reading is a foundational skill for successful learning at every level of schooling; to succeed academically students need to become active, engaged, critical readers. The ability to read critically – to analyze a text, understand its logic, evaluate its evidence, interpret it creatively, and ask searching questions of it – is essential for higher-order thinking. Skill in critical reading builds students' confidence, enriches their understanding of the world, and enables their successful educational progress. Critical reading informs academic writing, particularly analysis and argument, inquiry and exploration – modes of writing required across academic disciplines.

In this essay I explain what critical reading involves, demonstrate applied critical reading in practice, and provide an approach to teaching students how to become critical readers. Framing this work, contextualizing and amplifying it, are discussions of responsible, responsive, and reflective reading.

We begin, though, by considering what critical reading is and is not, identifying some common student misconceptions.

Critical Reading Across the Curriculum, Volume 1: Humanities, First Edition.
Edited by Robert DiYanni and Anton Borst.
© 2017 John Wiley & Sons, Inc. Published 2017 by John Wiley & Sons, Inc.

Being Critical

Students sometimes think their goal in reading is to agree or disagree with a text – to argue and take a stand vis-à-vis its author's idea or claim. Their understanding of "critical" is limited to "critique" and "criticism," to judging a text, to showing what's wrong with it, identifying its limitations and biases. That more complex work, important as it is, however, comes later, after the initial effort to comprehend what a text says. The first goal of critical reading is to understand. Students achieve understanding through learning to analyze texts carefully and thoroughly. They demonstrate understanding of texts by summarizing and paraphrasing them accurately in writing. These representations of texts need to be done respectfully and responsibly before students engage in any kind of critical challenge to them.

Critical reading focuses not only on what a text says but also on how it says what it does. In teaching our students to read critically, we first teach them to analyze a text's language and selection of detail, its genre, imagery, and form. We teach them to see how sentences and paragraphs are connected grammatically and conceptually, how writers create meaning through their selection of diction and detail, through their choices with respect to organization and development of idea. This fundamental work, however, though necessary, is not sufficient. We must teach our students something more as well.

The larger goals of critical reading include recognizing a writer's purpose, understanding his or her idea, identifying tone, evaluating evidence and reasoning, and recognizing a writer's perspective, position, and bias. Our teaching strategies should focus on helping students see what a writer says through how it is said. And those strategies should also include how well a writer's evidence supports his or her claims. These considerations are fundamental for reading critically in all disciplines.

To do this analytical work well, however, students need to overcome initial resistance to a text, the impulse to contradict, counter, or otherwise challenge it. To develop into effective and productive critical readers, students need at first to remain open to what a text offers. The performance artist/actor Matthew Goulish provides one approach to this kind of textual receptiveness. In his essay "Criticism" from *39 Microlectures* (2000), Goulish suggests that when we encounter any work of art, including imaginative works of all kinds (and by extension any verbal text), we should look for "moments of exhilaration." These special moments of textual encounter may be provoked by something exciting, engaging, or striking in a text, something that stirs our feelings, spurs our thinking, sparks our imagination. Here is how Goulish puts it:

> We may then look to each work of art not for its faults and short-comings, but for its moments of exhilaration, in an effort to bring our own imperfections into sympathetic vibration with these moments, and thus effect a creative change in ourselves. These moments will, of course, be somewhat subjective, so that if we don't find one immediately, we will out of respect look again ... In this way we will treat the work of art, in the words of South African composer Kevin Volans, not as an object in this world but as a window into another world. If we can articulate one window's particular exhilaration, we may open a way to inspire a change in ourselves, so that we may value and work from these recognitions. (p. 45)

This way of engaging with a text requires avoiding the tendency to find something wrong with it, something to criticize. Instead, we seek something that's right with the work, something exhilarating, anything at all that might prove useful – a vivid detail we admire, a discernible pattern that aids our understanding, an assertion that provokes our thinking, a question we begin answering for ourselves. Through these "moments of exhilaration" we establish a personal relationship with the text in ways that can lead to "a creative change in ourselves." The kinds of "recognitions" that arise from openness to a text or work are recognitions as much about ourselves as they are about what we read.

The concept of "moments of exhilaration" can stimulate students' engagement with a text, animating their thinking about it, opening for them metaphorical "windows into other worlds." Students' moments of exhilaration can provide ways into a text for them, a start toward finding something of value in it, something to extend their thinking, deepen their feeling, enrich their experience. By inviting students to identify, explain, and explore their exhilarating moments reading texts, we highlight their responsibility and validate their textual engagements.

We can and should demonstrate for our students the experience Goulish describes by sharing with them our own exhilarating moments of reading. What excites us about a text we have assigned? What have we ourselves found exhilarating about it? Why did we choose to read it in the first place? What possibilities for creative change might it offer our students when they read it in the open and attentive way Goulish suggests?

Responsible Reading, Responsive Reading

Goulish's advocacy of receptiveness to a work's promising possibilities constitutes one aspect of what we might call "responsible reading," an attitude toward texts and works that goes beyond responding to them subjectively, one that moves, instead, toward being accountable to them, toward a standpoint that Robert Scholes, in *Protocols of Reading* (1990), describes as "an ethic of reading" (p. 90). Part of this reading ethic involves the responsibility to give a text and its author their due. Our students need to hear out authors and texts, letting them have their say, whether they agree with an author's views or not, whether a text's ideas are accessible or difficult, regardless of who wrote a text, when it was written, or why. We need, in short, to encourage students to respect the integrity of texts, to read them responsibly. Henry David Thoreau, perhaps, has said it best: "Books must be read as deliberately and reservedly as they were written" (*Walden*, 1854/1983, p. 403).

This is a foundational principle of critical reading.

In reading responsibly we assume that a text possesses meaning. We give it, from this perspective, the benefit of the doubt. Our goal as ethical readers is to understand what a text means and to accurately represent that meaning in verbal or written form. In reading responsibly we try faithfully to follow an author's line of reasoning and to understand his or her perspective even when – especially when – the author's ideas, concepts, values, and perspectives differ from our own.

Once students have learned to read responsibly by attending carefully to texts, they can begin to assume authority over their reading, exercising power by talking back to the texts they read. They can balance giving texts a fair hearing with offering a judgment and critique earned through thoughtful, reflective analytical reading. In first listening and then responding to texts, students make them their own.

To produce something both respectful of the text and responsive to it that is distinctively the reader's own, George Steiner advocates writing in response to the texts we read. In "The Uncommon Reader" (1996), he suggests that reading responsibly requires that we be "answerable to the text" (p. 6). Our answerability includes both our response to the text and our responsibility for it; it requires an "answerable reciprocity" (p. 6) such that our critical engagement with a text results in a form of commerce with it, a textual dialogue, which can be best established through annotation and marginalia. Steiner suggests that in writing annotations, readers become servants of the text. Through annotation we attempt to elucidate the text for ourselves, to understand it, comprehend it. Marginalia, on the other hand, allow us to talk back to the text, replying to it rather than simply representing it. When readers annotate they are "servants of the text," and when they write marginalia, they are the text's "rivals" (p. 6).

In writing marginalia, we augment the author's text, perhaps disputing aspects of it, perhaps extending its significance through amplification, relating it to other texts we have read and other experiences we have had, finding new applications of the text as we consider its implications. The process is dynamic, collaborative, re-creative, and results in an inter-textual web of meanings – those provided by the authors we read and those we make ourselves in the process of reading them critically.

In having students write increasingly extensive marginal comments about a text, we can show them how to begin constructing texts of their own that both respect and rival those they read. We can demonstrate how marking texts in these ways can serve as points of departure for their own thinking. Teaching them to annotate effectively and to write thoughtful marginalia aids their development as critical readers and thinkers. These aspects of critical reading prove essential for our students' learning, whatever subject we teach. Moreover, through producing annotations and marginalia students become acculturated into the community of critical readers, such that reading critically becomes for them purposeful, meaningful, and habitual.

In helping students to become both responsive and responsible readers who balance openness to a text with resistance to it, we prepare them for the rewards of academic study. In getting them to listen to texts carefully before talking back to them, we encourage their development of empathy and discernment. And in having them write annotations and marginalia as preparation for more fully developed academic essays and papers, we allow them to experience for themselves the productive relationships among critical reading, writing, and thinking. These relationships are "critical" in a number of ways. Reading critically, asking questions of texts, stimulates reflection; writing about texts prompts careful attention to reading them; thinking about texts via annotations and marginalia prompts deeper reading, thoughtful reflection, and purposeful writing.

These critical reading practices are foundational for critical thinking.

A Framework for Critical Reading

One way to help students become responsible critical readers is to teach them to apply the following critical reading framework:

- *Making observations* about a text.
- *Establishing connections* among observations.

- *Making inferences* based on observations and connections.
- *Drawing conclusions* from the inferences.
- *Considering values* the text embodies and possibly endorses.

Making Observations

All interpretation begins with observation. We can't say about a text more than we can see in it. This is true whether we are observing a poem or a person, a movie or a monument, an artifact or an architectural structure, a laboratory experiment, a mathematical proof, a musical performance, a museum exhibition, a theatrical production, a social or political event, anything at all to which we may devote our attention. We learn to look at, and we learn to look for specific details, aspects, elements – of novels and of buildings, for example, of films and fashion photographs, of advertisements and popular songs, of all manner of "texts." In observing a painting, for example, we learn to notice how the artist creates line, uses volume, blends and balances color, creates perspective, employs smooth or thick brush-strokes, arranges the overall composition, to cite a few elements. In reading poems, we observe how the poem is structured, what kinds of sound patterns it uses, how sentences spill over or are contained within lines and stanzas, what its various voices convey in terms of tone and mood and implied meaning. Through learning to notice and attend – to look and listen with care – our students develop discernment; they come to understand *how* texts mean, not just *what* they mean.

There can be no discussion, no commentary, no productive interpretation of any work of any art without this bedrock noticing. The seeing and saying are reciprocal and mutually reinforcing. Careful, attentive, respectful noticing is fundamental to successful critical reading and writing. Our approach to critical reading is grounded in observation, with the active give and take between noticing and recording what we notice – writing it down. Regardless of the discipline we teach and our students' level of preparation, giving them repeated practice in making careful observations, both verbally and in writing, is an essential first step to critical understanding. They can't say more than they can see. Seeing more, they have more to think about, and ultimately more to say and write about what they think.

The scientist Samuel Scudder testifies to the power and importance of observation in recounting his study of fossils as a graduate student of Louis Agassiz, the Harvard professor of paleontology. Agassiz required him to look at plant and animal specimens for long periods of time without telling him what to look for. After staring at a single fossil specimen for a few hours, Scudder thought he was finished, only to be told by Professor Agassiz, "You have not looked very carefully … look again, look again!" (1874, pp. 369–370).

Only after spending days and then weeks examining that single specimen was Scudder allowed to compare it with others that Agassiz brought him. Along the way, Scudder learned how to look with scrupulous attention to detail, and how to prepare himself to see things he didn't expect to see. There are lessons here, for sure, not the least of which is that learning to look requires persistence and perseverance. Patient, deliberate noticing gives students a chance to see more, think about what they see, and thus have something more to say about it.

Establishing Connections

Observing textual details and features, whatever the nature of our "text," however, is not enough. To read critically, students must also make connections among the details they notice. We should encourage them to look for two kinds of connections: (1) connections among textual details; (2) connections between the writer's text and their own lives and world. (And, of course, for non-verbal texts, connections among their basic elements, whether visual or aural, experiential or conceptual.)

For example, in reading the following couplet, which concludes Shakespeare's Sonnet 29, we would invite students to look for connections between and among the details of its two lines:

> For thy sweet love remembered such wealth brings,
> That then I scorn to change my state with kings.

And so, they connect the "I" of the second line with the "thy" of the first. They relate the speaker's self to his beloved, whose "sweet love" he remembers. They relate the past tense of "remembered" to the present of "scorn to change." They contrast the literal wealth of kings with the metaphorical wealth of the speaker's love. From these related details, which also include rhyme and iambic pentameter, students can begin to think about meaning. We might ask them to explain the relationship between the couplet's two lines as a guide to its meaning, and to consider the couplet's meaning in relation to the meaning of the sonnet overall.

The connections we establish among observations move us toward meaning; those connections provide the basis for preliminary thinking about implications – about what those observed details might suggest or signify. Establishing and understanding relationships between and among details, and then between and among parts of a text, is crucial for critical reading.

Considering connections between text and world authenticates the work of critical reading, making it personally meaningful and valuable. And so with Shakespeare's couplet, students might think about how their experience of being unhappy or even depressed can change dramatically with the remembrance of someone they love, with the evocation of the beloved's image, such that nothing can compare with the value and power of that love.

Making Inferences

Establishing connections among textual details prepares us to make inferences about texts. One of the most important things we can do for our students is to help them make reliable inferences. We need to encourage them to make the inferential leap from the details they notice and connect. And we need to remind them that their inferences should be grounded in and supported by the details they observe and the connections they establish – textual evidence in short. When they make inferences, students should reasonably conclude that something is the case based on evidence – on what they have observed, and on connections between and among their observations. They need to learn that their inferences, however, may be correct or incorrect, or partly correct, and that inferences are hypotheses that need to be tested.

All disciplinary study requires making sound inferences. Scientists are expert inference makers. The scientific theories they develop out of the laws they devise are based upon their observations, which they test and confirm or disconfirm. They are inference-based extrapolations into the unknown from the observed data. In *The Meaning of It All* (1998), Richard Feynman calls them good guesses that have held up as true so far. Those good-guess inferences that determine the theory could be proven inadequate; they might be shown later to be slightly or even completely wrong. But they are the best inferences that can be made at the time – and thus they constitute current scientific knowledge. The guessing and estimating, the extrapolations from observation – the inference-making leading to laws and theories – all are essential for doing science.

Historical investigation follows an analogous process, mostly using primary and secondary source documents, rather than experiments, as evidence upon which to develop conclusions through reasoning inductively about particular instances and arriving at general principles. The particular details of history – historical facts, data, and other forms of information – provide the evidence for the development of inferences and theories of historical explanation.

Both scientific experimentation and historical analysis, however, may begin, and often actually do begin, with a theory or an idea – that is, with a generalization the investigator sets out to test by finding evidence that either supports or falsifies it. In this case, the process of thought moves from a general idea or concept to specific supporting evidence. Thus, thinking, including scientific and historical thinking, typically involves interplay between inductive and deductive reasoning, moving back and forth between them repeatedly in a looping, recursive process.

Our students need to understand this reciprocal process of investigative thinking. They need to know that they themselves do this in their everyday lives, and that this thinking process is formalized and deepened through academic study. We might suggest to them, in fact, that gaining confidence and competence in making inferences is essential for critical reading and critical thinking. Inference-making is a turning point in the critical reading/ thinking process, one that pivots from the basic skills of observing and connecting to the deeper skills of concluding and evaluating.

Drawing Conclusions and Considering Values

Thinking about the inferences we make in analyzing a text leads us toward developing a conclusion about it, an interpretation. We should help students understand, first, that an interpretation must be grounded in textual evidence – in the observations and connections they make about it and in the inferences they draw from what they have noticed and related. We also need to help them understand that the interpretive conclusions they make are tentative and provisional. Their interpretations can change. Like the theories scientists develop and the theoretical models historians employ, a textual interpretation is subject to revision. It can change based on the re-reading of a piece, on a reader's having thought more about it, on having discussed it with others, on relating it to other texts and life experiences. Textual interpretations are always subject to modification.

So, too, are evaluations of texts. Students are inclined to evaluate. They like to offer opinions, to judge. We can capitalize on those tendencies by helping them understand what evaluation can mean for critical reading.

Evaluation consists of two different kinds of assessment: (1) a judgment about a work's achievement, including the power and persuasiveness of its ideas; (2) a consideration of the values the work reflects and/or embodies. In the first sense of evaluation, in evaluating an idea, for example, we consider its accuracy as a description, its validity as an argument, its persuasiveness and interest as a proposal, its credibility as an imaginative construction. Evaluation depends on interpretation, on understanding. Our understanding of a work's idea influences our evaluative judgment of it. That's why understanding a text is so important and why we need to work our students hard to determine what a text means, signifies, suggests for them.

In another type of "evaluation," we assess the social, cultural, political, religious, and other values reflected in a work; in the process, we bring our own values into play. Considering those kinds of values in a work brings students to a better understanding of their own. We need to help students understand that their social values reflect their beliefs and customs, that their cultural values are shaped by their racial, ethnic, and family heritage, and that these values are also affected by gender and language. These aspects of evaluation can help students move beyond thinking of evaluation as making a judgment about a text's quality, whether it is "good" or "interesting" – or not – to think more deeply about how texts endorse or reflect a wide range of cultural and other values.

An additional point about values is that as our values change, the ways we evaluate particular texts, objects, processes, artworks, and the like can change as well. We may have found Hawthorne's or Melville's fiction, for example, or the paintings of Picasso, unappealing when we were high school or college students only to discover their allure later in life. The history of taste represents one large-scale example of evaluative shifts. The music of Johann Sebastian Bach was not appreciated nearly as fully in his lifetime as it is today. The work of many women writers, painters, and religious and philosophical thinkers was long neglected. We need to help students understand that evaluation is dynamic rather than static, provisional rather than final.

Demonstration – E. B. White on the Moonwalk

We can demonstrate the process of responsible, reflective critical reading with a close look at E. B. White's paragraph about the first moonwalk, written for *The New Yorker* in 1969. White read his sixth and final draft over the phone to the magazine's editor. All six drafts can be found in the appendix to a biography of White by Scott Elledge (1986). We will use the critical reading framework to demonstrate how students might engage with a text, and what we could help them notice about White's achievement in his nine-sentence paragraph. The sentences have been numbered for ease of reference.

Notes and Comment

E. B. White

[1] The moon, it turns out, is a great place for men. [2] One-sixth gravity must be a lot of fun, and when Armstrong and Aldrin went into their bouncy little dance, like two happy children, it was a moment not only of triumph but of gaiety. [3] The moon, on the other hand, is a poor place for flags. [4] Ours looked stiff and awkward, trying to float on the breeze that does not blow. [5] (There must be a lesson here somewhere.) [6] It is traditional, of course, for explorers to plant the flag, but it struck us, as we watched with awe and admiration and pride, that our two fellows were universal men, not national men, and should have been equipped accordingly. [7] Like every great river and every great sea, the moon belongs to none and belongs to all. [8] It still holds the key to madness, still controls the tides that lap on shores everywhere, still guards the lovers who kiss in every land under no banner but the sky. [9] What a pity that in our moment of triumph we did not forswear the familiar Iwo Jima scene and plant instead a device acceptable to all: a limp white handkerchief, perhaps, symbol of the common cold, which, like the moon, affects us all, unites us all.

White – Observations

We can begin by asking students what they see on the page: a single paragraph that begins with a brief sentence and ends with a much longer one. We might invite them to notice the length of White's sentences throughout the paragraph. They will find that his sentences vary quite a bit in length, that White intersperses his three very short sentences between longer ones. The varied sentence lengths avoid monotony, while aiding the paragraph's fluency. The longer sentences make room for complexity of thought.

We can ask about the function of White's opening sentences. "What do those initial sentences do?" we should ask them. The first sentence does two things: it makes an assertion; it creates surprise. Who would have thought (the surprise) that the moon (of all places) is "a great place for men"? Reading this sentence attentively, we wonder why White says what he does. We ask ourselves: "How" is the moon great for men? White's second sentence answers that question by positing two explanations: first, it is a place of "triumph"; second, it is a place of "gaiety," with White describing the two astronauts, Armstrong and Aldrin, as "happy children" doing a "bouncy little dance."

These first two sentences, our students should notice, are closely linked. The second provides specification for the first; it answers the question raised by the first, and it begins to suggest how, in White's view, the moon is "a great place for men." We might additionally help students notice that White compares the bouncy way men move on the moon (due to its significantly lower gravity than earth) to a "dance," illustrating their "gaiety."

White's opening differs in emphasis from what most other commentators of the time highlighted, focusing on the astronauts' walk on the moon as "one small step for [a] man" and "one giant leap for mankind" (Armstrong's own famous formulation). Triumphant it certainly was, though White chooses to emphasize something other than that triumph, and something more than gaiety, something, paradoxically, both humbler and more ambitious, which he develops later as the paragraph progresses.

White – Connections

Toward what connections might we direct our students' attention in analyzing White's paragraph? One thing we might lead them to see (and hear) is a shift – a change of tone as the paragraph proceeds. In sentences 3, 4, and 5, White shifts from the men's apparently happy movement – their "bouncy little dance" – to the American flag they planted on the moon's surface. The flag's stiffness, White suggests, is an indication of its awkwardness, its being out of place. The moon's atmosphere lacks the breezy force to make the flag wave in celebration of the Americans' triumphant walk on its surface. The fifth sentence's parenthesis injects a note of humor into its fundamental seriousness. White will develop the "lesson" he alludes to here in successive sentences.

We might direct our students' attention in these sentences to a shift from the celebratory tone of the paragraph's first two sentences to something graver that follows. We could point them to White's contrast between the active men and the static flag to detect this shift in tone. And we would hope they might take up White's invitation to consider the lesson implied by the paragraph's first five sentences – particularly as it is implied in sentences 3 and 4.

We might invite our students to look through the paragraph, noting words and details that are related and/or repeated. White repeats the word "flag," for example, in the plural "flags" and echoes it again in the word "banner." He uses the word "plant" (or a variant) twice – in planting an American flag and in planting a handkerchief on the moon.

Other connections they might notice include the references to nature – to river, sea, and sky, as well as to the moon. Considering the implications of these connections and repetitions leads students to begin thinking about meaning, initially through the inferences they begin making about those repeated terms and the references to the natural world.

But there is yet another element to making connections, one involved with analyzing the component parts of a text. In reading critically, students attempt to understand how a text – whatever its length or its genre – breaks down into parts. Students need to identify the parts. They need to understand what each part contributes to the whole; they need to identify each part's function or purpose. In short, they need to understand relationships – the relationship of part to part and of part to whole. The process of re-reading a text, focusing on its overall structure, solidifies and deepens students' understanding. Without understanding a text's structure, students can achieve no real understanding of its governing idea. Connecting the parts is essential for this understanding. On the basis of those connections, students can begin to think about implications. They are now ready to make well-grounded inferences.

White – Inferences

How might we help our students make inferences as they analyze White's paragraph? What inferences might be made from their observations and connections? What initial thoughts might they infer from them?

Making inferences leads us back to the text – for yet another look at (and listen to) its language and structure. Making inferences forces readers into scrupulous textual observation; it prompts them to make yet another pass at the text to reconsider it, ideally, perhaps, reading it aloud to hear what it suggests, to ascertain what its rhythms contribute to its meaning.

We might encourage our students to look carefully at (and listen carefully to) White's language as he builds out sentence 6, which is longer and more complex than the five sentences that precede it. We would ask students what work this sentence does, and why White might have made it as long as he did. We would help them see the contrast White develops there between admiration and national pride for the astronauts' achievement, on one hand, and a more expansive sense of awe for their accomplishment, something beyond patriotic fervor, on the other. We could encourage them to see the moon landing as more than an American triumph. The moon, as White notes, "belongs to all," while, paradoxically, belonging to no one.

Our critical reading goal is to help students develop the inferential habit, a habit of speculating about implications and possibilities, less to determine fully, finally, and definitively what they think than to provoke their thinking. Making inferences leads them to ideas.

White – Conclusions and Values

What conclusions might our students make about White's paragraph? Foremost, we would want them to understand (from sentence 7) that it's not just the moon that provokes this paradoxical idea, but nature more generally: "every great river and every great sea." This universalizing concept is further developed and illustrated in sentence 8, which relies on familiar associations of the moon with madness and love, while recognizing as well the moon's physical influence on the watery tides "everywhere." We should help students see how White brings back the image of the flag in an implied comparison with the sky, the "banner" under which lovers kiss "in every land." We are given, thus, another kind of banner, a universal banner of blue, to contrast with the national banner of the stars and stripes.

White's final sentence is a tour de force in its range of reference, its re-collection of images and ideas that come before, and in its stunning control of phrase and rhythm. Those images and that rhythm collect and connect earlier descriptive details, enforcing and solidifying White's notion that in emphasizing the moon landing as a human triumph, we miss a chance to see its larger human implications, that it remains an exciting yet imperfect achievement for humankind. In emphasizing its national American accomplishment, we miss an opportunity to see its universal human significance.

White's paragraph about the moon landing acknowledges the amazing accomplishment it was. White sees the moon landing as a tribute to human ingenuity as well as to American triumphalism. And yet for all the feat's triumphant success, White adduces other considerations beyond the values associated with either a national or a broader human achievement. He invites his readers, instead, to consider another way of thinking about the meaning of the moon landing.

He conveys these larger ideas with two related details at the end of his paragraph: his reference to the "familiar Iwo Jima scene" and his suggestion to replace the American flag with a white handkerchief, symbol of "the common cold." White refers to the iconic picture of American soldiers hoisting the flag after defeating the Japanese in World War II on the strategic Pacific island of Iwo Jima. He connects the moon landing to the important American victory only to suggest that there are other values at stake in the moon landing, and that there are other ways to think about the significance of what was achieved that day in 1969, different symbols by which that achievement might be represented, remembered, and revered.

An additional aspect of critical reading is thinking about the author's idea and evidence – whether or not we accept what is said and why, whether we agree or disagree, and why. In reading a text critically, we consider whether to accept, reject, or qualify what the writer says – and what form that qualification might take. The following exercise invites students to engage in this process of critical evaluation: to consider the extent to which they find White's argument persuasive and the extent to which it stimulates them to think about the larger issues he raises about nationalism and universalism.

Exercise: Further Considerations of White's Moonwalk Paragraph

1   Consider the historical context of the paragraph, first in relation to White's reference to Iwo Jima, and then in relation to the time in which it was written. How was White's little piece received at the time? How did it compare with the many other pieces written about the moon landing, in newspapers and magazines and books? What larger cultural and political implications does White's moon landing paragraph have for thinking about nationalism and internationalism? How have the issues of nationalism and internationalism played out historically since 1969?

2   Why do you think White included the sentence in parentheses: "(There must be a lesson here somewhere.)"? How would you characterize the tone of this sentence? How effective is this sentence? What "lesson(s)" do you draw from White's paragraph? To what extent do you agree with the lesson(s) the paragraph presents? Why?

3   In her book *Leaving Orbit*, Margaret Lazarus Dean notes that when they landed on the moon, Neil Armstrong and Buzz Aldrin not only planted an American flag, but also left a plaque with these words: "Here men from the planet Earth first set foot upon the moon July 1969, A.D. We came in peace for all mankind." How does this information affect your interpretation of and response to White's moon landing paragraph?

4   What title might you provide for White's piece? Explain why you gave it that title.

Application – Lincoln's Gettysburg Address

We can apply our critical reading approach and framework – observation, connection, inference, conclusion, and values – to Lincoln's Gettysburg Address. The paragraphs are numbered for ease of reference.

The Gettysburg Address

[1] Four score and seven years ago our fathers brought forth, upon this continent, a new nation, conceived in Liberty, and dedicated to the proposition that all men are created equal.

[2] Now we are engaged in a great civil war, testing whether that nation, or any nation so conceived, and so dedicated, can long endure. We are met on a great battle-field of that war. We have come to dedicate a portion of that field, as a final resting-place for those who here gave their lives, that that nation might live. It is altogether fitting and proper that we should do this.

[3] But, in a larger sense, we can not dedicate, we can not consecrate – we can not hallow – this ground. The brave men, living and dead, who struggled here, have consecrated it far above our poor power to add or detract. The world will little note, nor long remember what we say here, but it can never forget what they did here.

[4] It is for us, the living, rather, to be dedicated here to the unfinished work which they who fought here have, thus far, so nobly advanced. It is rather for us to be here dedicated to the great task remaining before us – that from these honored dead we take increased devotion to that cause for which they here gave the last full measure of devotion – that we here highly resolve that these dead shall not have died in vain – that this nation, under God, shall have a new birth of freedom – and that government of the people, by the people, for the people, shall not perish from the earth.

A Bit of Context

A few basic facts. First, Lincoln's speech was delivered in approximately two minutes. Second, there are five versions of the speech extant in various US libraries, including the Library of Congress, which owns two of these versions. The variant copies include minor differences in wording and punctuation. Some versions use dashes in places that others use commas. Some add a word here and there – for example in the last sentence where the version reprinted here has "that government of the people," one of the other variant versions adds the word "this": "that this government of the people." And third, a number of books have been written about this speech – its writing, delivery, rhetoric, and reception.

A Suite of Exercises

The following set of exercises employs the framework we applied to E. B. White's moonwalk paragraph. The exercises that highlight observations and connections invite a close look at Lincoln's language, especially his diction and syntax. The exercises on inferences and conclusions raise questions about his religious and historical allusions and also about his omissions. The exercises on conclusions and values include further variants on these topics, while inviting consideration of the rhetorical appeals of Lincoln's speech and the moral and cultural values it espouses. Using the framework of observations, connections, inferences, conclusions, and values, students can work productively through the Gettysburg Address. We can begin by asking students what they notice in Lincoln's language, especially his syntax and diction.

Exercise – Observations

1   What effect results from the varied lengths of Lincoln's sentences? Why might it be important for him to keep some sentences short – given the occasion of his speech and the fact that it is a speech?
2   Read the speech aloud, one paragraph at a time, slowly. What is noticeable about Lincoln's diction, or choice of words? At what level of formality does he pitch his language? Why?
3   What pronouns are emphasized? Who are the "we" and "us" that Lincoln refers to?
4   What historical references does Lincoln include and why do you think he includes them?
5   What does Lincoln avoid mentioning in his speech? What does he leave out, and why, given the historical context of the speech, the place where Lincoln delivered it, and what happened there? Consider the larger historical context and implications of what could have been included but wasn't.

Exercise – Connections

1   What patterns of repetition (and variation) does Lincoln employ? What effects do those repetitions of word, phrase, and clause create? More specifically, which particular words are repeated – and with what effects? Which single word (in various forms) occurs most frequently in the speech? Why is that word so important to Lincoln?
2   What negative words are included in the speech? What is their function, their purpose? What point does Lincoln make by means of negation?
3   Consider the importance of the words "conceived," "consecrate," and "devotion." What was conceived? What is being consecrated? What kind of devotion is Lincoln advocating? With what concepts – what ideas – does Lincoln link these three terms?
4   How do the connections made between these words and the concepts Lincoln evokes convey the spirit and the values Lincoln celebrates in the speech?

5   What other kinds of connections can you see and make among the details and/or the language of the speech?

Exercise – Inferences

1   What inferences might be made from the observations and connections we have made?
2   Why might Lincoln have kept the speech exceedingly brief?
3   Why might he have invoked the founding fathers and Declaration of Independence?
4   Why might he have chosen to avoid mentioning contentious political issues?

Exercise – Conclusions and Values

1   How does reading the speech aloud help you notice things not readily apparent when it is read silently? How does what you notice through listening to yourself or someone else read it aloud nudge your thinking about its purpose and its meaning?
2   What ideas begin to form as you make inferences about the speech?
3   What is the value of contrast and analogy for Lincoln in the speech? Why do you think Lincoln valued an ability to use language effectively?
4   What political, cultural, and religious values does the speech reflect?
5   What kinds of appeals does Lincoln make to his audience? What ultimate value drives Lincoln's rhetorical purpose?

These guided questions use the critical reading framework to direct students' attention to the formal diction and balanced syntax of Lincoln's speech and to repetitions of phrase and clause, which, taken together, create its majestic tone. Students can work in pairs or small groups, perhaps after doing some preliminary independent work on the exercises. They can share their observations and their questions, their inferences and provisional conclusions about the purpose, concepts, and effects of Lincoln's speech.

It's important for them to notice that Lincoln omits references to northerners and southerners, to victories and defeats, to slavery and states' rights. It's also important for them to see how often the word "dedicate" is used, and why. They need to see how the association of "dedicate" with religious language such as "consecrate" and "hallow" emphasizes reconciliation and a high moral purpose. It's important, as well, for them to discover the references to the Declaration of Independence that serve Lincoln's rhetorical and historical purpose to preserve the union and its form of government.

Our role is to guide students' critical reading – their understanding and interpretation, as well as their reflection about the significance and the implications of the speech – without directly telling them what we think it means, says, suggests, or implies rhetorically and historically. Our goal is to help students develop the requisite skills to do their own critical reading, to arrive at their own interpretive conclusions, and to consider the values enlisted, embodied, and enshrined in the text in relation to their own personal values.

We need to help students become independent readers, getting beyond their need for us. We serve as conduits for them, as guides, as ladders to be pushed away once students have developed the critical reading skills and associated habits of mind we demonstrate and embody for them with our own reading and in our teaching.

Reflective Reading – Reading and Living

In his essay "The American Scholar," Ralph Waldo Emerson writes: "There is then creative reading as well as creative writing" (as cited in Richardson, 2009, p. 7). For Emerson, reading is active and purposeful; it bears fruit in original thinking and writing. "First we read," he notes, "then we write" (p. 7). The sequence is natural, even inevitable. Out of our reading we generate ideas and develop our thinking. We reflect and make meaning.

In reading reflectively and imaginatively, readers do their own thinking, which they develop in writing. In doing that work faithfully and deliberately, readers demonstrate an ethic of reading that requires being both responsive and responsible to the text. Good critical readers balance how they respect texts and how they rival them, how they listen carefully to what texts say and how they challenge those texts. As George Steiner notes, "[T]he relation of the true reader to the book is creative. The book has need of him as he has need of it," as the reader brings the text to life in "dynamic reciprocity," with every act of genuine reading "collaborative with the text" (1996, p. 17).

In "History," Emerson urges the student to "read history actively and not passively; to esteem his own life the text, and books the commentary" (Richardson, 2009, p. 7). Reflecting on our reading leads us to connect it with our everyday lives. Emerson's ideas strengthen the reader's authority and weaken the authority of the text. Alberto Manguel, in *A Reader on Reading* (2010), describes this process in terms of "a commitment that is both political and private," one that can result in making us "better and wiser," because reading involves a quest for truth (p. 10). Manguel sees the ideal reader as "an inventor, who subverts the text," and as one "who does not take the writer's word for granted" (p. 152). The ideal reader exercises power over what he or she reads.

As Peter Mendelsund (2014) suggests, the act of reading "feels like, and is like, consciousness itself: imperfect; partial; hazy; co-creative" (p. 403). It's the "co-creative" aspect that links reading with the act of perception, which is always subjective, selective, and interpretive. Our unique response reflects our particular form of textual engagement, a response from which we make something new and personal, each book we read becoming part of our intellectual life.

Reading critically and creatively in these ways, we acknowledge how books influence our lives. The reciprocity between reading and thinking, along with the dynamic interchange between responsible and responsive reading, suggests the relationship between reading and living. We need to help our students experience how critical reading enriches and guides their lives, and, conversely, how reflecting on their lives enables and enhances their reading. We need to help them experience the impact critical reading can have on their thinking in relation to their living. They need to feel as well as understand the exhilaration of critical reading for their lives overall.

Reading and living animate and invigorate one another in reciprocal interplay. The books we read speak to one another and affect each other, combining in various ways in our minds and hearts. They form an inter-textual web that includes not only their relationships among themselves, but also their relationships with us, who engage in life-long conversations with them. We need to help students see how reading is related to their lives outside books, how their reading lives are entangled with their other lives. Thoreau suggests as much when he writes, "What I began by reading, I must finish by acting" (*Journal*, February 19, 1841).

Critical reading, like critical thinking with which it is inextricably intertwined, leads to additional questions, to further investigation, deeper exploration. Every text, as Kafka noted and demonstrated, remains unfinished. A poem, said Valéry, is never finished, only abandoned. If writers abandon texts, leaving them unfinished, then readers have room to enter them. Readers continue reading the texts that writers relinquish. And yet the reader's work, too, is never finished. We leave off reading rather than definitively conclude it. The texts we read critically become part of our consciousness, part of who we are. We become what we critically read, and as we continue to evolve as individuals, so too do the books that have become part of us. We never finish with them, nor they with us. This is one of the wondrous pleasures and the unending challenges of critical reading.

These notions highlight both the need for and the demands of critical reading. They suggest that to do it well requires, in Thoreau's words, "noble exercise ... that will tax the reader more than any exercise which the customs of the day esteem. It requires a training such as the athletes underwent, the steady intention almost of the whole life to this object" (*Walden*, 1854/1983, p. 403). Laying the foundation for that kind of critical reading for our students begins with us. When we are successful in helping them grow as critical readers, our students develop the skills and habits of mind that enable them to become responsible, reflective readers, critical thinkers, and life-long learners. What more can we teachers do for our students than this?

References

Dean, M. L. (2015). *Leaving orbit.* New York: Graywolf Press.

Elledge, S. (1986). *E. B. White: A biography.* New York: Norton.

Feynman, R. (1998). *The meaning of it all.* New York: Perseus Books.

Goulish, M. (2000). *39 microlectures.* New York: Routledge.

Lincoln, A. (1989). The Gettysburg address. In *Speeches and writings: 1859–1865* (p. 536). New York: Library of America.

Manguel, A. (2010). *A reader on reading. New Haven, CT*: Yale University Press.

Mendelsund, P. (2014). *What we see when we read.* New York: Random House.

Richardson, R. (Ed.) (2009). *First we read, then we write: Emerson on the creative process.* Des Moines: University of Iowa Press.

Scholes, R. (1991). *Protocols of reading.* New Haven, CT: Yale University Press.

Scudder, S. H. (1874). In the laboratory with Agassiz. *Every Saturday*, 16 (April 4), 369–370.

Shakespeare, W. (1987). Sonnet 29. In *Shakespeare's sonnets.* Ed. K. Duncan-Jones. London: Thomas Nelson and Son.

Steiner, G. (1996). The uncommon reader. In *No passion spent* (pp. 1–19). New Haven, CT: Yale University Press.

Thoreau, H. D. (2009). *The journal of Henry David Thoreau, 1837–1861.* New York: New York Review Books Classics.

Thoreau, H. D. (1854/1983). *Walden.* New York: Viking/Library of America.

White, E. B. (1969). Notes and comment. *The New Yorker* (July 26).

2

Reciprocal Acts

Reading and Writing
Pat C. Hoy II

A Story of Necessity

Almost a decade ago, I discovered that students were paying primary attention only to the *personal* connections they made when reading assigned written texts; they showed little interest in the larger body of ideas or the way those ideas were presented. It's almost as if the writers' ideas weren't important – didn't matter to the students. They were interested only in "cherry picking" something they could immediately and directly connect with their own experience or with the requirement at hand. Their habits led to hasty conclusions about meaning – to an erasure of central parts of the text under consideration. Diverted by a single-minded effort to find one defining *point*, they routinely ignored the larger *network of complementary ideas* inherent in the text.

Instead of learning to reason from evidence, most students had learned to take shortcuts, moving habitually from thesis to highly selected evidence – leaving out contradictions, challenges, complications. The learned emphasis had been not on rigorous analysis and interpretation of evidence but on a fact-based, highly structured response: thesis, propositions, examples.

All of us know that the examination of evidence rarely leads to certainty or to a thesis that can, out of necessity, be proved; it leads instead to discovery, to ideas that must, like the evidence itself, be continually reassessed and re-conceptualized to represent more accurately whatever truth the evidence

Critical Reading Across the Curriculum, Volume 1: Humanities, First Edition.
Edited by Robert DiYanni and Anton Borst.
© 2017 John Wiley & Sons, Inc. Published 2017 by John Wiley & Sons, Inc.

suggests to the researching writer. At the heart of this *inductive process* of discovery lies the complex business of reading complex written texts that do not reveal themselves to cursory examination.

The most fascinating thing about inductive reasoning is this fact: it never leads to certainty; the conclusions are never guaranteed. So the reader of evidence (whether written, visual, or sonic), is always searching for the unknown, always creating in his or her mind a necessary notion about the meaning of what is being gathered, sorted, analyzed, interpreted – so that that evidence can be turned into ideas and persuasive writing.

For the practicing writer, grappling with lively ideas leads eventually to clarification and the use of nuanced language, to a more complex form of expression than a formulaic set of declarations and a series of examples can provide. The act of writing – writing itself – is central to learning, just as the act of reading is central to writing. So we would do well to clarify for our students this entwining relationship, reminding them day in and day out that the most persuasive writing is predicated on acts of clear-headed critical reading.

Such reading will be our primary consideration in this essay because almost all serious writing is predicated on acts of serious reading. We read critically, seeking to understand a subject or, better yet, a body of collected information that will lead to discoveries about meaning. Our sources might be many different kinds of texts, the nature and variety of which will, of course, depend on the nature of our investigation. Whatever those sources may be, we must learn to *read* them because only reading can unleash their power; only reading can lead us to meaning, to fresh ideas.

We read so that we have something to write about. We also read to move beyond what we know at any given moment. Reading sets our minds, our inquiring minds, in motion as we pursue a deeper understanding of our lives and the world we live in.

Acts of Conception

The ability to *conceive* is central to this exciting, complex process of turning evidence into ideas and then into texts of our own making. It is difficult to say which comes first: conception or reading, reading or conception. When we teachers read a coherent sentence or paragraph in a printed text, we are unlikely to pause over what makes it coherent. As seasoned readers, we expect written texts to be coherent. But when we read an incoherent sentence in a draft, we know right away that it makes no sense, that something is amiss, and we suspect almost immediately that the paragraph following from that sentence will be nonsensical as well. The pleasure of reading is interrupted by incoherence.

Many of our students, even the better ones, cannot so easily make these distinctions between coherence and incoherence, and their flawed reading habits cause them to glide over what makes little sense or what does not interest them. So they have to learn quickly from us that the relationships among the words of a single sentence are crucial to *critical reading* – just as the relationships among paragraphs are also crucial. Coherent sentences – sentences whose words make sense in relation to one another – lead to coherent essays and arguments.

But teaching students about coherence the old-fashioned way from a good handbook is less effective than having them practice conception. Learning to think clearly about the meaning of evidence establishes the foundation for coherent expression. I want to exercise the muscles of my students' minds as a way of emphasizing the importance of rigorous reading, want them to see eventually that reading really is a word-by-word process; so too is writing. And yet we cannot teach them to read and write well one word at a time. Melanie Stangl, a student writer, reminds us about the importance of creativity and conception; this excerpt comes from her longer essay about reading and learning, an essay that ends with this observation: "the struggle to make meaning is what makes us human":

> The word "conceive," according to the *Oxford English Dictionary*, means "to take into, or form in, the mind." But ... humans are not receptacles of experiences; we don't simply and faithfully "take in." Understanding is not merely an act of reception. It is also an act of creation. We craft and we form all we experience in order to understand: we are literally trying to make sense. (Stangl, 2011, p. 18)

As we take new information into our minds, we endeavor to understand what it means, not only to us but to others. This creative endeavor leads eventually to our own attempts, as Stangl reminds us, to craft and form this new material so that we can understand it, reception and creation working together as enabling acts of mind. These acts of understanding can and should lead our students to a strong desire to tell others what they have discovered.

Working from Images

I begin conceptual work with provocative images, seeking always to find an image that my students may not have seen, something challenging. I want the image to excite them, but I also want it to lead to a series of discoveries about the larger world of ideas beyond it. Carl Jung, the depth psychologist, suggests that we know everything we know by way of image, so learning to *read* images stands us in good stead for other reading work. Images call us to be creative and conceptual; there are often no words to confound or limit us. So the relationship between reader and image is direct and immediate. One of the earliest lessons we learn from images is that what we think we see is not always what it seems. Images are gutsy, full of energy; they harbor untold delights.

The reading methodology is simple – two leading questions – but the consequences are most often profound. The exercise is interactive, involving the whole class. My job is to steer and moderate the discussion, not to interpret. Success depends, of course, on my choice of image and on my orchestration of a playful, but serious, investigation. Figure 2.1 below is a typical image from my trove. I project it on a screen so that its details will be enlarged and easier to discern.

Figure 2.1 René Magritte, *The Human Condition.*
© 2016 C. Herscovici/Artists Rights Society (ARS), New York.

I do not tell students anything about the image. My first easy question puts them right to work: *Each of you tell me one thing that you can actually see in this painting, something that you can point to – can physically verify in the painting.*

Naming usually begins immediately without additional prompting. I point as they name. Occasionally, someone will begin to interpret, so I have to step in. *I want only what you can see in the painting, only what you can point to and verify.* The idea behind this work is to enable everyone to see the whole of what's there before we move forward.

The second question elevates thinking. *Now, tell me what you can see because of this painting that you cannot point to and verify in the painting itself.*

This is often, at first, a silencing question, because it asks for both conceptual and creative work. The stakes are higher, and the answers put the students at risk. "I" is always involved in this interpretive work. With this question, I'm not asking for the more rigorous interpretive work that will come in later classes. I'm not asking for an interpretation of the painting that will have to be substantiated with evidence. I'm not at this stage even asking them to justify what they can see. I want them to learn that there is a difference between *seeing and naming parts* and *seeing something because of the parts*. The naming prepares them for the second kind of seeing; it also ensures that they learn to see what others can verify in the painting that they might miss. So the naming part of the exercise begins to highlight the benefits of *collaboration*. The difference between seeing parts and seeing what the parts suggest is crucial, but students need not understand right away all of the ramifications of that conceptual act. This foundational work will be repeated many times over the course of a semester; it will, if all goes well, become second nature, even as the process of reading, analyzing, interpreting, and reflecting becomes more complicated.

What I'm doing is establishing a reading *rhythm*; that's what I call it, a rhythm – an essential, foundational, repetitive reading practice. Deeper interpretation, justification, and reflection will eventually ride on this double rhythm – reading to account for what's physically there in the text, accompanied by reading that depends on conceptual creativity and risk-taking.

To facilitate and complicate the conceptual work in these early reading and thinking exercises, I sometimes pair various texts. In class, image work is almost always followed by work with a written text. Most often these written texts are excerpts that I have chosen from the previous night's assigned reading or excerpts that I have chosen because they emphasize some idea about reading or writing that is germane to the day's work.

Here is one tried and true excerpt – pertinent to our evolving sense of critical reading. Without an understanding of the concept Frank Kermode introduces in this passage, students will have trouble not only interpreting a text but also creating one of their own. Try to hear Kermode's voice as you read his clarifying words about the nature of conception.

> We understand a whole by means of its parts, and the parts by means of the whole. But this "circle" seems to imply that we can understand nothing – the whole is made up of parts we cannot understand until it exists, and we cannot see the whole without understanding the parts. Something, therefore, must happen, some intuition by which we break out of this situation – a leap, a *divination*, [Schleiermacher] called it, whereby we are enabled to understand both part and whole. (1993, p. 23)

Right away, we can begin to have fun with these words and their relationship to one another. This complementary reading exercise begins just as our work with images did. *Tell me what you see that you can physically point to and verify.* Give students free rein to play with words, sentences, and relationships during this second game of naming. It will be more difficult than the image game because it is more difficult to say and explain what they see in a printed text. It is also more difficult to stay with the naming.

Some possibilities – things students might say: I see Kermode establishing at the outset a relationship between the words *whole* and *parts* – a relationship that persists through the whole paragraph. I see the word *circle* in quotation marks and notice too that we are not told why. The word *imply* calls on us to do interpretive work. In just two sentences Kermode has put us, the readers (and potential writers), in a bind, giving us something to figure out. And then he gives us a solution, with just one italicized word: *divination.* To help us understand that important word, he provides two other helping words: *intuition* and *leap.* The word *understand* in some form is repeated five times in the passage.

The next question should come naturally given all this preliminary work. *Tell me what you understand about understanding that you cannot see spelled out in this paragraph. What meaning or understanding arises out of the paragraph's specific words – meaning that you cannot point to explicitly?* Let students work out what Kermode means by *divination* and what the process helps us do.

Often, you can also achieve beneficial interpretive results in these kinds of exercises if you pair the first image with a second image, or the written text with another written text – or pair the initial image with a seemingly

Figure 2.2 René Magritte, *Evening Falls.* © 2016 C. Herscovici/Artists Rights Society (ARS), New York.

unrelated text that has the potential to stimulate a more interesting reading of the image. Imagine the image in Figure 2.2 placed side by side with Figure 2.1.

Designing this kind of work is perhaps our most important task as teachers. If we design possibilities for this conceptual work before class, we can have fun *listening* to the students learn as they play. Inevitably, we will have to modify the design (add images, add texts, provide facts) on the basis of their responses. Part of the fun with these conceptual reading games is being at risk with the students; we never know what they will come up with, so we too have to be attentive and creative as we listen, question, modify, and orchestrate.

As a general rule, it is wise to begin these interactive exercises with no explanations, keeping in store other meaningful information that might stimulate further thought. Many students, for example, will likely not know who Magritte is, so when you give them a second image, when you set the two images side by side, you can provide just a bit of information about him; titles are almost always evocative and helpful. Such information might be given after the initial responses have quieted down. Then, see what the added information does to stimulate discussion, and be prepared that it might shut down responses. Sometimes too much information offered too soon, or in the wrong way, closes the mind, intimidates, suggests that there's nothing more to say.

Remembering Spontaneity

As we move, day-to-day, from these foundational rhythmic exercises to more rigorous and systematic approaches to reading and writing, we should remember the spirit of play and experimentation that accompanied the early rhythmic work. A spirit of playfulness keeps students from feeling the weightiness of risk. Playing and making mistakes becomes an enabling part of their creative work. Without that combination, they're likely to spend more time trying to get right answers than they spend exploring and leaping.

Thirty-five or so years ago when I first began asking students to read and summarize, it never occurred to me that summarizing required both advanced thinking and writing skills that we were not teaching them. And the handbooks and rhetorics had little to say about developing student minds so that they could do this serious conceptual work. Our methodology was informed by a series of imperatives: summarize this story in 150 words or less; compare and contrast this story with one of the two we read last week; develop a thesis for a short argument about the film clip we saw in class today; compare and contrast these two novels. It has taken, is still taking, a long time for writing teachers and the writers of textbooks to think clearly and systematically about just how to prepare students for these kinds of complex assignments. The imperatives ask for, actually demand, all at once, a *final* performance whose brilliance depends on our students knowing how to conceive, how to conceptualize, how to capture wholes, how to express in clear language what has been captured, and how to conceive a product that will convey what has been learned. Doing all of this work is heady business requiring rigor and persistence.

We found that students learn faster when we design work that allows them to practice over time the many essential skills required for the final-form work; that preliminary work needs necessarily to be progressive, so we do well to develop exercises designed to complement and build on one another as they lead students to the desired kind of product. Repetition, variation, and recursion are essential to the design and practice.

On the one hand, I am calling emphatically for slowing down the process of helping students learn to read and write, asking you to consider the importance of helping students learn preliminary skills so that eventually they can create persuasive products (essays, arguments, laboratory reports, surveys of literature, proposals). But with this emphasis, I do not want to mislead teachers or students about the power of the mind to grasp things *suddenly*, to do intuitively some of the essential preliminary work of reading and thinking. So I want to begin this deeper investigation of a systematic set of exercises with another game of sorts, a game that invites students and teachers to deal imaginatively with not only the language of a text but also its sounds.

The late Gabriele Rico wrote a fascinating book called *Creating Recreations* (2000). I had the pleasure of sitting in once or twice with a group of teachers at conferences where Gabriele put us through her paces. We were, along with her students, her research pool; the book had not been written. Years later, she asked me to introduce the book. What follows is some of what I said in my foreword, "Minds Aquiver." Her methodology is simple – as in absolute, fundamental. Those gathered in a classroom or in a workshop begin with a poem, a visual image, or even a snippet of prose. Someone reads a selected text aloud or projects an image on a screen, while others in the room practice the art of listening and seeing. A second reading of the text elicits a *mind map* from each participant – a medley of associations recorded around a blank circle on a sheet of paper. And then, perhaps, a nudge in the direction of meaning – a notion jotted in the center of the circle that will account for the recorded associations, something tentative. And finally, a creative task: *In just two and a half minutes **re-create** what you have just heard or seen, any way you'd like.*

Under the impress of this methodology, students become participants in the creative process; it takes them to the center of sense-making activity. They become agents. Imagining and conceptualizing accompany listening and reading and writing. But students do not have to learn these processes one at a time, nor do they have to take them up in a linear sequence. Instead, they experience them simultaneously as they write under the constricting but liberating impress of time. This process moves the cognitive mind slightly to the side so that uninhibited work can be done with the primary material – the spoken and visual texts. This is what Gabriele tells us about the process:

> The process that emerged [from my experiments], which I call Recreations, is the result of a marriage between the resonant voice and writing. Students listen, really listen, with the knowledge that they can reconfigure what they have heard in any way they want – in writing. However, rather than being a purely random process, Re-creations build on what they have only heard but not seen in print. What they

have heard is the pattern of someone else's words. This pattern circulates in the listener's mind generating associations, triggering memory, and activating the pattern-seeking brain. Then, in the space of two-and-a-half minutes listeners transform what they have heard into patterns of meaning unique to them. (p. 2)

Patterns of meaning unique to them. This is, of course, what we do always when we try to tell others what we have discovered during our reading and researching. But this way, Gabriele's way, teaches students something crucial about the power of their brains, alerts them to something the brain can do without our giving it instructions – if only we can get out of the way and let what E. M. Forster (1951) once called the "underside" of the brain do its work. When students learn almost instantly how to participate in this kind of generative playfulness, they actually begin to ask for more and more of these opportunities. Gabriele began almost all of her writing classes with the reading of short poems, prose passages, or images.

Students should do one reading just to listen (carefully, attentively, deliberately), and another to jot down associations and a tentative sense of meaning (where they begin to connect and associate) – all followed by the $2^1/_2$ minutes of re-creation. In response, students can write poems, capture essences, draw pictures – anything at all that attempts to capture the whole of the object (writing, image, sculpture, even film clip) under consideration.

Once, in a second-semester writing course, I read only a short passage from a longer essay by anthropologist Clifford Geertz, "Deep Play: Notes on the Balinese Cockfight," an essay that had been assigned reading for the night before. At the end of our re-creations, I asked for volunteer readers. A young woman's hand shot up, and she gave us a single sentence that captured the essence of Geertz's complex essay, including subtle details that were worthy of one of Geertz's own sentences. Others offered their own variations of re-recreations and by the time the discussion ended, students had a comprehensive understanding of the whole text that normally would have taken days to unravel. Such re-creation work is always partial at the outset, but by the time a number of students have responded, the class will have benefited significantly from an initial investment of $2^1/_2$ minutes. Students are often eager to read what they have written, and many students who have re-created by drawing a pictorial image of some sort will want to go to the board rather than trying to put words to the image. Often, I ask the whole class to put their work on the board, whether word or image.

In my own writing classes, I use re-creations occasionally, rather than routinely. I use them when I want to inspire students to come to terms fast with a new reading assignment, or I spring a re-creation requirement on them in class when I see that they have become lost in the details of a different kind of reading exercise that requires a narrow focus on a *part* of a text. Re-creations tend to inspire the kind of *divination* that aims to capture wholeness.

Getting More Systematic

I find that pairing re-creations with more systematic work helps a broader range of students enjoy success. A few years ago in our writing program, a young poet named Anthony Carelli joined us as a new teacher. Early in his first term, he designed a brilliant methodology that captured our spirit of play and instilled a thought-provoking rigor into our reading strategies. We called it the Carelli Chart; he called it a Reading Workbench (Table 2.1).

Study the instructions within the chart, and as you do, remember that this chart should be an active, electronic Word document so that students can add and delete rows to accommodate the number of paragraphs in the essay or article under consideration – one row for each paragraph. The instructions for each of the three columns are clear, but students will need some help understanding what is required before they first use the chart. I tell my students to fill out only the first and third columns during their first reading of the chosen or assigned text. The first column requires that they notice what the writer is actually doing in the paragraph: describing, listing, introducing the ideas of another writer, creating a transition. The third column asks them to identify key words in each paragraph, a task that's quite difficult until they become better readers; they will almost always choose too many words trying not to leave anything out. I usually limit their choices to three words. I want them to see, as they get deeper into the text, that key words repeat and vary throughout a good piece of writing.

Filling out the middle column is the most fun; doing so is also challenging. Students must be willing both to play and be rigorously imaginative. They're being called on to *become* the writer of the piece under consideration. They must, in practice, be mask-wearers. I encourage them to say to themselves, *I am Joan Didion or James Baldwin or Ann Zwinger or E. B. White, and my job is to translate each of my own paragraphs into a single sentence so that my readers will have a clearer sense of what I'm saying in each paragraph.* Obviously, as the paragraphs become more complex, the task for the student becomes more challenging, and the sentences become more complex. It will not be possible to reduce every paragraph to a single declarative sentence, so students have to experiment with form and punctuation. Putting the extra white space between sections of paragraphs helps students learn

Table 2.1 A Reading Workbench

Author's Action	1 Single, Complete Sentence Distillation of Paragraph Spoken *in Author's Voice*	Key Words
A (*First letter of Author's Name*) represents text Y/A tells story Y/A reports from Y/A analyzes Y/A reads Y/A speculates Z/A argues Z	Strive to retain all images. Your goal when writing these paragraph distillations is <u>not</u> to simplify the paragraph, but rather to gather as much meaning and complexity as is possible to gracefully organize in a single, clear sentence. If this column is filled out properly and thoroughly you should be able to read it from top to bottom as an accurate distillation of the whole essay. Review and amend earlier distillations for accuracy and coherence as you go.	List key words. Review and amend earlier groups of key words as you go.
	First, number the essay's paragraphs. Then create one table row per paragraph.	
1	A represents and begins to analyze Z	Here you are trying to speak from inside the author's mind. You should use the "I" pronoun when referring to the author: "I think …" or "When I stood there looking at …" or …
2		
3		
	Leave meaningful breaks between groups of rows to represent important structural seams in the essay.	
4		
5		
6		
7		
8		

Now, in your own voice, write a rich paragraph that represents the whole essay – especially the author's strangest new thinking – to someone who has never read the essay. Your job is to show your reader the uneasy exhilaration (confusion, disturbance, thrill) you encounter in your reading.

how clusters of paragraphs work together to create meaning; seeing these *hidden structures* is something we begin to work on early in the semester – as soon as we move beyond a consideration of excerpts to a concern over whole texts.

The final requirement, the one stated at the end of the Reading Workbench, asks for a holistic, written representation of the entire selection. Students and other readers should be able to read those middle-column sentences from top to bottom and, by so doing, have a clearer sense of the entire selection. Then, following that review of their work, students must revert to their own voices and write a rich paragraph that accounts for the entire piece. This final requirement presents a good opportunity for students to practice related writing skills: introduction of writer and text, citation (summarizing), documentation, and reflection. Before we look at such a paragraph, let's see what a completed chart looks like.

The chosen text is John Berger's brief essay "The White Bird" (1993). Berger asks us to think seriously about the relationship among three of his favorite concepts: aesthetics, hope, and evil. His approach to their relationship takes us in a pleasing, roundabout way *from* a consideration of man-made white birds *to* nature's duality (its persistent indifference and its occasional offerings of beauty) and, finally, *to* a complex image of actual birds freezing outside while the man-made birds waft in the warm breezes stirred by the kitchen fires inside the cottages. The work in the middle section of the chart reveals both the movement of Berger's mind and the complexity of his thought (Table 2.2).

In order to write a rich, summarizing paragraph about this text, students will need to be taught the rudiments of representation – how to introduce a text, how to quote and summarize, how to reflect (when reflection is appropriate), and how to ensure that the reader, who has not read the text, will be able to understand the rich paragraph. They need to know too that this representational work will often exceed one paragraph if the audience and the essay itself warrant it. I like to tell students that the representation of the text is a gift that we as writers offer to our readers; it is in fact our re-creation of the essence of the text and its ideas.

> In his essay "The White Bird," John Berger calls our attention to a small, crafted bird that flies often in the homes of people in Europe; these birds are made simply from basic materials, but they are made with care and somehow manage to evoke human feelings that correspond to those evoked by real birds in nature. Berger eventually uses these birds to highlight the sharp distinction between art that tries to capture certain essences of the larger world and nature itself, which

Table 2.2 Completed workbench for John Berger, "The White Bird"

	Author's Action *A presents text Y/A tells story Y/A reports from Y/A analyzes Y/A reads Y/A speculates Z/A argues Z*	1 Sentence Distillation of Paragraph Spoken in Author's Voice *If this column is filled out properly and thoroughly you should be able to read it from top to bottom as an accurate distillation of the whole essay. Review and amend earlier distillations for accuracy and coherence as you go.*	Key Words *List key words. Review and amend earlier groups of key words as you go.*
	First, number the essay's paragraphs. Then create one table row per paragraph.		
1	B tells a story; introduces the w. bird	I am fascinated with the fairly widespread practice of making white birds from wood because the making of these birds—the creation of something so simple and beautiful—makes me clarify the relationship among the concepts of aesthetics, hope, and evil.	Aesthetics, hope, evil
2	B tells how the birds are constructed, step by step	I am intrigued by the process by which the white birds are made from simple materials, without glue, to create a thing of beauty that can be mounted inside a house and ride on the currents of wind circulating among the rooms.	Skill, art, completeness, lightness
3	B qualifies his classification	I do not want my claims about the artistic qualities of the birds to seem absurd, yet I want to be clear that they are beautiful in their simplicity, which results in their being both pleasing and mysterious.	Simplicity, artful, pleasing, mysterious, traditional pattern
4	B enumerates and explains two qualities of the birds	These birds are figurative, representing both a particular bird and the natural world in which they live, but they are inside and therefore symbolic, evoking at the same time a more general cultural symbolism associated with real and mythical birds	Figurative representations, world of birds, world of nature, symbolism, cultural
5	Continues enumerating, dealing with three qualities	I turn now to the birds' artistic qualities— the lightness and pliability of the wood, how the wood becomes bird yet remains an art object unified by formality and economy, how the bird provokes a kind of astonishment—to try to get you to see how the bird's qualities make you want to hold it and discover the secret behind its making.	Lightness, pliability, texture, simple complexity, astonishment, secret

(continued)

Table 2.2 (Continued)

	Author's Action	1 Sentence Distillation of Paragraph Spoken in Author's Voice	Key Words
6	Sums up the qualities	Look at the undifferentiated whole now, consider that you are standing before a mystery: a piece of wood has become a bird, actually more than a bird, a mysterious thing that has been worked with a mysterious skill under the influence of love.	Undifferentiated whole, a made thing, mysterious skill, love
7	B explains the limitations of what he has done	My enumeration of the qualities of the bird has been an attempt to isolate what creates an aesthetic emotion, an emotion in this case that is predicated on holding the self in abeyance, yet my definitions reduce aesthetics to art while saying nothing about the relationship between art and nature, or even art and the World.	Emotion, aesthetics, art, self, nature, World
		Leave Meaningful breaks between groups of rows to represent important structural seams in the essay.	
8	B transitions to nature	So we have to begin again because one can also experience an aesthetic emotion before nature (just as we can with the art object).	Aesthetic emotion, man-made object, nature
9	B clarifies what he means by nature	I do not hold to the sentimental view of nature as a place of freedom; rather, nature is a place of struggle and energy, a place where we encounter evil, the need for shelter, where we learn of nature's indifference and our human need for protection, where we experience pain and begin to question whether the Creation itself was purposeful, and if so, also hidden from our view so that we have to depend on signs to understand.	Nature, struggle, energy, pain, arena, evil
10	B returns to beauty	Never mind the bleakness, we can also encounter beauty in Nature that comes to us of a sudden, an unpredictable beauty that is always an exception and that is why it moves us.	Bleak natural context, beauty, sudden, unpredictable, encounter, exception, in spite of

Table 2.2 (*Continued*)

	Author's Action	1 Sentence Distillation of Paragraph Spoken in Author's Voice	Key Words
11	B counters a common held perception about beauty	Some might argue that the origin of the way we are (or were first) moved by beauty was functional, but that is a reductionist way of looking at the origin of beauty, and besides much of beauty is useless.	Functional, beauty, useless, reductionist
12	B considers difference between cultural notions of beauty	A given community's notions of beauty can depend on its means of survival, its economy, its geography, its ideology, its reaction to nature at a given moment in history.	Community, beauty, history, economy, geography, ideology
13	B finds constants among cultures	But no matter what I have just said, there are certain constants which all cultures have found beautiful.	Beauty, culture, constants
14	B begins to complicate his argument	And now, I want to complicate this explanation of our response to beauty and tell you that we can see what we can see of the natural world because our perception has evolved to produce what I like to call "the phenomenon of a potential recognition" that amounts, on occasion, to a double affirmation: we affirm what we see and are affirmed by what we see, giving us a god-like capability of affirming that what we have seen is *good*, and it is from this recognition of good that the aesthetic emotion from nature derives.	Aesthetic emotion, potential recognition, double affirmation, good (as opposed to evil)
15	B brings good and evil together through the Fall	So my major terms—aesthetic emotion, good, hope, mystery, and evil—come together now in my mind, and I must begin to own up to my major idea: that we live after the Fall, that evil is rampant, that we must resist it with all our might, that the world does not confirm our Being, but we are nevertheless afforded hope by these instantaneous glimpses of beauty where the energy of our perceptions becomes inseparable from the energy of creation.	Phenomenological, untranslatable message, aesthetic moment, less alone, energy

(*continued*)

Table 2.2 *(Continued)*

	Author's Action	1 Sentence Distillation of Paragraph Spoken in Author's Voice	Key Words
16	B returns to the white bird	The aesthetic emotion we feel before a man-made object is derivative of the emotion we feel before nature, and with that recognition we begin to understand that all the languages of art have been developed to make the instantaneous permanent; art presumes that beauty is the basis for an order; beauty is not *in spite of*, it is.	Aesthetic emotion, emotion before nature, beauty, order, making the instantaneous permanent
17	B begins the ending	As I begin to close, I want you to know that I still hold to a previous judgment of mine that it is reasonable to evaluate a work of art according to whether or not it helps us in the modern world claim our social rights, and now I claim that art's other face (its transcendental one) raises the question of man's ontological right.	Historical face of art, transcendental face of art, social and ontological rights
18	B again collects his concepts	Art does not imitate nature; it imitates a creation aimed toward various ends: to propose an alternative world, to amplify, confirm, and make social the brief hope offered by nature—all of which is to say that art is an organized response to those occasional glimpses that nature sometimes affords us, transforming that potential recognition into something permanent that gives us corresponding glimpses of hope.	Imitation, creation, confirmation, hope, art and nature in unison, transformation, recognition, permanent
19	B brings back the bird	All I can tell you now is this: the white birds waft on the warm air inside, while the real birds freeze outside.	Rising, drinking, dying; artistic bird, man, real bird

can be indifferent not only to us but also to the other creatures that inhabit it. This indifference troubles Berger so much that he considers it evil. But nature can also bestow gifts of beauty on us, can surprise us at odd, unpredictable moments with glimpses of nature that astonish us. What fascinates Berger about such glimpses of beauty is this: they evoke similar feelings of hope in peoples of all cultures, and when we humans think about them, these glimpses remind us of our common humanity; they give us hope against the bleakness that we so often face in our daily lives. When we catch these glimpses, they provide what Berger calls a *double affirmation* for us; we affirm what we see, and what we see affirms us, giving us a kind of god-like quality that allows us to see the *good*, and from such affirmations, the aesthetic emotion arises. We sense our kinship with one another and can begin to see as well that our art is not an imitation of nature but an effort to make permanent those glimpses of beauty that draw us together, giving us hope and a deeper understanding of the world's complexities.

Merging What and How

To complete this section on systematic reading, I want to offer a relatively simple way to help students learn to understand and represent the *hidden structures* that we find in all good writing. I call them hidden because they are not always set off with labels, titles, and reminders as they are in this longer essay of mine. We have to learn to read in two ways at once, paying attention to what is being said and how it is being said. As critical readers interested in understanding the whole text, we are concerned not only with *what* the text means, but also with *how* it means. Understanding the how gives us a sense of possibilities for our own writing.

Again, the reading exercise itself is simple in concept but sometimes complicated to execute. The requirement to conceptualize lies at the heart of students' initial difficulty, and conceptualizing is often complicated by what they have learned in the past about argument. If students have been taught to depend on a relatively rigid structure – introduction, body, con-clusion – with a predictable number of paragraphs for each of those three sections, they will falter when approaching an essay like "The White Bird" that calls on the reader to follow a more subtle and less predictable path of reasoning. Figuring out what is being said is often made difficult by pre-conceived notions of form. Expectations get in the way of reception. So I want students to learn to *see* and *diagram* that more subtle, less predictable chain of reasoning they sometimes encounter in compelling, unpredictable texts.

The first step when reading a written text this way is to number all of the paragraphs; the second step is to figure out where the **Beginning (B)** of the piece ends and where the **Ending (E)** begins. Everything else in the text constitutes the **Middle (M).** Students learn, with our help, that the number of paragraphs in the *Beginning* and in the *Ending* vary from piece to piece; those divisions depend more on function and clarity than they do on a specified or predetermined number of paragraphs. The work in the *Middle* depends on the evidence being presented and on the writer's way of organizing and responding to that evidence, just as it depends on how the writer decides to help readers understand the evolving ideas. Every good writer reveals the logic of his or her imagination, trying to do so in a way that allows readers to understand that logic and the ideas it advances. As critical readers, we have to be attuned to the development of those ideas, alert to the way paragraphs work separately and together to create a coherent piece of writing. We have to be alert to clusters of paragraphs working together, just as we have to be aware of how individual paragraphs can work independently.

The Reading Workbench, when done correctly, also considers structural divisions, but I want students to present the findings of their investigation of hidden structures in yet another form. Here is another way to *see* "The White Bird," nineteen paragraphs distributed and grouped according to function and meaning across the essay's Beginning, Middle, and Ending (Figure 2.3).

Slowing the process of reading with this kind of exercise gives students an opportunity to see how other minds work as they develop ideas. Students investigating the process of thinking this way will see too that declaration (typical of much argumentative prose) can be less persuasive than

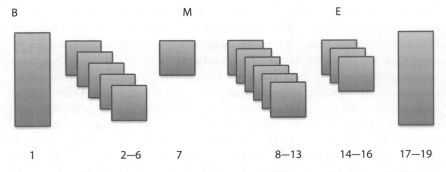

Figure 2.3 Visualizing hidden structures: Beginning, Middle, Ending paragraph groupings.

exploration and inquiry. Often after students have completed these rudimentary diagrams, I ask them to work in small groups (two or three students), to try to reach a consensus about their own differences, to put their final group solution on the board, and to be prepared to present their reasoning to other students. As a way of clarifying their thinking about the various clusters of paragraphs, I often ask them to give each of those clusters a two-word title that captures the idea-work of the paragraphs in the cluster. All of this reading work prepares students, over time, for the writing they will be doing in the course. They learn to see possibilities for themselves – possibilities for their writing – as they read and study the work of others.

Consider now yet another variation on a different exercise, one that can be used effectively to achieve different reading emphases. When I sense that students need more help recognizing how texts work – how they work to say (and suggest) what they mean – I use these variations in combination with the other exercises. Whereas the Reading Workbench emphasizes meaning (given the work of that middle column) and the diagrams that we just considered emphasize hidden structures, this chart variation emphasizes words and their relationship to both evidence and meaning.

Often when I'm helping students learn to read a given written text, I will have them create a three-column chart, asking them to select the three most important words they can identify across the whole text; these words or their variants likely appear in several places – repeated and varied as the writer of the text uses them to develop his or her ideas. Assume again, for illustration, that the reading assignment is "The White Bird." Berger introduces these three crucial words in the first paragraph of the essay (see Table 2.3).

I might select two words and ask the students to select a third. As they gain more experience, I give them more latitude. I also allow them to select, instead of a word, an image from the text, if the writer has introduced an important one. Once students have collected evidence, I ask them to study it to see what it tells them about the text they are reading. I'm always interested in having them think about ideas. *What is this text really trying to tell us? How do these words and the evidence in general help me and you better understand the writer's point of view about the subject?*

After considering such questions in a class discussion or in small group collaborative sessions, I ask students to "reveal" to me, in a well-developed paragraph, what the chosen words (and their relationships) tell us about the writer's ideas. I most often tell students that they can use the words themselves only one time in their paragraphs. I can, of course, see from the chart and the collected evidence whether the words are well chosen and important, but what I want to know in the paragraph is what those

Table 2.3 Compiling evidence in "The White Bird"

Aesthetics	Hope	Evil
The students' task in each column is to copy into the appropriate column evidence from the text that justifies the selection of the word. It is important to have them type out the evidence (direct quotation or summary); typing brings the language into their minds, while leading to deeper understanding.	Evidence should be selected from across the whole essay. The word *hope*, for example, may appear in the evidence, or the evidence may suggest something about the concept of hope. All of the appropriate evidence should be entered in the column.	It may turn out that the evidence does not justify the selection of a particular word. In that case, the student should select another word based on a closer reading of the text. It follows that the evidence must justify the selection. Eventually, the student must decide whether the three selected words are crucial to the writer's development of ideas.

words *and* the evidence mean. I'm looking for the essence of meaning that is justified by the selected evidence.

In another variation on this chart, I want students to think about *style, content, and significance*. This work is a bit more sophisticated but no less fundamental than the other work. I prefer to introduce this chart in class so that group participation can reveal a range of interesting responses. When students begin to select important details from the text for the first two columns, they are already dealing unknowingly with significance. But eventually we will want to focus on the *significance* of what has already been recorded under the *content* and *style* columns.

Initially, you might begin this exercise with an excerpt from a longer text. What we're trying to do is encourage close, intensive reading while keeping meaning ever present in the students' minds. Beginning with a shorter text can reveal to them just how much pleasure and knowledge can be derived from savoring important textual detail. This brief excerpt from George Steiner's essay "Real Presences" (1996) is particularly good for this kind of work because what he says is also germane to the idea about reading that we're trying to convey: close reading yields fascinating revelations. Listen to Steiner's words as they play in your head:

> We must read as if the text before us has meaning. This will not be a single meaning if the text is a serious one, if it makes us answerable to its force of life. It will not be a meaning or *figura* (structure, complex) of meanings isolated from the transformative and reinterpretive

pressures of historical and cultural change. It will not be a meaning arrived at by any determinant or automatic process of cumulation and consensus. The true understanding(s) of the text or music or painting may, during a briefer or longer time-spell, be in the custody of a few, indeed of one witness and respondent. Above all, the meaning striven towards will never be one which exegesis, commentary, translation, paraphrase, psycho-analytic or sociological decoding, can ever exhaust, can ever define as total. Only weak poems can be exhaustively interpreted or understood. Only in trivial or opportunistic texts is the sum of significance that of the parts. (p. 34)

Because this is a difficult text – what I would call a text fit for teachers – I want to follow our earlier lead and pair it with another of Steiner's texts (one that includes a painting). I do this to suggest how a less difficult text can help us read and interpret a more difficult one.

In this second text, an excerpt from a longer essay titled "The Uncommon Reader" (1996), Steiner is interpreting Chardin's painting, *Le Philosophe lisant*, to help us understand how ceremonial and ritualistic the act of reading ought to be. The reader in the painting is dressed for the occasion (formal cloak and hat) and is surrounded by the necessary accouterments (book, quill, hourglass). We see immediately that the act of reading calls for both preparation and commitment. In this brief passage, Steiner, focusing on the quill, reminds us about our own obligations as readers:

Immediately in front of the medals and hourglass, we observe the reader's quill. Verticality and the play of light on the feathers emphasize the compositional and substantive role of the object. The quill crystallizes the primary obligation of response. It defines reading as action. To read well is to answer the text, to be answerable to the text, "answerability" comprising the crucial elements of response and of responsibility. To read well is to enter into answerable reciprocity with the book being read; it is to embark on total exchange ("ripe for commerce" says Geoffrey Hill). The dual compaction of light on the page and on the reader's cheek enacts Chardin's perception of the primal fact: to read well is to be read by that which we read. It is to be answerable to it. The obsolete word "responsion," signifying as it still does at Oxford, the process of examination and reply, may be used to shorthand the several and complex stages of active reading inherent in the quill. (pp. 5-6)

Let's now be answerable to Steiner's text (Table 2.4).

Table 2.4 Responding and interpreting: Steiner, "The Uncommon Reader"

Content	Style	Significance
*The quill and light interest S. *Reading seems to be something of a sacred act to S; the reader in the painting is dressed for the occasion, and S's attitude (the tone of the piece) suggests that we are talking about a serious act. *He is also interested in mystery, the way the *light* on the reader's cheek tells us something about the effect of the text on him. *S is, himself, coming to terms with the act of reading. *"Responsion" is crucial to our understanding of what S has to say.	*The repetition of *r* seems to interest S: responsibility, response, reader. *In fact he relies heavily on repetition and variation to convey his thoughts. *Introduces some odd but telling terms: *primary obligation of response*; *primal fact*; *process of examination and reply*; *stages of active reading inherent in the quill.* *Uses the colon and the semicolon well. *Cites very little evidence from the painting, so what we are reading is S's reflection on what the painting suggests to him about the act of reading.	What S seems to be doing is setting us up for more information about the use of the quill; in this paragraph he is primarily interested in making us understand the sought-for relationship between the reader and the text. He wants us to understand our obligation as readers; we bring the text to life for our own readers just as S brings the painting to life for us. We see that he is using the painting to give us a visual impression of a process. My guess is that he has much more to say about the use of the quill – what we do with it as we read, something about the work *inherent* in it.

Following this exercise and the discussion about it, I ask students to look back at the first Steiner excerpt. I want them to follow suit with the chart, filling in only the first two columns. I reserve *significance* for a class or for a small group discussion. In preparation for the initial chart work for the more difficult passage, I want students to think about these questions: *How does the* **style** *tell you that the same writer has created both texts? How can what you learned earlier about* **content** *help you understand this more complex passage? What is Steiner telling us about reading in this passage that he did not tell us in the other one?* I want students to grapple with the notion that we must read as if the text has meaning and that there is something inexhaustible about a serious text, something that makes us eager to interpret it, puzzling out its meaning. As readers we must learn to be comfortable with the fact that everything we need to know about a challenging text is not always spelled out. The meaning and the effect of the text call us to be responsive. I want them to see and understand that we can only grasp the essence of the text if we are rigorous, critical readers who want badly to come to terms with the whole text (all the words and sentences) – what is there and what is suggested. I want them to know that we cannot grasp everything all at once, that a rich text offers a cause for investigation rather than a reason for turning away in frustration.

Writing as Representation, Writing as Composition

Our prescribed written work during this essay about reading has necessarily focused on ways writing can help us learn; writing in this sense is inherent in all of the reading exercises we have considered. Often we're simply writing down words, keeping track of evidence, making notes about associations, but on other occasions we have been required to write one-sentence translations of whole paragraphs, or even one-paragraph representations of whole essays. When we move *from* functional writing associated with listing and cataloguing *to* writing that embraces and reveals our thinking, we move directly into the realm of conceptualizing – the kind of higher-order thinking we first saw as we moved naturally from physical verification of detail in a Magritte painting to a representation of what the painting allowed us to see in our mind's eye but could not see explicitly in the painting itself – something of value that could not, and cannot, be reduced to mere summary or paraphrase.

The more demanding and comprehensive critical reading and writing that we're aiming to teach our students encapsulates the work of the investigative, analytical mind working in conjunction with imaginative and creative powers to express not only what a given text (or body of texts) says to us, but also what we think of those discovered ideas. It is not the aim of this essay to work out a set of maps for the kind of work that turns our critical reading into a corresponding final form (essay, argument, article, laboratory report) worthy of our own serious reading, but it should follow from the methodology of our reading that we need a repertoire of exercises that can lead students not only to read critically a given body of work, but also to bring that body of work into a form that will do justice to the reading that we have done. That form can take many shapes, but it will almost always depend on the tripartite structure (Beginning, Middle, and Ending) that has given both shape and meaning to the texts we have been reading. Just how those final products work within the tripartite structure depends on many variables, but the one constant that informs all of our writing is relatively simple: what we have to say about our investigative reading must be developed so that our intended audience will know what we have learned and what we have to say about that body of evidence. We know too that if we are to delight in that written work of our own, we have to learn to write sentences and paragraphs that often mean more than they say explicitly. We have to help our students learn, through a series of well-designed exercises, how to create their own provocative structures of meaning.

Reading stirs our minds, gives us information about a given subject, fosters our own ideas, and entices us to express those ideas in intriguing ways. As Anne Carson reminds us in *Eros* (1986), reading sets us on a chase that "emits a light like knowledge"; it creates in us, under the best of circumstances, a charged desire to know more and to translate that light into imaginative and persuasive language that will both delight and persuade our readers.

References

Berger, J. (1993). The white bird. In *Sense of sight* (pp. 5–12). New York: Random House.

Carson, A. (1986/2014). *Eros: The bittersweet*. Princeton, NJ: Princeton University Press.

Forster, E. M. (1951). Anonymity: An inquiry. In *Two cheers for democracy* (pp. 77–88). New York: Harcourt.

Kermode, F. (1993). Divination. In *The ordering mirror: Readers and contexts* (pp. 21–41). New York: Fordham University Press.

Rico, G. (2000). *Creating recreations*. Spring, TX: Absey & Co.

Stangl, M. (2011). When Tom sees Jerry. In Pat C. Hoy II et al. (eds.), *Mercer Street: A collection of essays from the expository writing program* (pp. 13–19). Mechanicsburg, PA: Fry Communications.

Steiner, G. (1996a). Real presences. In *No passion spent* (pp. 20–39). New Haven, CT: Yale University Press.

Steiner, G. (1996b). The uncommon reader. In *No passion spent* (pp. 1–19). New Haven, CT: Yale University Press.

3

A Shared Horizon

Critical Reading and Digital Natives
Anton Borst

Is critical reading under threat in the digital age? Does microblogging spell the eventual end of longer-form analysis and argument as dominant cultural forms? Will tomorrow's "digital natives" be unable to construct a thought longer than 140 characters? However hyperbolic such questions may sound, teachers have reason to worry about the future of learning when students increasingly turn to the Web for information instead of the library, and too often appear to pay more attention to their smartphones than to what is said in class. What can a teacher do, particularly when the trend among school and university administrations today is to *increase* rather than diminish the presence of technology in the classroom?

Among instructors who share these concerns, a common tactic is to issue prohibitions, two of the most common in my experience being to forbid the use of devices in class and to forbid the use of Wikipedia or other Web-based sources in conducting research. As a college instructor I have employed variations of both policies, and while I would not question the need for them in certain contexts, I do question the reasoning behind them when issued reactively, as seemingly the only solution to technology's distractions. I have come to believe that while such blanket prohibitions may serve the teacher in the short term, in the long term they do not serve the student, because they do not help students become more critical readers and users of digital technology.

Critical Reading Across the Curriculum, Volume 1: Humanities, First Edition.
Edited by Robert DiYanni and Anton Borst.
© 2017 John Wiley & Sons, Inc. Published 2017 by John Wiley & Sons, Inc.

Before I describe my approach to promoting critical engagement with technology in the classroom, it will help to examine some of the broader assumptions that may already shape our view of how digital technology impacts reading. Too often, in the discourse surrounding technology and education, we are left with only two positions from which to engage the issue: technophile or Luddite. A necessity or a distraction; an essential means for engaging students or a desperate attempt to cater to shortening attention spans; an investment in the future or a wasting of already tight budgets: depending on the educators you ask, and depending on their mood that day, the role of technology in higher education might be classified under any – or all – of these categories. They have all felt true to me at one time or another, sometimes virtually all at once, even though I've worked in the field of instructional technology for half a decade and incorporate digital media in my literature and writing classes. Despite my enthusiasm for technology in the classroom, my views on the topic thus remain unsettled. F. Scott Fitzgerald once described a "first-rate intelligence" as "the ability to hold two opposed ideas in the mind at the same time, and still retain the ability to function" (1945, p. 69). In the present case, five or six or a dozen notions may be held in mind at once, but I am, for the time being at least, still functioning.

Fitzgerald's words touch on a crucial aspect of "critical thinking," namely the ability to fully inhabit arguments and their counter-positions so that a deeper understanding – if not a settling of the argument – might evolve. Many education reformers identify the development of critical thinking skills as an essential but too often neglected outcome of education at all levels, and apologists for the humanities and liberal arts often cite it as the special domain of those disciplines. But as much as our institutions of learning may aim to cultivate critical thinking, they must also be made its object, and in few areas is such critical self-appraisal as urgently needed as that of education and technology. With its potential to impact institutional policy, determine the allocation of funds, and alter the very nature of the teaching profession, the evolving relationship between education and technology inspires precisely the kind of pervasive, public, and inflated rhetoric that requires critical intervention and, more specifically, *critical reading*.

Beyond the latest-trend stories covering the issue in national news outlets, beyond the sales pitches of new edutech vendors, the discourse surrounding education and technology can become overheated even among those authorities whose presumed role is to set the standard of critical analysis: academics themselves. Given the fact that our students will be living and striving in a world ever more saturated with technology, it is crucial that we not only foster their critical reading skills, but also show them how to apply those skills to the new technologies that increasingly mediate their learning and their socializing. Moreover, because we, as teachers, instructional technologists, administrators, and education professionals generally, unavoidably have a vested interest in how technology may change the nature of what we do, it is equally important for us to read critically our own assumptions about the role of technology in our classrooms.

To provoke such engagement, I will walk through a critical reading of one major theme of the discourse surrounding the topic of education and technology. Because the term "digital native" is so rhetorically loaded and immediately relevant to students (it purports to define them), analyzing the concept can provide a productive discussion and writing prompt for students in composition, new media composition, and digital writing courses. Aimed at teachers as well as learners, the following discussion demonstrates how I model critical analysis for my first- and second-year university students, particularly in the context of reading and writing.

Critically Reading the Digital Native

Education and technology as a topic, of course, already demands the kind of critical intervention I emphasize whenever students begin new projects in my writing classes. The topic is much too broad to have any real meaning. What is meant by "technology," for example? Blogging platforms and digital video tools? Social media? The MOOC? Or technologies that have so long been regarded as essential components of the classroom that we no longer recognize them as technology: projectors, email, pen and paper, writing itself?

To focus on the discourse surrounding education and technology, I would tell my students, is a start, but nowhere near where we need to be to articulate a cogent and productive statement on our topic. Something much more specific is needed: a particular concept or theme limited enough to allow for thorough scrutiny, but rich enough to suggest further-reaching implications. The "digital native" is a fine candidate in this regard: a single phrase, a single idea that has been repeatedly invoked and debated in discussions of the general relationship between education and technology. Moreover, as the phrase so often slips into conversation (or sales pitch) with the unexamined air of common sense, it begs for critical examination.

Marc Prensky is often associated with the term, which he popularized in 2001 in a two-part article titled "Digital Natives, Digital Immigrants." In the digital age, that may as well be a century ago, and yet, as his critics continue to point out, his arguments are still waiting for supporting, research-based evidence. Prensky posits the now familiar idea that today's students have different brains than those of previous generations as a result of growing up alongside computers, video games, cellphones, and many other digital technologies. According to Prensky, these new brains, which are accustomed to receiving "information really fast," tend to "parallel process and multi-task," and prefer "random access (like hypertext)" over linear delivery of information, as well as "games over 'serious' work" (2001a, pp. 3–4). Consequently, traditional forms of education fail to reach students who have been shaped by what Prensky refers to as the "twitch speed" of "video games and MTV" (2001a, p. 4). This disconnect between old modes and new minds, asserts Prensky, is the "most fundamental cause" of "the decline of education in the US" (2001a, p. 1).

As the last claim illustrates, "Digital Natives, Digital Immigrants" at times approaches the register of jeremiad. "A really big *discontinuity* has taken place" between the generations, he states, and on the order of a "singularity" (2001a, p. 1). The profound cognitive changes between the digital generation and its analog predecessors "very likely" betoken corresponding physical changes in the brain (2001a, p. 1). In the second installment of his article, he asserts again that, "almost certainly," today's brains are "*physiologically different*" than those of people born before the diffusion of digital technology (2001b, p. 4)

The deployment of claims so sweeping, yet at the same time so subtly measured, allows Prensky to launch arguments that are never fully substantiated. He marshals recent research showing how the brain changes in response to stimuli throughout life, notes that social psychologists have demonstrated how people growing up in different cultural contexts think differently, and observes persuasively enough that students born since 1980 have grown up in a digitally saturated environment different from what their parents and teachers experienced. He does not provide clear evidence that connects these three facts, however: we are simply meant to conclude from these separate premises that the brains of digital natives have been shaped in fundamentally different ways than the brains of their predecessors because those predecessors inhabited a fundamentally different environment during development, and, further, that the changes in the brains of today's students necessitate a radical transformation of educational methods. (In the essay, Prensky's chief recommendation in this regard is to use video games for learning.)

Though certainly not the first or last to assert a generational digital divide (kindred theorists have written of the Net generation and millennials), Prensky remains a touchstone in criticism of the "digital native" concept as applied to education, having been one of its most significant disseminators (Smith, 2012). Scholars critical of his and similar arguments point out the lack of empirical evidence for such claims, as well as the emergence of empirical evidence undermining the notion of a universally tech-savvy age demographic (Bennett, Maton, and Kervin, 2008). Numerous focused research studies have indicated that students born in the last decades of the twentieth century are not a homogenous population in terms of the degree to which they use technology or the skill with which they use it (Jones, Ramanau, Cross, and Healing, 2010). Indeed, as Bennett et al. have argued, "It may be that there is as much variation *within* the digital native generation as *between* the generations" (2008, p. 779). Numerous studies have also cast doubt on the notion of an innate proficiency and enthusiasm for technology among millennials (Salajan, Schonwetter, and Cleghorn, 2010). Margaryan, Littlejohn, and Vojt (2011) found that the students they studied primarily used "established technologies," including Google and Wikipedia, with very few engaged in social media, blogging, or gaming. Researchers have also discovered significant digital divides along racial, gender, and socioeconomic lines within millennial populations (Hargittai, 2010). Consequently, a radical transformation of education that caters to the digitally privileged might have the unintended effect of reifying such social inequities.

Unlike Prensky, these empirical studies make limited and provable claims about precisely defined populations within the digital native cohort – populations limited by particular age group, academic discipline, and region of the globe. My own experience teaching and working as an instructional technology consultant within an urban, public university system corroborates their findings, as my millennial students have run the gamut of technological know-how. A minority of them appear more adept than me (sometimes considerably more so), and a handful appear to be already engaged in online content creation apart from the online activities I assign for class. The majority of the students are more or less adept at learning new digital platforms, but have limited knowledge of their availability. More significantly, today's students generally do not think critically about their use of technology, or about its impact on life and learning in the twenty-first century. A case in point that I suspect many college and high school instructors can relate to: unless otherwise instructed, many students misjudge and misuse Internet sources when conducting research. Often, it seems, students are not critical readers of the information they consume through digital media.

Responding to the Digital Native

To inspire students in a writing class to reflect on their place in the digital landscape, I may ask them to write, either in class or in a blog post, a response to the following prompt: "Are you a digital native? Why? What does that phrase mean to you?" I am careful not to define the term myself before they offer their own views. We will then spend ten minutes discussing their responses. If the writing took place online, they may have also commented on the posts of other students, giving us even more to work from in our in-class conversation. I will collect their responses in a list on the board, or in a blog post on the course website, so that we can keep the richness of their responses in mind as we move to the next step in critically engaging the category of "digital native."

This second step is to read Prensky's essay, either at home or in class, paying particular attention to the claims he makes, the evidence he provides for these claims, his implied assumptions, and his rhetorically charged word choices. Because the piece is so heavily laden with assumptions and claims, it may help students to fill out a table, listing his claims in one column, the evidence he provides for them in a second column, and the student's evaluation of that evidence in a third and final column ("strong," "weak," "indirect," or "nonexistent").

Asking students to consider the dearth of evidence for the claims surrounding the "digital native," while reminding them of the pervasive use of the term, may lead them to recognize that Prensky's persuasiveness, albeit superficial, lies largely in how he shapes his message in language: his tone, his diction, his appealingly clear and sweeping analogies. We might pull apart his central analogy of native versus immigrant and ask about its implications: whether Prensky's comparison between native speakers of a language and nonnative speakers, on the one hand, and young and old users of technology, on the other, is just. We might even ask students to consider what Prensky must think of immigrants, who, according to the logic of his analogy, are never able to adapt fully to their new homeland like their children, and are thus, in some sense, inescapably obsolescent. Looking at one of the studies mentioned earlier, such as Bennett et al., which includes a substantial literature review, provides a stark contrast to Prensky's mode of argumentation.

The initial writing activity leads students to think about who they are in relation to technology before encountering the frequently strident generalizations of "Digital Natives, Digital Immigrants," thus preparing them to read the essay critically. They have a stake in the argument, because the argument is about them. They may have reactions to the fact that they have been defined, in essence, as consumers of technology, and that this idea is shaping how they learn by influencing educational policy. They also may largely agree with the general notion that they're more capable of using technology than their parents or grandparents, that they prefer video to text, interactivity to passivity. But they may have their own ideas about how they would like technology to shape or not shape their learning; these activities and discussions will prompt them to reflect upon and voice those ideas. And, as a culminating activity, students may write short posts in which they develop their own analogies – illuminating and intellectually responsible analogies – to describe their relationship to digital technology (or some aspect of digital technology) and its effect on their learning and writing; or, better yet, what they would want that relationship to look like.

A Shared Horizon

In *What the Best College Teachers Do* (2004), Ken Bain examines the qualities of college instructors whose teaching has had a deep, lasting, positive impact on their students' thinking, perspective, and interest in the discipline being studied. Among the outcomes he looked for as evidence of such teaching was whether "students [had] developed multiple perspectives and the ability to think about their own thinking" (p.10). We want our students not only to learn what we are teaching them, but also how to learn on their own, which requires self-reflection and self-assessment. This may seem obvious to some – even the most practical and applied subjects are constantly updated with new information – but the "transmission of information" model of education continues to persist in certain quarters. Because thinking and reading are increasingly digitally mediated, facilitating critical conversations about student reading practices at key junctures throughout the semester has become part of my effort to cultivate self-reflective learners in the courses I teach. These conversations often involve sharing my own practices and experience as a reader and researcher.

Having been born just on the other side of the digital divide in the mid-1970s, I sometimes wonder whether my own age demographic does not hold a certain advantage over the so-called "natives." I grew up playing Nintendo and watching MTV, but I also watched these things come into being, and glimpsed the world that had gone on before without them. This perspective in time, therefore, has the potential to prevent these media from appearing completely naturalized to me, whereas children growing up today will never know a world without tablet computers and smartphones (at least until they are superseded). As media theorist Marshall McLuhan once wrote, "One thing about which fish know exactly nothing is water, since they have no anti-environment which would enable them to perceive the element they live in" (1989, p. 175). From this perspective, the "natives" have as much to worry about as the "immigrants" in terms of their relationship to technology: they may be lulled into uncritically using the technology with which they are bombarded, relinquishing not so much their choice of whether or not to use emerging media as their choice of *how* to use those media – and especially their choice not *to be used by* those media.

But this line of thinking still lends too much credence to some of the more reductive – and divisive – implications of the "digital native/immigrant" analogy. I would like to offer a different, more generative analogy that invites collaboration between teachers and learners, one that blends digital and analog classroom practices, and that acknowledges millennials (and whoever may follow them) as individuals rather than an oversimplified demographic unit: digital media as a "shared horizon." Students and instructors face an ever-approaching, ever-receding, horizon of emergent media, digital or otherwise. While individual students and instructors may appear closer to or farther from that line relative to one another, relative to the horizon itself their differences in position are negligible. Moving one's position is far from impossible, though some may find themselves more advantageously placed than others for many reasons in addition to age. More important, the line itself is always moving and the nature of what is emerging always changing. We are left collectively – teacher and student alike – to question, adapt to, and shape the course of future developments in media. Students need to expend as much effort, and need as much help, keeping up with their digital world as instructors do.

The multi-part exercise previously described is thus intended to help locate both learners and teachers within the digital landscape. It provides students with a critical distance from which to examine their current relationship to digital media; and, ultimately, it gives them the opportunity to define for themselves what they want that relationship to be or become. It also benefits the teacher, doing what every well-designed, effective assignment does: provides the instructor with a means of assessment – not only to evaluate students, but to calibrate the instructor's teaching. It gives the teacher a snapshot of her students' digital literacy, as well as of their ability to evaluate arguments, think creatively, and write with agency, all of which contribute to critical reading skills.

Devices, Screens, and Digital Native Reading Practices

"Devices" – laptops, smartphones, tablets – place the collected knowledge of the world at students' fingertips, yet have the capacity to drain completely the powers of attention and concentration that would make any of that information meaningful. When teaching literature, I frequently ask students to look up difficult words online as we work through texts in class, rather than give them the definitions myself, in order to inculcate the long-term habits that will make them better readers and writers. This practice also serves to guide and encourage their use of invaluable online resources, both Web-based (e.g. *Dictionary.com*) and library-curated (e.g. the *Oxford English Dictionary*). But I also recognize the potential for distraction inherent in "screens," how students checking social media on their laptops distract not only themselves, but also those sitting around them. Though I would not argue with any teacher who therefore chooses to prohibit devices in class, or, more strategically, regulates when students may and may not have their laptops open to take notes, I currently allow my students to use their devices, largely because they may be using digital versions of the class readings (some of which I provide as PDFs or links), and because I want to help them become critically engaged users of technology in and outside the classroom.

But why read on screens to begin with? Studies suggest that reading on screens promotes scrolling, skimming, and scanning at the expense of comprehension and deep thinking; the presence of links, and the inherent overabundance of information online, compounds the problem of speed with distraction (Konnikova, 2014). According to other studies, reading onscreen requires more mental and physical effort than reading the printed page, and thus detrimentally affects comprehension; experiments found that extended periods of reading on the brightly lit screens of smartphones and tablets, for instance, "can cause eyestrain, headaches and blurred vision" (Jabr, 2013).

As a teacher as well as a reader, I am primarily concerned by digital texts for their potential effect on deep and critical reading. The mere sight of links, regardless of whether a reader intends to click any, has been shown to impede comprehension by constantly requiring the brain to make micro-judgments about whether to click them (Carr, 2011, p. 122). I also worry about the inability to annotate electronic texts, annotation being a vital component of critical reading. I treat the physical books in my personal library like notebooks, covering their pages with marginalia, underlining, and asterisks. Though I read many academic articles as PDFs onscreen, if I plan to write about them or otherwise seriously engage them, I print them out to mark them up. Moreover, like so many of us, I simply prefer reading physical books.

But I have been cautious about imposing my predilection for print on students. If I am skeptical about the "digital native" concept in its more extreme incarnations, I am nevertheless circumspect about the fact that, yes, I have not grown up in the same way, in the same environment as my millennial students. In fact some research suggests that, barring access to the Internet, onscreen reading does not differ from print reading in its impact on comprehension (Konnikova, 2014). And some theorists claim that online reading – to the extent that it does encourage habits of skimming, scanning, and keyword-searching potentially at odds with close reading – fosters skills essential for navigating the unprecedented scope of today's digital archive – skills that can be (and have been) productively applied to the print archive as well. Citing James Sosnoski's notion of "hyperreading," which he describes as "reader-directed, screen-based, computer-assisted reading" (quoted in Hayles, 2010, p. 66), as well as her own related notion of "hyperattention," Kathleen Hayles argues:

> Deep attention is essential for coping with complex phenomena such as mathematical theorems, challenging literary works, and complex musical compositions; hyperattention is useful for its flexibility in switching between different information streams, its quick grasp of the gist of material, and its ability to move rapidly among and between different kinds of texts. (p. 72)

The problem may not be hyperattention itself, but hyperattention to the exclusion of deep attention. Deep attention is, of course, essential to my teaching and reading of literature, but my work as a scholar and teacher also relies considerably on "hyperattention," not only to keep up with the deluge of daily news, but to conduct research, to familiarize myself with new fields of knowledge, and to pursue interdisciplinary projects. Both sets of skills need careful articulation and validation for students, and may not have been part of their previous formal education. Even if they have been, emerging technologies will continue to challenge and complicate what it means to read, critically or otherwise, for teachers as well as students, requiring new articulations of effective reading practice in the classroom.

Consequently, I continue to reflect on, modify, and experiment with my own reading practices, several years ago acquiring an e-reader and more recently making an effort to read book-length texts from my smartphone. The former's annotation tools increasingly impress me, assuaging many of my concerns about students being able to annotate digital texts. In addition to highlighting and note-taking, certain settings add entirely new layers of information to the reading experience, such as a function displaying what other readers have underlined, providing a glimpse of a book's reception by the larger reading public. While possessing essentially the same functionality, my smartphone has proven less satisfying for reading books, largely because of the size and illumination of the screen, though it serves as my primary source for news journalism. Despite my openness to reading on devices, I still favor printed texts for longer and more intellectually engaging books, and almost always for books I plan to write about. But if my students, regardless of age, prefer e-books, who am I to argue as long as they read the books and come to class ready to discuss them?

Some scientific evidence suggests that my predilection for the printed word may be more than a matter of personal preference, and may actually have a basis in how the physical features of the book aid comprehension and memory. As Ferris Jabr in *Scientific American* explains:

> When we read, we construct a mental representation of the text. The exact nature of such representations remains unclear, but some researchers think they are similar to the mental maps we create of terrain – such as mountains and trails – and of indoor physical spaces, such as apartments and offices. Both anecdotally and in published studies, people report that when trying to locate a particular passage in a book, they often remember where in the text it appeared. Much as we might recall that we passed the red farmhouse near the start of a hiking trail before we started climbing uphill through the forest, we remember that we read about Mr. Darcy rebuffing Elizabeth Bennet at a dance on the bottom left corner of the left-hand page in one of the earlier chapters of Jane Austen's *Pride and Prejudice*. (Jabr, 2015)

The phenomenon of mentally mapping physical texts is not restricted to digital immigrants, and research surveys indicate that digital natives actually prefer distraction-free printed books to e-texts. While covering such seemingly counter-intuitive research results, a *Washington Post* reporter recorded one college student explaining that print texts allowed him to build "a physical map in my mind of where things are" (Rosenwald, 2015). Of course, whether a college student would make the same response ten or twenty years from now remains to be seen.

Conclusion

Such findings have not led me to ban devices from my classroom. On the contrary, I find my trust in the capacities of my students and myself to reflect productively on our own reading practices confirmed. Developing abilities to use reading technology effectively will not be any more automatic than developing those needed to read print, and the quality of reading may be different or require different kinds of effort. All reading is effortful and demanding, and talking with students about their reading practices, whether in print or on screen, online or off, helps ensure that deep, critical reading happens, regardless of medium. Sharing and demystifying our reading practices can prompt students to reflect more critically on their own, and to develop practices that work best for them, even if these practices don't ultimately mirror ours. Simply prohibiting the use of certain media or methods ends critical engagement; it fails to equip students with tools they will need to read attentively online or onscreen when they inevitably must, and to remain mindful in distraction-filled digital environments.

As a consequence of discussing modes and means of reading in class, students may be moved to read everything in hardcopy, or they may read on their tablets but disconnect from the Internet and take more careful notes than they had previously, or they may discover the potential of their e-reader's word-search function. By prioritizing the principles of critical reading, while keeping those principles in dialogue with a variety of practices for realizing them, students can develop the skills needed to navigate a digital environment that will continue to change rapidly after they graduate. As instructors, we too must constantly calibrate our teaching to navigate the ever-changing classroom, whether those changes relate to broad cultural and technological trends, or to the fact that, every semester, a different set of human beings sits before us. Listening to students will provide the only accurate picture of how they read today. And reflecting, with them, on our own reading practices will help teacher and learner alike begin to reckon with what it means to be a digital native.

References

Bain, K. (2004). *What the best college teachers do*. Cambridge, MA: Harvard University Press.

Bennett, S., Maton, K., and Kervin, L. (2008). The "digital natives" debate: A critical review of the evidence. *British Journal of Educational Technology*, 39(5), 775–786. doi: 10.1111/j.1467-8535.2007.00793.x.

Carr, N. (2011). *The shallows: What the Internet is doing to our brains*. New York: W. W. Norton.

Fitzgerald, F. S. (1945). *The crack-up*. New York: New Directions Publishing.

Hargittai, E. (2010). Digital na(t)ives? Variation in Internet skills and uses among members of the "net generation." *Sociological Inquiry*, 80(1), 92–113. doi: 10.1111/j.1475-682X.200900317.x.

Hayles, N. K. (2010). How we read: Close, hyper, machine. *ADE Bulletin*, 150, 62–79. doi: 10.1632/ade.150.62.

Jabr, F. (2015). Why the brain prefers paper. *Scientific American*, 309(5), 48–53.

Jones, C., Ramanau, R., Cross, S., and Healing, G. (2010). Net generation or digital natives: Is there a distinct new generation entering university? *Computers & Education*, 54, 722–732. doi: 10.1016/j.compedu.2009.09.022.

Konnikova, M. (2014). Being a better online reader. *The New Yorker* (July 16). http://www.newyorker.com/science/maria-konnikova/being-a-better-online-reader (accessed September 27, 2016).

Margaryan, A., Littlejohn, A., and Vojt, G. (2011). Are digital natives a myth or reality? University students' use of digital technologies. *Computers & Education*, 56, 429–440. doi: 10.1016/j.compedu.2010.09.004.

McLuhan, M. (1989). *War and peace in the global village*. New York: Touchstone.

Prensky, M. (2001a). Digital natives, digital immigrants, part 1. *On the Horizon*, 9(5), 1–6.

Prensky, M. (2001b). Digital natives, digital immigrants, part 2: Do they really think differently? *On the Horizon*, 9(6), 1–6.

Rosenwald, M. S. (2015). Why digital natives prefer reading in print. Yes, you read that right. *The Washington Post* (February 22). https://www.washingtonpost.com (accessed September 27, 2016).

Salajan, F. D., Schonwetter, D. J., and Cleghorn, B. M. (2010). Student and faculty inter-generational digital divide: Fact or fiction? *Computers & Education*, 55, 1393–1403. doi: 10.1016/j.compedu.2010.06.017.

Smith, E. E. (2012). The digital native debate in higher education: A comparative analysis of recent literature. *Canadian Journal of Learning and Technology*, 38(3), 1–18.

Part II

Critical Reading in the Disciplines

4

Critical Reading and Thinking

Rhetoric and Reality
Lawrence Scanlon

To read and think critically is to read and think rhetorically. While students may not at first realize it, whenever they look and listen, whenever they read and think and respond, they engage the world rhetorically. Another way of saying this is that the rhetorical world confronts them everywhere they go – on the bus or train, in their cars or school corridors, at the movies or in a museum, at the checkout line at the store. On their laptops and on their smartphones in the "privacy" of their homes, they enter rhetorical transactions with their culture. As they negotiate these transactions, they respond with "the faculty of observing in any given case the available means of persuasion," as Aristotle defined rhetoric so long ago (1984, p. 2155). Or, as Kenneth Burke puts it, they attend to "the use of words by human agents to form attitudes or induce actions in other human agents" (1962/1969, p. 41). While that "faculty of observing" might not always be conscious, it is nonetheless present in ordinary situations. A brief passage from literature provides an example of the process at work.

In "Dead Confederates," a contemporary short story by Ron Rash, a character named Wesley Davidson attempts to bring the narrator of the story, a co-worker on the DOT road crew in need of money, into collusion on what looks to be a questionable enterprise. Wesley draws him in:

Critical Reading Across the Curriculum, Volume 1: Humanities, First Edition.
Edited by Robert DiYanni and Anton Borst.
© 2017 John Wiley & Sons, Inc. Published 2017 by John Wiley & Sons, Inc.

"I ain't hearing a word till tomorrow," he says. "Think about how a thousand dollars can put some padding in your wallet. Think about what that money can do for your momma."

He says the words about Momma last for he knows that notion will hang heavy on me if nothing else does.

The narrator agrees. He says to Wesley:

"When?" I ask.

"Night, of course," he says, "a clear night when the moon is waxed up full. That way we'll not give ourselves away with a flashlight."

Him thinking it out enough to use moonlight gives me some confidence in him, makes me think it could work. Because that's the other thing bothering me besides the right and the wrong of it. If we get caught we'd be for sure doing some jailhouse time.

"I've done thought this thing out from every which angle," Wesley says. (2014, pp. 274–275)

Our students often find themselves in the positions of Rash's characters. Surely Wesley wouldn't be able to explain his rhetoric – doubtless he would not even know that he is practicing it. Nor would the narrator realize he's performing rhetorical analysis in recognizing and indicating the appeals to pathos, logos, and ethos that the speaker, Wesley, employs. But we do see that the narrator is thinking critically. In this story, as in the lives of our students, rhetoric's use and rhetorical analysis both are natural processes, for rhetoric is rooted in *"the use of language as a symbolic means of inducing cooperation in beings that by nature respond to symbols"* (Burke, p. 43).

Of course we wish to bring our students to a place of understanding beyond that of Rash's narrator, to a place where they can think, read, speak, and also write clearly and cogently about rhetoric and argument. We want them to understand and talk intelligently about the natural processes of rhetoric and criticism. Simply stated, we might say that rhetoric is the art of persuasion and argument the practice. As Hepzibah Roskelly puts it, "We employ rhetoric whether we're conscious of it or not, but becoming conscious of how rhetoric works can transform speaking, reading, and writing, making us more successful and able communicators and more discerning audiences" (p. 7). Once students come to see that *rhetoric* is not an abstruse historical term but an everyday practice, they not only begin to understand rhetoric in the works they read and the messages they receive, but they may also begin to practice the art of rhetoric themselves in the writing they produce. The more conscious their understanding of rhetoric becomes, the more clear their reading and thinking will be – and increasingly so as they shape their writing to express this new understanding. Moreover, through this process, they will come to see that "shape itself has persuasive force" (Crider, 2007, p. 58).

Rhetorical Challenges

Of course, before we continue, we need to be clear about what we mean by "critical." The very word "critical" may be misunderstood by many of our students, who know its negative associations only, i.e. those having to do with faultfinding or with serious injury. They have to come to understand a critical attitude as one based on reasoned deliberation and characterized by careful judgment. And as with the word "critical," the very idea of "rhetoric" is new if not mysterious or misleading for students at first. They may think rhetoric is some esoteric subject beyond their experience, or – at least those among them who attend to political speech – that it refers to obfuscation, deception, or manipulation. But as Kenneth Burke reminds us, "the basic function of rhetoric … is certainly not 'magical'" (p. 41). The less "magical" or mysterious rhetoric becomes for students, the better.

Part of the difficulty students face is the language in which the subject comes to them. At first, many students think (and may even be taught) that rhetoric is about terms. "There's a metaphor," they will report, "and here's a juxtaposition." Such a "Where's Waldo?" approach to rhetorical analysis will not help students who do not know how to connect those features to meaning and purpose.

Still, why is it that students should have difficulty with what should be a natural process? One reason is that they have been taught for years that English, as a subject in school, means reading poems and stories and novels and plays – works of *belles lettres* – and discussing and writing about them. They learn fast that they have to "interpret" them. We teach our students in English classes as if we are preparing them to be literary critics. In Gerald Graff's characterization of our enterprise in *Professing Literature*, "the very phrase *teaching literature* is misleading, since what teachers and students produce in literature courses is not literature, but *criticism* – that is, discourse about literature" (2007, p. 19).

Another reason is that our students have spent years trying to write almost exclusively in a genre they have not read and do not read, namely the essay. For them to write intelligently about written texts, should we not provide models for them to read? Since most of the reading they have done has been of *belles lettres*, why not have them read writing about written works – for example Samuel Johnson or Virginia Woolf on Shakespeare, Orwell on Dickens, D. H. Lawrence on Hawthorne or Twain, or Alice Walker on Zora Neale Hurston? We teachers have to help our students read rhetorically, whatever texts they encounter. For as even the *McGuffy Reader* of 1921 states: "there may be eloquent *readers*, as well as eloquent *speakers*" (p. 59). And ultimately, perhaps, those readers and speakers may become eloquent *writers*. Stephen King opens his essay, "Reading to Write": "If you want to be a writer, you must do two things above all others: Read a lot and write a lot" (2014, p. 221). "The more you read," he later elaborates, "the less apt you are to make a fool of yourself with your pen or word processor" (p. 225). Reading, reading, reading, yes, and writing, writing, writing, as well. As our students do both, they can benefit immensely from our guided instruction.

I often tell my students, I am teaching you to write *not the way students write but the way writers write*. Or as David Jolliffe has frequently said in many contexts, students should produce "essays and not exam responses." To effect such a result, students need models – examples of writing about writing. The best models for students are not necessarily works of literary criticism, but rather discursive and argumentative writing about literature. Since those texts more nearly resemble the kinds of writing that we demand from our students, they will serve as better models than literary criticism. They also serve as excellent prompts for student writing.

One method for moving students away from their accustomed approach to analyzing literature is to have them use their reading to support an argument that responds to what another writer says. Here are two examples of such assignments, based on a classroom reading of Anton Chekhov's "Gooseberries" and D. H. Lawrence's "The Rocking Horse Winner."

[1] Based on your reading of Anton Chekhov's "Gooseberries," write an essay in which you defend, challenge, or qualify the following observations by Virginia Woolf. As evidence, use specific references to the text of the story.

Our first impressions of Chekhov are not of simplicity but of bewilderment. What is the point of it, and why does he make a story out of this? we ask as we read story after story ... But is it the end, we ask? We have rather the feeling that we have overrun our signals; or it is as if a tune had stopped short without the expected chords to close it. These stories are inconclusive, we say, and proceed to frame a criticism based upon the assumption that stories ought to conclude in a way that we recognise. In so doing, we raise the question of our own fitness as readers. Where the tune is familiar and the end emphatic – lovers united, villains discomfited, intrigues exposed – as it is in most Victorian fiction, we can scarcely go wrong, but where the tune is unfamiliar and the end a note of interrogation or merely the information that they went on talking, as it is in Chekhov, we need a very daring and alert sense of literature to make us hear the tune, and in particular those last notes which complete the harmony. (Woolf, 1948)

[2] Write a well-reasoned essay that supports or qualifies the following observation that Aldous Huxley makes about D. H. Lawrence. Refer specifically to the text of "The Rocking Horse Winner" as you support your argument.

Lawrence's special and characteristic gift was an extraordinary sensitiveness to what Wordsworth called "unknown modes of being." He was always intensely aware of the mystery of the world, and the mystery was always for him a numen, divine. Lawrence could never forget, as most of us almost continuously forget, the dark presence of the otherness that lies beyond the boundaries of man's conscious mind. This special sensibility was accompanied by a prodigious power of rendering the immediately experienced otherness in terms of literary art. (Huxley, 1959)

Such assignments demand that students read closely and critically both the primary texts and the commentary by other writers. Essays written in response to such prompts must incorporate the literary analysis students are familiar with into their rhetorical analysis of the commentary, and then use that information in the arguments they develop. Close critical reading and thinking are key, as Barnet and Bedau (2014) suggest, for "critical thinking means questioning not only the assumptions of others but also questioning your own assumptions" (p. 5). Students will have to understand the assumptions held by Woolf or Huxley as they read, and interrogate their own assumptions about reading and literature as they write. Students will need to bring their understanding of the short story to their consideration of the commentary on that story. In effect they will create their own metacommentary as they ask themselves questions such as, What do I understand of the story? What do I understand of the commentary? What assumptions do I share with Woolf (or Huxley)? Do I disagree? Why? How does my view differ? Has my view of the story changed? Has it been modified or enhanced or augmented? Such a process makes students critical of their own first responses as they think about their own thinking.

Ways of Reading

It is important to recognize several ways of reading a text: semantic, syntactic, aesthetic, thematic, and pragmatic. If we regard these different approaches as levels, the first would be the semantic, which asks what the text says. Students will report their comprehension; they will engage in summary and paraphrase. Next is the syntactic level, which addresses how a text is formed, and requires recognition of genre and stylistic analysis of tropes and schemes. An aesthetic reading then considers a text's pleasures and a thematic reading explores its significance, requiring reader response and literary analysis. In general, we find that students are quite accustomed to these approaches – especially to the first four, which have been the stuff of their English coursework for years. They know or at least recognize them, especially from their considerations of poetry.

But there is an additional approach with which students will be less familiar – the pragmatic. Considering a text on the pragmatic level addresses not what it says or how it says what it says, or how we like or value it, or even what its theme is, but *what it is doing*. Literature on the pragmatic level performs work in the world as it expresses itself through "performative utterances" as well as constative ones, i.e. utterances that perform as well as state (Austin, 1962/1977, pp. 32–46).[1] Considering writing this way, George Orwell speaks of his "desire to push the world in a certain direction, to alter other people's idea of the kind of society that they should strive for" (1946/2002, pp. 1082–1083). Similarly, Toni Cade Bambara says, "Writing is one of the ways I participate in struggle … Writing is one of the ways I do my work in the world" (1990, p. 322). When we take a pragmatic approach to texts, we look at what they do, that is, at what work they perform in the world.

Logos, Ethos, Pathos

The first rhetorical concern we have with any text, whether it is a written work, a painting, a cartoon, a billboard – whatever the text may be – is its *logos*, or "embodied thought." So a student should ask first: What is it about? What is its content? What does it say? What ideas does it express or suggest? Later considerations will address, of course, its organization, its reasoning, and its argument. Once a student has answered these questions, the next feature to consider is *ethos*. The student asks: Is this speaker trustworthy, credible? How can I tell? Does the speaker present good sense and good will? Does he or she begin with an automatic ethos (Abraham Lincoln,

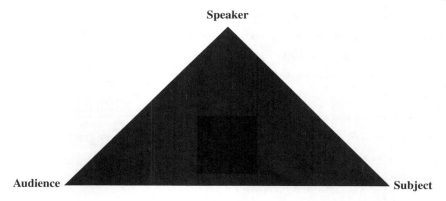

Figure 4.1 Aristotle's Rhetorical Triangle.

say, or Toni Morrison, or the American Medical Association)? If so, how is that credibility maintained? If not (an unfamiliar speaker, or a student), how is credibility established? How much does the ethos depend on the subject, context, and audience? What are the speaker's intentions? What is the text's apparent purpose? Then on to *pathos*: how does the speaker appeal to the audience? To what emotions, values, beliefs, and interests does the speaker appeal? What assumptions does the speaker hold regarding those? Do I share them? How objective or disinterested is the speaker? Does he or she have a stake involved, so to speak: something to gain or lose? With these questions in mind, the student comes to see that a text is not an "autonomous artifact," a free-standing object for analysis from a New Critical approach, but rather that its purpose, meaning, and effect all depend on the relationships indicated in Aristotle's rhetorical triangle (Figure 4.1).[2]

Demonstration: Annotating a Speech

As students bring these questions and concerns to a text, they should take notes and annotate. Since their audiences are clearly identified and their rhetorical situation is clearly evident, letters and speeches offer perfect texts for students to analyze. The passage in Figure 4.2, a speech delivered before the National American Woman Suffrage Association, Philadelphia, on July 22, 1905, by Florence Kelly, has been annotated for an analysis of its argument. The marginal annotations demonstrate the kind of attention to text that we would like to see from our students.

Having read the Kelly speech carefully and attending to the analysis in the annotations, students would be ready to perform the same tasks. I would

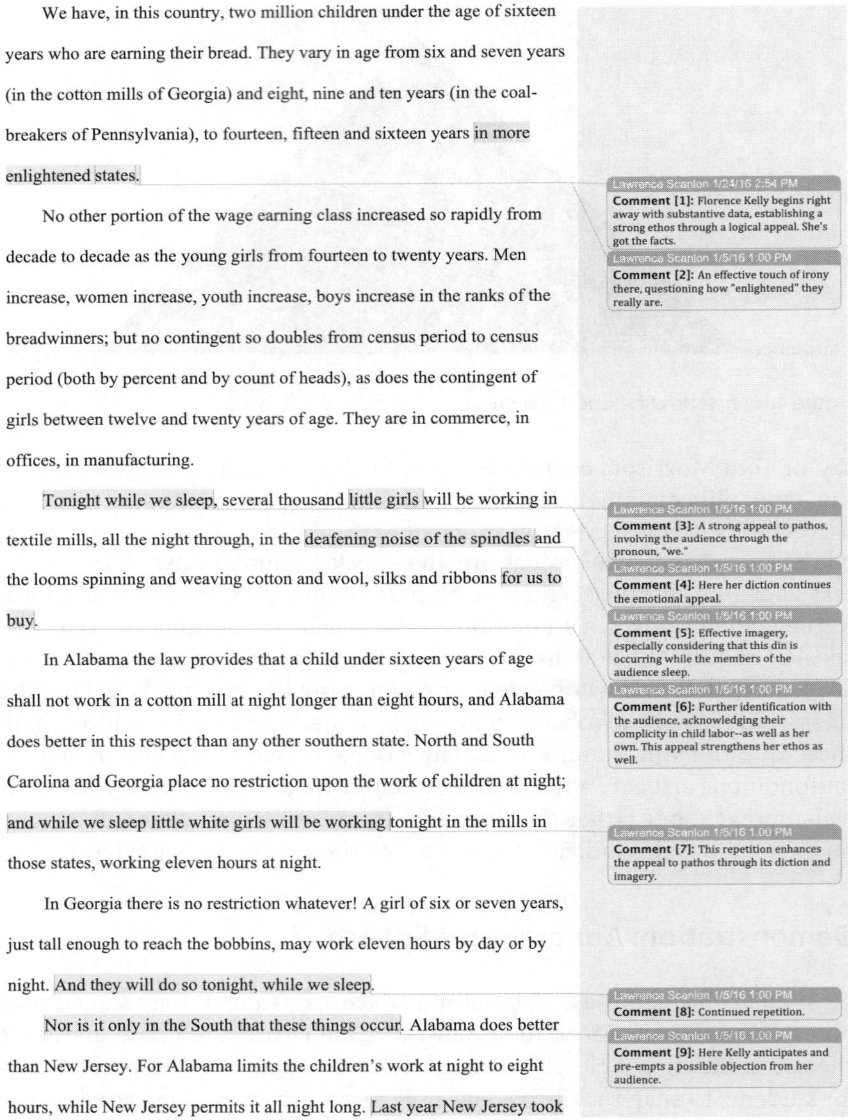

We have, in this country, two million children under the age of sixteen years who are earning their bread. They vary in age from six and seven years (in the cotton mills of Georgia) and eight, nine and ten years (in the coal-breakers of Pennsylvania), to fourteen, fifteen and sixteen years in more enlightened states.

No other portion of the wage earning class increased so rapidly from decade to decade as the young girls from fourteen to twenty years. Men increase, women increase, youth increase, boys increase in the ranks of the breadwinners; but no contingent so doubles from census period to census period (both by percent and by count of heads), as does the contingent of girls between twelve and twenty years of age. They are in commerce, in offices, in manufacturing.

Tonight while we sleep, several thousand little girls will be working in textile mills, all the night through, in the deafening noise of the spindles and the looms spinning and weaving cotton and wool, silks and ribbons for us to buy.

In Alabama the law provides that a child under sixteen years of age shall not work in a cotton mill at night longer than eight hours, and Alabama does better in this respect than any other southern state. North and South Carolina and Georgia place no restriction upon the work of children at night; and while we sleep little white girls will be working tonight in the mills in those states, working eleven hours at night.

In Georgia there is no restriction whatever! A girl of six or seven years, just tall enough to reach the bobbins, may work eleven hours by day or by night. And they will do so tonight, while we sleep.

Nor is it only in the South that these things occur. Alabama does better than New Jersey. For Alabama limits the children's work at night to eight hours, while New Jersey permits it all night long. Last year New Jersey took

Comment [1]: Florence Kelly begins right away with substantive data, establishing a strong ethos through a logical appeal. She's got the facts.

Comment [2]: An effective touch of irony there, questioning how "enlightened" they really are.

Comment [3]: A strong appeal to pathos, involving the audience through the pronoun, "we."

Comment [4]: Here her diction continues the emotional appeal.

Comment [5]: Effective imagery, especially considering that this din is occurring while the members of the audience sleep.

Comment [6]: Further identification with the audience, acknowledging their complicity in child labor--as well as her own. This appeal strengthens her ethos as well.

Comment [7]: This repetition enhances the appeal to pathos through its diction and imagery.

Comment [8]: Continued repetition.

Comment [9]: Here Kelly anticipates and pre-empts a possible objection from her audience.

Figure 4.2 Florence Kelly's speech to the National American Woman Suffrage Association, annotated.

a long backward step. A good law was repealed which had required women

and [children] to stop work at six in the evening and at noon on Friday.

Now, therefore, in New Jersey, boys and girls, after their 14th birthday,

enjoy the pitiful privilege of working all night long.

> Comment [10]: Kelly admonishes her audience to be on guard, since on social issues if we are not alert we can even move backward!

In Pennsylvania, until last May it was lawful for children, 13 years of

age, to work twelve hours at night. A little girl, on her thirteenth birthday,

could start away from her home at half past five in the afternoon, carrying

her pail of midnight luncheon as happier people carry their midday

luncheon, and could work in the mill from six at night until six in the

morning, without violating any law of the Commonwealth.

> Comment [11]: Nice ironic touch, alliterative too

> Comment [12]: Powerful imagery. Effective comparison, and sad irony at the end.

If the mothers and the teachers in Georgia could vote, would the

Georgia Legislature have refused at every session for the last three years to

stop the work in the mills of children under twelve years of age?

Would the New Jersey Legislature have passed that shameful repeal bill

enabling girls of fourteen years to work all night, if the mothers in New

Jersey were enfranchised? Until the mothers in the great industrial states are

enfranchised, we shall none of us be able to free our consciences from

participation in this great evil. No one in this room tonight can feel free from

such participation. The children make our shoes in the shoe factories; they

knit our stockings, our knitted underwear in the knitting factories. They spin

and weave our cotton underwear in the cotton mills. Children braid straw for

our hats, they spin and weave the silk and velvet wherewith we trim our

hats. They stamp buckles and metal ornaments of all kinds, as well as pins

and hat-pins. Under the sweating system, tiny children make artificial

flowers and neckwear for us to buy. They carry bundles of garments from

the factories to the tenements, little beasts of burden, robbed of school life

that they may work for us.

> Comment [13]: Effective rhetorical question introducing Kelly's main idea and central thesis. It's nice the way one rhetorical question leads to the other, emphasizing her point. Effective geographic juxtaposition of Georgia and New Jersey. Kelly suggests that geographical distinctions are rendered null when talking of mothers of children. Strong appeal to pathos.

> Comment [14]: Kelly's thesis statement, asserting her central claim.

> Comment [15]: Powerful phrase.

> Comment [16]: Direct address, again addressing the audience's complicity in the "great evil." Wow, she's serious!

> Comment [17]: Very particular. The specificity makes the listener *see*.

> Comment [18]: Effective imagery

> Comment [19]: Occurrence of "our" six times and "us" twice. Again, including her audience, appealing to pathos.

We do not wish this. We prefer to have our work done by men and

women. But we are almost powerless. Not wholly powerless, however, are

citizens who enjoy the right of petition. For myself, I shall use this power in

every possible way until the right to the ballot is granted, and then I shall

continue to use both.

> Comment [20]: "We" three times, again identifying with the audience: We're all in this together!

> Comment [21]: Interesting qualifiers. The first qualification, "almost" powerless, is itself qualified: "Not wholly powerless..." Here she begins to make a distinction, moving from "we" to "I," posing a challenge to her audience before resuming the use of "we." She is suggesting that if she can do it, then so can they; they can separate themselves from and fight against the "great evil" of child labor if they strive to gain the vote.

Figure 4.2 *(Continued)*

What can we do to free our consciences? There is one line of action by which we can do much. We can enlist the workingmen on behalf of our enfranchisement just in proportion as we strive with them to free the children. No labor organization in this country ever fails to respond to an appeal for help in the freeing of the children.

For the sake of the children, for the Republic in which these children will vote after we are dead, and for the sake of our cause, we should enlist the workingmen voters, with us, in this task of freeing the children from toil!

Lawrence Scanlon 1/5/16 1:00 PM
Comment [22]: If we apply the Toulmin model of argument analysis to Kelly's argument, we might state it thus: "Because children are suffering from unfair and oppressive working conditions, we need to work for women's suffrage, since only women, and especially mothers, will vote to end such a 'great evil.'"

Lawrence Scanlon 1/5/16 1:00 PM
Comment [23]: As she concludes, she makes two strong appeals to pathos. First she suggests cooperation between men and women, and secondly, through repeated references to "the children" she enlists her audience in a noble enterprise, that of saving them.

Figure 4.2 *(Continued)*

give them a speech to analyze, such as Martin Luther King, Jr.'s "I Have a Dream" speech, Lincoln's Gettysburg Address, J. F. Kennedy's Inaugural Address, George W. Bush's 9/11 speech, or Mayor Michael Bloomberg's Ground Zero Mosque speech.

Everything's an Argument: No It's Not! Yes It Is!

If "everything's an argument," as Andrea Lunsford says in her book of that title (Lunsford and Ruszkiewicz, 2013), then useful texts are abundantly available. Letters and speeches offer excellent texts for analysis since their rhetorical situation is clear. Narrative essays are also fine choices. Three of my favorites, George Orwell's "A Hanging," Barry Lopez's "The Stone Horse," and Annie Dillard's "Living Like Weasels," present arguments, respectively, against capital punishment, for natural and artistic preservation, and for living an individual life. These texts are of particular interest because they use narrative and personal experience effectively to develop their arguments.

Once students become more adept at reading texts critically, they will be more open to making connections among texts as well. Reading works in conversation has become a common practice, thanks in part to the work of Gerald Graff and, before him, Kenneth Burke. Let's consider a few texts that address a similar subject or theme, beginning with the following passage from chapter 28 of Samuel Johnson's *Rasselas*:

On necessary and inevitable evils, which overwhelm kingdoms at once, all disputation is vain; when they happen they must be endured. But it is evident that these bursts of universal distress are more dreaded than felt; thousands and tens of thousands flourish in youth and wither in age, without the knowledge of any other than domestic evils, and share the same pleasures and vexations, whether their kings are mild or cruel, whether the armies of their country pursue their enemies or retreat before them. While Courts are disturbed with intestine competitions and ambassadors are negotiating in foreign countries, the smith still plies his anvil and the husbandman drives his plough forward; the necessaries of life are required and obtained, and the successive business of the season continues to make its wonted revolutions. (Johnson, 1968, pp. 66–67)

We could follow the *Rasselas* passage with the following pair of poems by Thomas Hardy and by W. B. Yeats:

In Time of "The Breaking of Nations"

I
Only a man harrowing clods
In a slow silent walk
With an old horse that stumbles and nods
Half asleep as they stalk.

II
Only thin smoke without flame
From the heaps of couch-grass;
Yet this will go onward the same
Though Dynasties pass.

III
Yonder a maid and her wight
Come whispering by:
War's annals will cloud into night
Ere their story die.

—Thomas Hardy

Politics

'In our time the destiny of man presents its meanings in political terms.'

Thomas Mann

How can I, that girl standing there,
My attention fix

On Roman or on Russian
Or on Spanish politics?
Yet here's a travelled man that knows
What he talks about,
And there's a politician
That has both read and thought,
And maybe what they say is true
Of war and war's alarms,
But O that I were young again
And held her in my arms!

—W. B. Yeats

With this group one might also include Breughel's painting *The Fall of Icarus* and E. B. White's essay "The Flocks We Watch By Night." The focus is on discovery, i.e. the students would have to discover and explain the common thread, and then write about that idea or theme with reference to the texts. They will notice that the Johnson and the Hardy texts share some common "characters," for example the farmer, the "husbandman" who "drives his plough forward" in Johnson's passage, and the "man harrowing clods" in Hardy's; they will also point to "kingdoms" in the former, and "dynasties" in the latter. They will see the opposition between war and strife on the one hand, and the continuation of everyday occurrences on the other.

They will suggest that the Johnson text could be taken as a statement of the "theme" of the Hardy. (I always love saying that this passage in *Rasselas* inspired Hardy to write the poem. Everyone – students and teachers alike – believes me, and starts writing it down. But the way the group did come together was simpler: reading *Rasselas*, I thought of the Hardy poem, which in turn brought the Yeats to mind.) A significant difference students will note is the romantic situation at the end of Hardy's poem between the "maid and her wight." That presence connects the Yeats poem to the Hardy, while politics and "war and war's alarms" connects all three texts. Students might see a common theme, stated thus: "We understand that in life there are sometimes great events and terrible hardships – we think of such tragic occurrences as war, disease, natural disasters – that threaten to overwhelm our lives. Impossible to resist, they must be faced. But while great events are of course important, indeed momentous, often it is the small and personal things in life – work, friendship, love – that seem to endure and enable us to carry on."

While students discover that the content (the what) and the themes (the why) might be similar in some respects from piece to piece, they also need to see how the form, genre, style, and rhetoric (the how) differ greatly from

Table 4.1 The WHY Chart: What? How? Why?

The writer (<u>verb/adverb</u>):	The writer (<u>verb/adverb</u>):	The writer (<u>verb/adverb</u>):
explains, analyzes / didactically	observes, presents, shows	reflects, considers, "sighs" / wistfully

one text to the other. As a final step in their analytical process, they would be given a template to complete for each of the three texts. Possible responses are shown in Table 4.1

Such a process aids students in thesis construction. After completing the templates, one student wrote as a thesis statement, "While Johnson explains didactically, Hardy observes and reflects. Yeats, though, sighs wistfully." A thesis statement for what turned out to be a splendid essay.

You could also group works by genre and purpose, for example, satires by Jonathan Swift or H. L. Mencken or Mark Twain with contemporary pieces, such as "Coyote vs. Acme" by Ian Frazier, or Anthony Lane's hysterically funny review of the Spice Girls movie from *The New Yorker*, or "Girl Moved to Tears by *Of Mice and Men Cliffnotes*" from *The Onion*. A third way a teacher might group texts is according to their rhetorical features or organization, which provides the basis for the following exercises.

A Suite of Exercises

Exercise 1

Students would read the entire texts from which the following excerpts are taken; they would then submit these key passages to close reading with a focus on irony, juxtaposition, and antithesis. This exercise helps students to recognize how antithesis works rhetorically, especially when they notice how different writers employ it effectively.

Here are three excerpts for student analysis:

[1] The nations of Asia and Africa are moving with jetlike speed toward gaining political independence, but we still creep at horse and buggy pace toward gaining a cup of coffee at a lunch counter.
—Martin Luther King, "Letter from a Birmingham Jail"

[2] Some writers have so confounded society with government, as to leave little or no distinction between them; whereas they are not

only different, but have different origins. Society is produced by our wants, and government by our wickedness; the former promotes our happiness positively by uniting our affections, the latter negatively by restraining our vices. The one encourages intercourse, the other creates distinctions. The first is a patron, the last a punisher.

—Thomas Paine, *Common Sense*

[3] Our moods do not believe in each other. Today I am full of thoughts and can write what I please. I see no reason why I should not have the same thought, the same power of expression, to-morrow. What I write, whilst I write it, seems the most natural thing in the world: but yesterday I saw a dreary vacuity in this direction in which now I see so much; and a month hence, I doubt not, I shall wonder who he was that wrote so many continuous pages. Alas for this infirm faith, this will not strenuous, this vast ebb of a vast flow! I am God in nature; I am a weed by the wall.

—Ralph Waldo Emerson, "Circles"

In this exercise, the students would discuss how these three writers develop their ideas through irony, juxtaposition, and antithesis. They would discover the surface features, the *what*, so to speak. It is then essential for the student to move from the *what* to the *so what*. Such a movement can be effected by using the following templates, the first of which begins with meaning, moves to surface features, and concludes with purpose or intent. The second template does the reverse. It's good practice to have students complete both templates, and then decide which is more rhetorically effective.

1 [Discussing, developing, introducing, stating …] the [idea, position, notion, thought, claim …] that _____ [name of writer or speaker] juxtaposes _____ with _____ in order to _____ .

2 In order to _____, [name of writer or speaker] juxtaposes _____ with _____, [suggesting, developing, positing, introducing …] _____.

Exercise 2

Yet another grouping of passages for rhetorical analysis may be put together by focusing on the differences between periodic and cumulative sentences. A periodic sentence withholds its independent clause until the end, after "building up" to it; a cumulative (or "loose") sentence begins with its main clause and then adds further, cumulative, information. Here are two sentences each from two different writers. In each case, the first is periodic and the second cumulative. Students would analyze each sentence and then rewrite it – if periodic, as cumulative, and if cumulative, as periodic – and discuss the effect of each. Then they would discuss the syntax as it affects the relationship of the sentence to the writer's meaning and purpose. Finally, students would discuss how sentence variety affects a writer's work.

[1] If we shall suppose that American slavery is one of those offenses which, in the providence of God, must needs come, but which, having continued through His appointed time, He now wills to remove, and that He gives to both North and South this terrible war as the woe due to those by whom the offense came, shall we discern therein any departure from those divine attributes which the believers in a living God always ascribe to Him?

—Abraham Lincoln, Second Inaugural Address

[2] It is rather for us to be here dedicated to the great task remaining before us – that from these honored dead we take increased devotion to that cause for which they gave the last full measure of devotion – that we here highly resolve that these dead shall not have died in vain – that this nation, under God, shall have a new birth of freedom – and that government of the people, by the people, for the people, shall not perish from the earth.

—Abraham Lincoln, Gettysburg Address

[3] Knowing that there exists in the minds of men a tone of feeling toward women as toward slaves, such as is expressed in the common phrase, "Tell that to women and children;" that the infinite soul can only work through them in already ascertained limits; that the gift of reason, Man's highest prerogative, is allotted to them in much lower degree; that they must be kept from mischief and melancholy by being constantly engaged in active labor, which is to be furnished and directed by those better able to think, &c., &c., – we need not multiply instances, for who can review the experience of last week without recalling words which imply, whether in jest or earnest, these views, or views like these, – knowing this, can we wonder that many reformers think that measures are not likely to be taken in

behalf of women, unless their wishes could be publicly represented by women?

—Margaret Fuller, *Woman in the Nineteenth Century*

[4] We will not speak of the innumerable instances in which profligate and idle men live upon the earnings of industrious wives; or if the wives leave them, and take with them the children, to perform the double duty of mother and father, follow from place to place, and threaten to rob them of the children, if deprived of the rights of a husband, as they call them, planting themselves in their poor lodgings, frightening them into paying tribute by taking from them the children, running into debt at the expense of these otherwise so overtasked helots.

—Margaret Fuller, *Woman in the Nineteenth Century*

Exercise 3

Students can learn a lot about the rhetorical effects of syntax by recognizing the power of the periodic sentence. Here are five effective examples of periodic sentences. Having students rewrite them as cumulative sentences will doubtless show them the advantage of the periodic.

[1] Now, if it is deemed necessary that I should forfeit my life for the furtherance of the ends of justice, and mingle my blood further with the blood of my children and with the blood of millions in this slave country whose rights are disregarded by wicked, cruel, and unjust enactments, I submit; so let it be done!

—John Brown, "Last Speech"

[2] By every consideration which binds you to your enslaved fellow-countrymen and to the peace and welfare of your country; by every aspiration which you cherish for the freedom and equality of yourselves and your children; by all the ties of blood and identity which make us one with the brave black men now fighting our battles in Louisiana and in South Carolina, I urge you to fly to arms, and smite with death the power that would bury the government and your liberty in the same hopeless grave.

—Frederick Douglass, "Secession and War"

[3] If you follow one arrow, if you crouch motionless on a bank to watch a tremulous ripple thrill on the water and are rewarded by the sight of a muskrat kid paddling from its den, will you count that sight a chip of copper only, and go your rueful way?

—Annie Dillard, "Seeing"

[4] When in the Course of human events, it becomes necessary for one people to dissolve the political bands which have connected them with another, and to assume among the powers of the earth, the separate and equal station to which the Laws of Nature and of Nature's God entitle them, a decent respect to the opinions of mankind requires that they should declare the causes which impel them to the separation.

—Thomas Jefferson, The Declaration of Independence

[5] Whenever I find myself growing grim about the mouth; whenever it is a damp, drizzly November in my soul; whenever I find myself involuntarily pausing before coffin warehouses, and bringing up the rear of every funeral I meet; and especially whenever my hypos get such an upper hand of me, that it requires a strong moral principle to prevent me from deliberately stepping into the street, and methodically knocking people's hats off – then, I account it high time to get to sea as soon as I can.

—Herman Melville, *Moby-Dick*

Conclusion

In a world increasingly dominated by digital media, our students are becoming so mediated by electronic middlemen they seem to be plugged in and tuned out. Daily we read news reports about the inimical effects of cellphones, the Internet, social media, and video games on attention spans. But even those of us who are inclined to bemoan the declining capacity of students to engage in focused attention must admit that deficits in student attention are not new. Interviewing candidates for government positions in 1962, Smith R. Simpson lamented in the *Foreign Service Journal*, "My initial surprise was to find among the candidates an abysmal ignorance of so elementary a subject as the geography of the United States. ... As with elementary geographic and economic aspects of the United States, so with historical, sociological, and cultural." Simpson reminds us of a passage in George Orwell's 1936 novel, *The Clergyman's Daughter*, which describes the experience of Dorothy, a new teacher who questions her pupils on their existing knowledge:

> When she had finished with history (and it took five minutes to get to the bottom of their historical knowledge) she tried them with geography, with English grammar, with French, with arithmetic – with everything, in fact, that they were supposed to have learned. By twelve o'clock she had plumbed, though not actually explored, the frightful abysses of their ignorance. For they knew nothing, absolutely nothing – nothing, nothing, nothing, like the Dadaists. (p. 226)

We teachers cannot depend on what our students should have learned, but did not; rather, we need to concentrate on what we have to teach, or at least, on what we think our students should learn. We have to confront the world that our students present to us. We need to provide experiences that will help them slow down that world so they can learn to focus and attend. The approaches to reading and thinking critically described in this chapter are designed to do those things; they can enliven any class and enlighten nearly every student. The more we help our students to read and think critically, the less likely we will be to undergo Dorothy's experience, and the less likely our students will be to validate her observations.

Notes

1 I owe much of my perspective on reading pragmatically, and also on the work of John Austin, to Mary Trachsel of the University of Iowa.
2 In addition to Aristotle's triangle, another highly useful approach to critical reading and thinking is found in the work of British philosopher Stephen Toulmin. It is too complex to go into here, but explanations are widely available.

References

Aristotle. (1984). Rhetoric. In *The complete works of Aristotle*. Ed. J. Barnes (vol. 2, pp. 2152–2194). Princeton, NJ: Princeton University Press.

Austin, J. L. (1962/1977). *How to do things with words*. Cambridge, MA: Harvard University Press.

Bambara, T. C. (1990). What it is I think I'm doing anyhow. In *Calling home: Working-class women's writing* (pp. 321–325). Ed. J. Zandy. New Brunswick, NJ: Rutgers University Press.

Barnet, S., and Bedau, H. (2014). *From critical thinking to argument*. New York: Bedford/St. Martin's.

Brown, J. (2015). Last speech. In R. Aufses, R. Shea, and L. Scanlon (eds.), *Conversations in American literature: Language, rhetoric, culture* (pp. 732–733). New York: Bedford/St. Martin's.

Burke, K. (1962/1969). *A rhetoric of motives*. Berkeley: University of California Press.

Crider, F. S. (2007). *The office of assertion*. Wilmington, DE: ISI Books.

Dillard, A. (1974/2012). Seeing. In *Pilgrim at Tinker Creek* (pp. 14–34). New York: Harper Classics.

Douglass, F. (2003). Secession and war. In *The life and times of Frederick Douglass* (pp. 240–252). Mineola, NY: Dover Publications.

Emerson, R. W. (1983). Circles. *In Essays and lectures*. Ed. J. Port (pp. 401–414). New York: Library of America.

Fuller, M. (1845/2015). Woman in the nineteenth century. In R. Aufses, R. Shea, and L. Scanlon (eds.), *Conversations in American literature: language, rhetoric, culture* (pp. 607–613). New York: Bedford/St. Martin's.

Graff, G. (2007). *Professing literature: An institutional history*. Chicago: University of Chicago Press.

Hardy, T. (1915/2001). In time of "the breaking of nations." In *The complete poems*. Ed. J. Gibson. New York: Palgrave.

Huxley, A. (1959). *Collected essays*. New York: Harper & Row.

Jefferson, T. (2013). The Declaration of Independence. In R. Shea, L. Scanlon, and R. Aufses (eds.), *The language of composition: Reading, writing, rhetoric* (pp. 120–123). New York: Bedford/St. Martin's.

Johnson, S. (1968). *The history of Rasselas, prince of Abissinia*. Oxford: Oxford University Press.

Kelly, F. (2015). Speech on child labor. In R. Aufses, R. Shea, and L. Scanlon (eds.), *Conversations in American literature: Language, rhetoric, culture* (pp. 980–982). New York: Bedford/St. Martin's.

King, M. L., Jr. (2013). Letter from a Birmingham jail. In R. Shea, L. Scanlon, and R. Aufses (eds.), *The Language of composition: Reading, writing, rhetoric* (pp. 281–294). New York: Bedford/St. Martin's.

King, S. (2014). Reading to write. In S. Cohen (ed.), *50 essays: A portable anthology* (pp. 221–225). New York: Bedford/St. Martin's.

Lincoln, A. (2015). The Gettysburg address. In R. Aufses, R. Shea, and L. Scanlon (eds.), *Conversations in American literature: Language, rhetoric, culture* (p. 692). New York: Bedford/St. Martin's.

Lincoln, A. (2015). The second inaugural address. In R. Aufses, R. Shea, and L. Scanlon (eds.), *Conversations in American literature: Language, rhetoric, culture* (pp. 695–696). New York: Bedford/St. Martin's.

Lunsford, A. A., and Ruszkiewicz, J. J. (eds.). (2013). *Everything's an argument*. New York: Bedford/St. Martin's.

McGuffy's sixth eclectic reader. (1921). New York: Van Nostrand Reinhold.

Melville, H. (1930). *Moby-Dick*. New York: Random House.

Orwell, G. (1936). *The clergyman's daughter*. New York: Harcourt Brace.

Orwell, G. (1946/2002). Why I write. In *Essays* (pp. 1079–1085). New York: Alfred A. Knopf.

Paine, T. (2015). Common sense. In R. Aufses, R. Shea, and L. Scanlon (eds.), *Conversations in American literature: Language, rhetoric, culture* (pp. 376–378). New York: Bedford/St. Martin's.

Rash, R. (2014). Dead confederates. In *Something rich and strange: Selected stories* (pp. 271–292). New York: HarperCollins.

Roskelly, H. (n.d.). What do students need to know about rhetoric? In *Special focus in English language and composition: Rhetoric*. New York: The College Board.

Simpson. R. S. (1962). Are we getting our share of the best? *Foreign Service Journal* (November), 25–27.

Woolf, V. (1948). The Russian point of view. In *The common reader* (pp. 243–256). New York: Harcourt Brace.

Yeats, W. B. (1983). *Politics*. In *The poems of W. B. Yeats*. Ed. R. Finneran. New York: Macmillan.

5

The Community of Literature

Teaching Critical Reading and Creative Reflection

Adrian Barlow

Ways of Reading

Just as there are ways of seeing, so there are ways of reading. We do not necessarily see things as they are: we see them as we are. A point of view may be shared, but it will never be universal. So it is with reading, and introducing students to the advanced study of literature involves two sometimes conflicting tasks.

First, we teach that reading is a complex undertaking in which texts ask questions of us as much as we ask questions of them, and these questions will vary from time to time and from person to person. Shakespeare's play *The Merchant of Venice*, whether acted on stage, adapted for screen, or read on the page, is not the same play from a post-Holocaust perspective as it was when first performed in the late 1590s. Today it questions our attitude towards Shylock and towards the anti-Semitism of the play's Christian characters in a way unimagined before Belsen.

At the same time, working with students nevertheless demands that we keep reminding ourselves that reading – how we read and what we

Critical Reading Across the Curriculum, Volume 1: Humanities, First Edition.
Edited by Robert DiYanni and Anton Borst.
© 2017 John Wiley & Sons, Inc. Published 2017 by John Wiley & Sons, Inc.

read – is fundamentally intended to give pleasure. Philip Larkin (1983) puts this well:

> at bottom, poetry, like all art, is inextricably bound up with giving pleasure, and if a poet loses his pleasure-seeking audience he has lost the only audience worth having, for which the dutiful mob that signs on every September is no substitute. (pp. 81–82)

Larkin is speaking as a writer, not as a teacher. But his "dutiful mob" is the students we teach, and they deserve our enthusiasm as well as our knowledge. Beatrice White (1955) would have agreed with Larkin, and her comments in "The Teaching of Literature" claim our attention at the start. Her views, and the way they are expressed, may belong to a more innocent age, but it is helpful to consider whether or not what she says is actually outdated. If so, how might our own, critical, reading differ from hers?

White begins by claiming: "Works of art speak with the tongues of angels and often in language too profound for the young, the ignorant, and the inexperienced to understand." She argues that "The bridging of the gulf between the artist's vision and the immaturity of the student is one of the most teasing problems we, as teachers, have to confront" (p. 134). White assumes her readers will treat "works of art" as synonymous with "works of literature." What is more, she expects they will assent readily to her view of literature as being in some metaphorical sense divinely inspired – the work of literature being created when the artist's "vision" is expressed in words uttered, in the biblical phrase, "with the tongues of angels." This is an idea articulated perhaps more helpfully by W. H. Auden (1935) – and others before him – as "memorable speech." Such language, she suggests, may be too "profound" for students to understand; if so, the teacher's job is to "bridge the gulf" between student and text.

White is clear, too, about how bridging the gulf may be achieved. She explains that "It is essential in teaching literature to grasp and pass on the richness and freshness of the writer's creative imagination, to keep the original inspiration white-hot, by direct and constant application to the text under study" (p. 135). You could almost say that critical reading evolved in opposition to the values and practices evident in White's account of the teaching of literature. Behind her reference to works of art lies the belief that literary texts are as instantly recognizable as Old Master paintings. A work of literature is, by this reckoning, self-evidently just that: like quality, you'll recognize it when you see it. But critical reading invites us to ask – and specifically expects us to ask our students – what, if anything, can justify calling one text literary and another non-literary.

There is also a cultural assumption behind what White writes. She presupposes her readers endorse her Christian frame of reference and, hence, that she and her readers share the same cultural values: she and we (it is implied) will approach texts with a common perspective. Critical reading, by contrast, challenges these assumptions, acknowledging that in the twenty-first century the community of literature – a phrase I shall shortly explore – is plural, diverse, argumentative, and unpredictable.

I am not trying to argue that critical reading stands in every respect for the opposite of what Beatrice White believed in; but as teachers today, we and our students face other and competing challenges, and the biblical and classical traditions no longer underpin most discussions of literature. For this reason, the importance of contexts of different kinds is at the heart of the reading and discourse practices in our age. So for all teachers the answers to the questions, What is literature? and What are literary studies? involve asking contextual questions and, at the same time, asking questions of context itself.

To take just one example: the publication of Harper Lee's novel *Go Set a Watchman* (2015) set critics and reviewers re-reading and revising their long-held judgments of *To Kill a Mockingbird* (1960). Suddenly, *Mockingbird* was no longer the book it used to be. Sarah Churchwell (2015) has described *To Kill a Mockingbird* as a "consoling fable" and a "racial parable" and as "a parable about America" (p. 6). However, *Go Set a Watchman*, Churchwell claims,

> is now forcing us to look more squarely at the racism lurking beneath [*To Kill a Mockingbird*], and we don't like what we see. Our horror at discovering that Atticus was really a racist may be genuine, but it is also the rage of Caliban, seeing himself in the mirror. (p. 6)

I take Churchwell to refer here to our own horror at discovering we had not seen what had been really there in the earlier book all along. Another critic, Helen Laville (2015), has developed this argument further:

> *Watchman* is a lot more honest. It doesn't feed white America the comforting version of civil rights history where the bad guys are easily identifiable ignorant hicks, the good guys are heroic and noble white men with impeccable manners, and the black people are all subservient, respectful and endlessly patient. *Mockingbird* is a child's book, told by a child. *Watchman* is for grown-ups. It asks serious questions about what racism is. And it comes at a time when America desperately needs a grown-up conversation about race.

Critical reading is essential because it gives students tools with which to confront texts, asking just such questions as are raised by these two reviews. Some media commentators over-hastily condemned *Go Set a Watchman* because its representation of Atticus Finch destroyed the image of the morally upright and non-racist lawyer they thought they remembered in *Mockingbird*. They have had to think again, not least because *Watchman*, they discovered, was in fact an earlier draft of *Mockingbird*. The discussion in which these two critics, Churchwell and Laville, became engaged raises questions about "honesty" in literature, and about what readers are entitled to expect from different novels aimed at different readers – adults and children. Laville challenges her readers to reconsider not just their own opinions but their own stereotypes; in so doing she forces them to ask how "honestly" they may have read *To Kill a Mockingbird* in the first place. She and Churchwell also demonstrate how our literary imaginations as readers can be expanded by reading, re-reading, and reflecting on one text in the light of another.

Here, then, are some questions we need first to ask ourselves, before asking our students:

- Have we, as teachers, tended wrongly to pigeon-hole *Mockingbird* as a novel for younger readers? (Compare the pigeon-holing of Swift's *Gulliver's Travels* and Orwell's *Animal Farm* as novels for children.)
- If so, why? Have curriculum pressures (recommended reading lists etc.) played a part?
- How far should the fact that *Watchman* was an earlier draft of what became *To Kill a Mockingbird* alter our perception of either novel?

Textual Conversations – Critical Dialogue

Texts exist not in isolation but in community. This is one of the key lessons we have to teach: there are conversations between books, as between readers and writers. Writers, readers, and texts themselves all exist within social, cultural, political, historical, and literary contexts. Engaged as we are in literary studies – the writing, reading, and reception of literary texts – we shouldn't lose sight of the literary contexts that bind us.

Here is one writer's perspective on this. Susan Sontag (2007) explains:

> A writer is first of all a reader. It is from reading that I derive the standards by which I measure my own work and according to which I fall lamentably short. It is from reading, even before writing, that I become part of a community – the community of literature – which includes more dead than living writers. (p. 213)

Sontag's statement that a writer is first of all a reader reminds us that, from childhood onwards, we start by *hearing* stories read or told to us, *watching* stories being acted out, then *learning how to read* stories – and all this before we can write with anything like the same fluency with which we speak. Reading precedes writing. And then, when we do start to write (and for all our writing lives thereafter) we learn to act as our own critics: our writing always involves rewriting, having second thoughts, pressing the delete button, starting over. Jonathan Bate (2010) reminds us that "literary texts are those in which language is used most cleverly, those that respond to a diversity of readings" (p. 24). The language is the writer's responsibility, the reading is ours. And neither does the writer write, nor the reader read, in a vacuum. "The creation of the literature of the future," Bate agrees with Sontag, "is dependent on a dialogue with the literature of the past" (p. 26). In teaching critical reading, we must help students to tune in to this dialogue, to join in, even challenging and reshaping the terms of the conversation. It is precisely by joining this conversation that students become members of the community of literature.

We can see what Bate means in a brief but powerful scene from *Wolf Hall*, the novel by Hilary Mantel (2009) about the court of King Henry VIII. Thomas Cromwell, the king's chief minister, is talking to the poet and courtier Thomas Wyatt about Anne Boleyn, whom Henry is determined to marry. Anne is a young woman with a reputation for having had previous lovers, and this is something about which the king seems for the moment willfully unaware. Cromwell is trying to assess the danger – to Anne herself and to men such as Wyatt – if, after her marriage and coronation as queen of England, Henry should discover her past affairs. During the conversation Wyatt betrays (as Cromwell intends him to) his own feelings about Anne and about the way she used to treat him:

> "She liked me, I think, or she liked to have me in thrall to her, it amused her. We would be alone, she would let me kiss her, and I always thought … but that is Anne's tactic, you see, she says yes, yes, yes, then she says no."
>
> "And of course, you are such a gentleman."
>
> "What, I should have raped her? If she says stop she means it – Henry knows that. But then another day would come and again she would let me kiss her. Yes, yes, yes, no. The worst of it is her hinting, her boasting almost, that she says no to me but yes to others." (p. 349)

Wyatt is hurt and scared, hurt by the way Anne has treated him in the past and by her indifference now, and scared about his own future safety. Although Mantel never says so (she does not have to), this scene is a commentary on the historical Thomas Wyatt's poem "They flee from me that sometime did me seeke".[1] Indeed, the scene could not have been written in the way Mantel wrote it, did Wyatt's poem not exist. Here are the relevant lines:

> Thanked be Fortune, it hath been otherwise
>   Twenty times better; but once especial –
> In thin array, after a pleasant guise,
>   When her loose gown did from her shoulders fall,
>   And she me caught in her arms long and small,
> And therewithal so sweetly did me kiss,
> And softly said, *"Dear heart, how like you this?"*
> It was no dream; for I lay broad awaking:
>   But all is turn'd now through my gentleness,
> Into a bitter fashion of forsaking;
>   And I have leave to go of her goodness;
>   And she also to use new fangleness.
> But since that I unkindly so am served:
> *"How like you this?"* – what hath she now deserved?

These lines, which conclude a twenty-one line poem, function like a sonnet, with a change of direction (the *volta*) between the eighth and ninth lines – "But all is turn'd now" – and a bitter final couplet, in which the woman's seductive words, *"How like you this?"* are thrown back, both at her and at the reader, in the last line. This is a poem in which the amorous invitation of "kiss ... this" precedes the rude awakening the poet receives (quite different from the "broad awaking" state in which he lay after being kissed) when he suddenly encounters her "bitter fashion of forsaking": his "gentleness" (his gentlemanly treatment of her) is suddenly opposed by her "new fangleness" (modish bad behavior toward him). And although these two words rhyme on the last syllable ("-ness"), what strikes the reader is the dissonance between "gentle-" and "fangle-." The poet's disgust at the unnatural ("unkind") cruelty she has meted out to him is reflected finally in the angry end-rhyme: "served" and "deserved."

This close reading of the poem not only reveals the layers of imbrication in Wyatt's fourteen lines but, in doing so, provides a commentary on the passage from *Wolf Hall*; in turn, Mantel's interrogation of Wyatt by Cromwell takes us back to one of the best-known poems of the early Tudor period. These two texts are written almost five hundred years apart, yet here they are in dialogue with each other: when Mantel puts into Cromwell's mouth the words "And, of course, you are such a gentleman," we as readers can reach back for the word "gentleness" in Wyatt's poem. We don't do this, however, simply for confirmation that the novelist has indeed been writing this passage with one eye on the poem: the unsuppressed sarcasm of Cromwell's statement accentuates a tone easily missed when Wyatt's poem is first read – that whine of self-justification, pleading with the reader to believe he is entirely the innocent party in this relationship, passive and ill-treated.

Re-reading and Creative Reflection

Thus the literature of the past shapes the way writers write, and readers read, today. Equally, what we read today can re-shape the texts we re-read from the past. It becomes an iterative critical dialogue: text to text and reader to reader. Literature, as John Carey (2005) points out, "is a field of comparisons and contrasts … whatever we read constantly modifies, adapts, questions or abrogates whatever we have read before" (p. 195). Re-reading[2] is indeed a central element in the practice of critical reading. So I want here to invoke two critics whose comments on the relationship between re-reading and critical reading have a direct bearing on the way we as teachers encourage and develop our students' confidence in reading critically and reflecting creatively. By "reflecting creatively" I mean the stages of reading through which students gain confidence in thinking for themselves and developing that reflexive personal response which turns classroom practice into a life-skill.

The first critic, Patricia Meyer Spacks (2011), rejects "an absolute division between 'recreational' and 'professional' rereading. Pleasure plays its part in both, whether or not we speak of it: pleasure provides a starting point for perception" (p. 166). This insight into the value of pleasure as part of the reading process takes us forward from Philip Larkin's remark, quoted earlier. Pleasure in reading, Spacks indicates, can be more than simple enjoyment: it can create a state of attentiveness which stimulates heightened responsiveness to what is happening in the text. But there is a difference between the way in which the professional reader, as distinct from the recreational reader, deals with this heightened responsiveness:

> Professional rereading assumes the importance of literature as artistic construct and as a way of knowledge and operates with the goal of understanding both. Recreational rereading takes place on the basis of diverse assumptions. Typically, I suspect, it is more open-minded than its professional equivalent. Both, however, are vital functions of cultural life and growth. (p. 185)

Spacks limits "professional rereaders" to teachers and academics. I would extend her label to students as well, arguing that as teachers we need to foster in our students that same open-mindedness she cherishes in (but restricts to) recreational re-reading. For this reason, to talk of the pleasure re-reading can provide is neither indulgent nor sentimental; on the contrary, it is something to be nurtured and protected throughout our teaching of literature, to students of whatever age.

This point is well made by my second critic. In his book *On Literature* (2002), J. Hillis Miller distinguishes not between professional and recreational reading and re-reading, but between reading *allegro*, "in a dance of the eyes across the page," and reading *lento*:

> Slow reading, critical reading, means being suspicious at every turn, interrogating every detail of the work, trying to figure out by just what means the magic is wrought. This means attending not to the new world that is opened up by the work, but to the means by which that opening is brought about. (p. 122)

Miller calls this process "demystification," and his use of the word "magic" to describe the action of the writer suggests that there must always be a certain tension between the writer weaving the magic and the critical reader wanting to discover how the trick is done. He argues that throughout the "tangled tradition" of literary studies there have always been two approaches to this work of demystification. First he identifies what he calls "rhetorical reading": "Such reading means a close attention to the linguistic devices by which the magic is wrought .... A rhetorical reader is adept in all the habits of 'close reading'" (pp. 122–123). By contrast, Miller presents a second type of reading, a form of cultural studies that demystifies the beliefs about class, race, and gender relations that books can mask. "These are seen," he argues, "as modes of vision, judgment, and action presented as objectively true but actually ideological" (p. 123).

Thus critical reading demonstrates that the words on the page cannot provide the last word on any text – though, as I have argued (following Spacks and Miller), one always starts with them. Indeed, critics and teachers of recent generations have often been distrustful of the very idea of close reading: no text, they argue, has a single meaning waiting patiently to be excavated without any reference beyond the text. Granted; but as Elaine Showalter (2003) has argued:

> The close reading process, or *explication de texte*, that we use in analyzing literary texts does not have to come with the cumbersome baggage of the New Criticism, or with political labels. Before or along

with attention to factors outside the text, students have to understand something about the verbal, formal, and structural elements of the words themselves. Close reading can be a neutral first step in understanding literature. (p. 56)

Demonstration – Hardy's "In a Museum"

In the early stages of working with students it may certainly be necessary to take this step-by-step approach. Here, by way of illustration, is an analysis of Thomas Hardy's poem, "In a Museum," which will proceed from close reading, filtered through biographical, literary, and historical contexts, to appraisal of the poem in the context of a modern critical response to the text:

> Here's the mould of a musical bird long passed from light,
> Which over the earth before man came was winging;
> There's a contralto voice I heard last night,
> That lodges with me still in its sweet singing.
>
> Such a dream is Time that the coo of this ancient bird
> Has perished not, but is blent, or will be blending
> Mid visionless wilds of space with the voice that I heard,
> In the full-fugued song of the universe unending.[3]

This poem needs some immediate context. In June 1915 Thomas Hardy visited Exeter with his second wife, Florence. They went to a concert and then, next morning, visited the local museum, where a particular exhibit caught Hardy's attention and spurred him to write this poem.

The exhibit Hardy writes about is a plaster cast ("mould") of a fossil of the earliest known bird, *archaeopteryx*. The original had been found in Germany only a few years after the publication of *On the Origin of Species*, and was hailed as evidence to support Darwin's theories because it was a transitional fossil, suggesting that birds may have evolved from dinosaurs. Extinct birds aren't unusual as museum exhibits. But this bird outdoes even the dodo: it was flying "over the earth" long before the appearance of *Homo sapiens*. "Winging" may sound slightly precious. However, Hardy needs it to prepare for the feminine rhyme "singing" at the end of the stanza; and the word also echoes the name of the bird itself: the Greek etymology of *archaeopteryx* is "ancient wing."

The fossil, though millions of years old, is present to the poet "Here" and now. Similarly, the beautiful voice he heard in the previous night's concert is simultaneously in the past – "There" – and present because it "lodges with me still." The poet is moved by song, whether it be the "sweet" contralto voice of the singer or the "coo" of the musical bird. He himself enjoys the music of poetry: he uses alliteration emphatically in the first line ("mould / musical … long / light") and the rhythms of the extended, leisurely lines are carefully modulated, no one line quite mirroring another.

But if Hardy in the first stanza focuses sharply on the here and now, in the second he adopts a longer perspective: "Such a dream is Time" – that past and present are arbitrary and elastic. The "coo" of the archaeopteryx has either been already "blent" into the song of last night's singer, or it "will be blending" in the future. Time is limitless, just as the prehistoric land-scape over which the bird flies is "visionless." It is as unimaginable and incommunicable as the strange arctic birds that appear in Hardy's *Tess of the d'Urbervilles*:

> gaunt spectral creatures with tragical eyes – eyes which had witnessed scenes of cataclysmal horror in inaccessible polar regions of a magni-tude such as no human being had ever conceived …. But of all they had seen which humanity would never see, they brought no account, the traveller's ambition to tell was not theirs. (ch. XLIII)

This is one of Hardy's bleakest images of man's cosmic insignificance. "In a Museum," by contrast, is more ambiguous. "The full-fugued song of the universe unending" recalls Keats's nightingale whose singing with "full-throated ease" draws the speaker toward "easeful death."[4] So is this really a poem about human insignificance in a universe as indifferent to man as the strange birds are indifferent to Tess? Or is "full-fugued" in fact an affir-mative epithet, pointing us toward the idea of celestial harmony and the music of the spheres – a harmony and a music of which man is part?

Besides, what exactly is unending: the song or the universe? Whichever it is, does the word invite us to contemplate bleak endlessness or hope-ful continuity? In "The Voice" (1912), written only three years before "In a Museum," Hardy had wondered whether the voice that was calling to him really was the voice of his dead first wife, Emma, or just a trick of the wind:

> You being ever dissolved to wan wistlessness
> Heard no more again, far or near?[5]

In the end, though, despite his doubts, he stubbornly insists the voice is that of "the woman calling." My own reading of "In a Museum" is that while Hardy leaves the question open, the positioning of "unending" as the last word of the poem, and the stress on the prefix "un-" allows at least the possibility of hope. "Un-" can indicate joy, after all: unconfined, unalloyed. "Unending" is a more positive word than "endless," carrying none of the desolation of "wistlessness" or "existlessness" (Hardy's original choice of word in "The Voice").

Not everyone agrees. Some critics see this poem as a clear statement of Hardy's pessimism. But the second line of the second stanza – "perished not ... blent ... will be blending" – seems to me affirmative, suggesting continuity. It is at this point that close reading moves decisively beyond the "neutral first step" described by Elaine Showalter. The next step is to test one's own reading against evidence elsewhere: here, the provisional optimism of my reading of this poem is reached after focusing closely on the poem's final word, "unending," before contrasting "In a Museum" with expressions of Hardy's famous pessimism found in *Tess of the d'Urbervilles* and in "The Voice." If one has pursued an analysis of a poem thus far with students, now is the moment to take the third step and to allow alternative views into the conversation.

Broadening Context

One such reading of the poem reaches a very different conclusion. Catherine Lanone (2010) has argued that "The fossil bird of 'In a Museum' may be taken as the relic, not so much of a prehistoric bird, as of romantic poetry and Platonic beliefs." She likens Hardy to the "blind watchmaker" – the metaphor used by Richard Dawkins for "a universe in which natural selection has no vision, no foresight, no sight at all. If it can be said to play the role of watchmaker in nature, it is the blind watchmaker" (1986, p. 5). Lanone contrasts the song of the fossilized bird with those of Keats's nightingale and Hardy's own darkling thrush. She suggests that, in the context of "The Darkling Thrush," the melancholy poet envies a bird that apparently has the key to a joy he himself cannot grasp. She therefore concludes:

> "In a Museum" thus becomes the mausoleum of dissolved romanticism, with its fossil standing as an empty shape beckoning amongst poems and novels dealing with loss and displacement. The Darwinian twist mocks the Romantic vision of the emblematic bird's eternal song, a transcendental presence connecting the poet with the higher forces of inspiration.

But does Hardy's poem finally "mock the Romantic vision of the emblematic bird's eternal song"? This question demands an understanding not just of a single poem, but of a broader literary and philosophical concept, Romanticism, and of its eventual rejection. The answer depends not simply on how one reads Hardy's second stanza, but on the way that reading of the poem is situated in a specific cultural context – the shattering impact of Darwinism, the rise of modernism, and the trauma of World War I.

Here is the point at which close and critical reading coincide. If our students are to engage with such questions, our responsibility is to encourage and teach them to broaden as well as deepen their reading. Only in the context of such broadening can the questions identified above be meaningfully assayed. But it is essential we keep a balance: students who lose the appreciation and enjoyment of individual works of literature just as their literary horizons start to broaden will have been failed by the teaching we have offered.

Application – *Middlemarch*, Chapter XXIX

George Eliot's *Middlemarch* (1871–1872) is one of the most highly regarded novels of the nineteenth century. Even if no longer read as widely as in the past, it is still reckoned among the greatest English novels. How one defines a "greatest," or even a "great," work of fiction is always problematic. If enough people claim that *Anna Karenina* is the greatest novel ever written, and go on saying so for long enough, then the claim becomes accepted, and ultimately axiomatic – as though self-evidently true. A critical reading of Tolstoy's novel (or of Eliot's) would quite rightly challenge such lazy assumptions, and it is one of the virtues of critical reading that it teaches students to take nothing for granted.

But authentic critical reading is always dependent upon just that, reading. If it simply leads to the replacing of one set of superficial judgments by another – that *Middlemarch*, for instance, is restricted by its narrow provincial perspective or that Dorothea Brooke (its central character) is ultimately exposed as a conventional heroine in search of a romantic happy ending – this is not a substitute for genuine reading. The danger here, as always, is that students and teachers may turn from close engagement with texts to criticizing them for what they do not say, looking only for *symptomatic* readings, readings which will expose the unspoken assumptions behind the text and its author's intentions. Is *Middlemarch* to be rated a lesser novel because it lacks the epic historical sweep of *War and Peace*? Is the focus on provincial life evidence of the author's own bourgeois ideology? Is *Middlemarch* itself symptomatic of the English novel's preoccupation with middle-class Middle England, a preoccupation stretching back at least to Jane Austen and creating a falsely romantic image of an England that only ever existed in the imagination of writers, most of whom lived comfortably in London?

Such symptomatic readings, and the questions they provoke, have their place; however, like all other readings they must be based upon close reading. Here, for instance, is a passage from *Middlemarch* describing the funeral of Peter Featherstone. His extended family gathers, all of them hoping he has left them something in his will, "most of them having minds bent on a limited store each would have liked to get the most of" (p. 365). The narrator enjoys describing the expectations and attitudes of those who follow the funeral procession:

> Solomon found time to reflect that Jonah was undeserving, and Jonah to abuse Solomon as greedy …. These nearest of kin were naturally impressed with the unreasonableness of expectations in cousins and second cousins, and used their arithmetic in reckoning the large sums that small legacies might amount to, if there were too many of them. Two cousins were present to hear the will, and a second cousin besides Mr Trumbull. The second cousin was a Middlemarch mercer of polite manners and superfluous aspirates. (pp. 365–366)

Chapter XXIX, from which this passage is taken, offers students scope to reflect upon the extent to which they are being coerced by the novel's first-person narrator into accepting a perspective on the characters and the situation they might not wish to share. Here are some questions designed to help students focus on these issues:

Exercise 1

- What subconscious effect, if any, does the choice of Old Testament Jewish names (Solomon, Jonah) have on you as the reader, especially when linked to adjectives such as "undeserving" and "greedy"?
- Does the second sentence invite you to endorse the idea that close family members are entitled to be "naturally impressed" (or, rather, unimpressed?) by the "unreasonableness" of cousins and second cousins?
- Is this an impartial description by the narrator of the way different people are thinking, even before the funeral is over and the dead man's will has been read? Or does it reflect a satirical and superior position adopted by the author and mediated through her narrator? What could the phrase "used their arithmetic" imply about Solomon and Jonah?
- Are you inclined, reading the last sentence of the passage, to share or reject the narrator's judgment on the Middlemarch mercer?

This last question, and the sentence to which it refers, illustrates the gap to be bridged between the nineteenth century in which *Middlemarch* was written and the twenty-first century in which we now read it. The "Middlemarch mercer of polite manners and superfluous aspirates," being a shopkeeper (as a mercer he sells cloths and fabrics), is in trade. This was a critical distinction in class-bound Victorian English society: his "polite manners" are therefore directed at those higher-class patrons who visit his shop. So, for "polite" read "deferential."

A nuance such as this will need unpacking with students to whom provincial Victorian England will, up to now, have been literally a closed book. But alerting students to the importance of social and historical, as well as literary and cultural, contexts is essential to the whole project of critical reading. Indeed, literary and cultural contexts overlap, and the analysis needs to be taken further, for what does George Eliot mean by "superfluous aspirates"?

An aspirate is a term in phonetics meaning "the sound represented in English and several other languages by the letter *h*" (*Chambers 21st Century Dictionary*). Sounding, or failing to sound, the letter *h* appropriately used to be a clear social marker in England: those who failed to sound the aspirate when it should be sounded betrayed themselves (it was assumed) as ill-educated. Some people, however, trying too hard, sounded aitches where they did not belong, and by so doing – using a "superfluity of aspirates" – betrayed their lack of social or educational confidence. This is what the Middlemarch mercer did, and it is what the narrator explicitly draws the reader's attention to.

If all this linguistic snobbery sounds absurd today, it is worth encouraging students to look at other instances in Victorian and early twentieth-century literature; by doing so, they will gain a clearer insight into a world of cultural discrimination that may be totally dissimilar to their own, but which was deeply embedded in the literature of the nineteenth and early twentieth centuries. The following task would support such student-based research:

Exercise 2

- Read "The Ruined Maid" by Thomas Hardy (1866) and "The Oxford Voice" by D. H. Lawrence (1928). In what ways, if any, do these poems enlarge your understanding of the issues of social class raised in the passage from *Middlemarch*, chapter XXIX?

Having examined this brief passage from *Middlemarch*, and explored within it the social nuances and implicit attitudes outlined above, it is open to students to extend this critical reading to the rest of the novel. They need further evidence in order to be able to make up their own minds, and the following graduated sequence of questions will focus their research:

1 Think of the narrator as a character, created by the novelist. What sort of person might the narrator (as you imagine him or her) actually be? From the way he/she intervenes in the narrative and comments on characters and events, what sort of personality does this narrator seem to you to have?
2 How well would you say this passage prepares us for the scene that follows immediately afterwards, the reading of Peter Featherstone's will?
3 Is the failure of the narrator to be open about his or her contempt for the people being introduced here *symptomatic* of a failure within the novel as a whole to treat the characters honestly?
4 And if this is so, is it a failure of the narrator, treated as a character who mingles, as it were, with the people of Middlemarch going about their daily lives?
5 Or does this, more seriously, betray a failure of *Middlemarch* itself to be honest (candid) in its depiction of a provincial world it treats with metropolitan condescension?
6 What are the dangers of using terms such as *honestly* and *honest* in any critical reading of a work of fiction?

Contemporary Contexts

Middlemarch is a novel about which much has been written. Students today probably have access to overmuch comment and criticism, more easily accessed online than on campus library shelves. I think that it is essential, therefore, for us and them to engage not just with canonical works but also with recent texts: the critical readers of tomorrow need to be articulate advocates of new writing. Not all teachers are confident enough to teach texts that have not already generated a body of critical or teaching resources. However, in the context of critical reading as I have described it, there is plenty of scope to interrogate the way a new text "inculcates beliefs about class, race or gender relations" (Miller, 2002, p. 123). Here, therefore, in conclusion is an illustration of one approach to teaching a complex recent novel and, through that novel, addressing some of the questions any close critical reading should raise.

The novel in question is *Cutting for Stone* (2009) by Abraham Verghese. The story spans thirty-two years, and has a back-story stretching as far away again. Geographically, the book moves from India to Ethiopia, where the major part of the story takes place, and then to New York. Some reviewers complained about the plot's dependence on coincidences. Almost all, however, found much to admire in the writing and structuring of the novel. The author, Abraham Verghese, is by training a surgeon, and the action of the story centers on two hospitals, one Ethiopian and the other American, each kept going by dedicated but under-trained and under-resourced doctors and nurses. Surgery itself becomes both a motif and a metaphor running through the novel; from the moment of their birth, it dominates the lives and careers of the twin protagonists. Their mother, a Carmelite nun, dies in the delivery room; their father, a humane British-born surgeon, disappears. One of the twins, Marion, is the chief narrator of the novel, and the author has sometimes a hard job persuading the reader that Marion can be simultaneously a character in the story and an omniscient narrator: Marion appears to have no difficulty in narrating events about which he knows nothing. Crucially, the novel's African section is set against the backdrop of rebellion and civil war in Ethiopia. Female genital mutilation is a topical taboo, but the representation of women in the story still raises concerns, as seen in a review by Aida Edemariam (2009) in the *Guardian*:

> This is a book narrated by a surgeon, and structured as a surgeon might structure it: after the body has been cut open and explored everything is returned to its place and carefully sutured up – which is not, in the end, how life actually works. And, like surgery, there's a certain brutality involved, particularly evident in the novel's gender politics. Of course the narrator arises from a patriarchal society, but it is difficult not to feel discomfited by the fact that the virgin/whore/mother/passive sufferer roles of the women (particularly the Ethiopian women, who are prostitutes, or servants, or simply available and, if not, righteously punished for their wilfulness) are so unquestioned.

A first reading of *Cutting for Stone*, followed by the review just quoted, raises questions that could prompt initial reactions and inform students' subsequent critical re-reading of the novel.

Exercise 3

- How justified is the reviewer's criticism of the novel's plot as being too neat to reflect the messiness of real life?
- To what extent, if any, do you share the reviewer's discomfort at the representation of women in the novel?

- To what extent is the relationship between the twins, as represented by the narrator, adequate to the story and convincing in its sequence of *intimacy > jealousy > rejection > estrangement > reconciliation > self-sacrifice*?
- Does the Ethiopian civil war feature strongly enough to justify its impact on the plot and on the characters who become its victims? What assumptions underlie the author's attitude to the armed struggle for Eritrea?
- Does the shifting of the action from Ethiopia to America create a fracture in the narrative too serious to be restored by the final resolution of the plot, the eventual unravelling of the back-story, and the return of the key survivors to Addis Ababa?

These questions are focused on a single novel. Several of them, however, can best be answered by comparing *Cutting for Stone* with other novels which have similarities of plot, structure, gender politics, social taboos, and issues of cultural displacement. An effective approach might be to have different sub-groups within a class or seminar each taking responsibility for reading one of these additional books (all written by women) and then re-reading *Cutting for Stone* in the light of the second novel. The recommended novels for comparison are:

- *The Memory of Love* (2010) by Aminatta Forna: a novel set in the aftermath of the civil war in Sierra Leone. One of the central characters, Kai, is a surgeon whose work involves trying to restore the bodies of those mutilated in the fighting. Another key character is a British psychotherapist, who cannot cope with the crisis of the country where he has come to work.
- *The God Of Small Things* (1997) by Arundhati Roy: set in India, and centering on twins whose relationships with their mother and with each other are disrupted, severed, and never fully restored, this novel reflects both the legacy of empire and the cruelties of the caste system.
- *White Teeth* (2005) by Zadie Smith: a novel set in London, bringing together two generations of West Indian, Bangladeshi, and English families. The Bangladeshi family has twin sons who become utterly dissimilar, one of them a radicalized Muslim, the other an atheist scientist.

Each of these novels offers starting points for re-reading and re-evaluating *Cutting for Stone*. Taken together, they provide a remarkable resource: four overlapping texts that ask questions about empire and its aftermath, about cultural complexity and the immigrant experience, radicalization, gender and gender politics, science and love – the latter figured particularly in issues of twinship, kinship, and separation.

What such a program of reading proposes is an approach to critical reading based on text, context, and intertext – with close reading and, specifically, re-reading at the heart of the exercise. At a time, and in a world, where reading itself is increasingly being reconfigured as a digital, adaptive activity, this is a model of literature teaching that remains committed to the notion of the book, to the possibilities of dialogue between books and their readers and hence, fundamentally, to the idea of a community of literature whose future will soon be in the hands of our students.

Notes

1 Several variant forms of this poem exist. The version quoted is taken from *The Oxford Book of English Verse* (1900), p. 63.
2 "Re-reading": throughout, I have included a hyphen to emphasize that *reading again* is an iterative process, not merely a repetitive one; however, I acknowledge that "rereading" is the approved usage, as adopted by Patricia Meyer Spacks.
3 From Hardy (1917).
4 John Keats, "Ode to a Nightingale," written in May 1819.
5 From "The Voice," in Hardy (1914).

References

Auden, W. H. (1935). *The poet's tongue*. London: Bell & Son.
Bate, J. (2010). *English literature: A very short introduction*. Oxford: Oxford University Press.
Carey, J. (2005). *What good are the arts?* London: Faber & Faber.
Churchwell, S. (2015). Moral ambition sabotaged. Review of Harper Lee, *Go Set a Watchman*. *The Guardian* (July 17). https://www.theguardian.com/books/2015/jul/17/go-set-a-watchman-harper-lee-review-novel (accessed September 29, 2016).
Dawkins, R. (1986). *The blind watchmaker*. Harmondsworth: Penguin Books.
Edemariam, A. (2009). Stitching up the surgeon's life. *The Guardian* (May 9). http://www.theguardian.com/books/2009/may/09/abraham-verghese-cutting-for-stone (accessed September 29, 2016).
Eliot, G. (1871–1872). *Middlemarch*. Harmondsworth: Penguin Books.
Forna, A. (2010). *The memory of love*. London: Bloomsbury.
Hardy, T. (1891–1892/1993). *Tess of the d'Urbervilles*. Ware, Herts.: Wordsworth Editions.
Hardy, T. (1914). *Poems of 1912–1913*. London: Macmillan.
Hardy, T. (1917). *Moments of Vision and Miscellaneous Verses*. London: Macmillan.

Lanone, C. (2010). Mechanical birds and shapes of ice: Hardy's vision of the "blind watchmaker." *Miranda*, 1. Retrieved from http://miranda.revues.org/676 (accessed September 29, 2016).

Larkin, P. (1983). *Required writing*. London: Faber & Faber.

Laville, H. (2015). Why *Go Set a Watchman* is a much better novel than *To Kill a Mockingbird*. *New Statesman* (July 16). http://www.newstatesman.com/culture/2015/07/why-go-set-watchman-much-better-novel-kill-mockingbird (accessed September 29, 2016).

Lee, H. (1960). *To kill a mockingbird*. Philadelphia, PA: Lippincott.

Lee, H. (2015). *Go set a watchman*. London: Heinemann.

Mantel, H. (2009). *Wolf Hall*. London: Fourth Estate.

Miller, J. H. (2002). *On literature*. New York: Routledge.

Roy, A. (1997). *The god of small things*. London: Flamingo, HarperCollins.

Showalter, E. (2003). *Teaching literature*. Oxford: Blackwell Publishing.

Smith, Z. (2005). *White teeth*. London: Hamish Hamilton.

Sontag, S. (2007). *At the same time*. London: Hamish Hamilton.

Spacks, P. M. (2011). *On rereading*. Cambridge, MA: Belknap, Harvard University Press.

Verghese, A. (2009). *Cutting for stone*. London: Vintage.

White, B. (1955). The teaching of literature. *English*, 10, 133–136.

6

Approaching Intellectual Emancipation

Critical Reading in Art, Art History, and Wikipedia

Amy K. Hamlin

Reconsidering Wikipedia

Several years ago I removed from my syllabi a sentence that conveyed what previously had been a given in my practice as an art historian: "Do *not* rely on Wikipedia to conduct your research." Wikipedia was, and arguably remains, a shibboleth among art history professors I know and admire, and for good reason. The information found on many Wiki pages related to art history is pre-digested at best or can be biased and outright false at worst. I was trained to be dismissive of sources autochthonous to the Internet, especially secondary sources not peer-reviewed by experts in the discipline. As a potential resource for students of art history and self-described as "a free-access, free-content Internet encyclopedia," Wikipedia represented a threat to the integrity of my field (Wikipedia, 2015c). I believed that the opportunity for anyone to create or edit articles on Wikipedia eroded the distinction between layman and expert that conditions so many academic disciplines. What kind of scholar and professor would I be were I not to warn my students against the dangers of unregulated knowledge? Better to bury their heads in the sands of sanctioned scholarship found in scholarly

Critical Reading Across the Curriculum, Volume 1: Humanities, First Edition.
Edited by Robert DiYanni and Anton Borst.
© 2017 John Wiley & Sons, Inc. Published 2017 by John Wiley & Sons, Inc.

monographs and peer-reviewed print journals. That was, after all, how I had learned to read art and art history.

Two experiences in 2014 forced me to reconsider Wikipedia. Fittingly, the first occurred in the classroom. It was one of those meta-teaching moments that oblige you to acknowledge and reckon with your own misguided assumptions in full view of your students. As a preface to a group discussion of the 1997 film *Artemisia* by Agnès Merlet about the seventeenth-century Roman painter Artemisia Gentileschi, I posed a general question: "How do we know what we know about this artist?" It was a question aimed at encouraging my students to consider ways in which the representation of an artist's life is not an unassailable truth but rather a complex construction. Shaped, in this case, by the filmmaker's ways of knowing, the life is reconstructed in a series of choices that determine staging, sequencing, and potential affect. I invited students to compare Merlet's cinematic account of Gentileschi's life to excerpts we read from Mary Garrard's essential monograph on the artist entitled *Artemisia Gentileschi: The Image of the Female Hero in Italian Baroque Art.*

I then offered for consideration Wikipedia's definition of "epistemology." More than the *Oxford English Dictionary*, it helped illustrate an understanding of knowledge as a human production created over time.[1] We perused the article's annotated history of the term as well as the page's revision history that originated on June 5, 2001, with a single line: "The branch of philosophy that deals with the nature of knowledge" (Wikipedia, 2015b). So far, so good, right? Then a hand went up. The student appeared vexed as she wondered aloud about my recourse to Wikipedia. Just a few weeks prior, she observed, I had stressed the Wikipedia warning in our syllabus review. Do as I say, not as I do, apparently. Charmed by the irony of the situation and embarrassed by my lack of self-awareness, I owned up to the contradiction but begged off an explanation. I needed to think this through. Upon reflection, I was astonished to realize that a double standard had indeed emerged in the PowerPoints I compiled in all of my classes; I regularly used Wikipedia for shorthand knowledge of persons, places, things, events, and concepts to elucidate some aspect of the art or artist under discussion. Less surprising but perhaps also reassuring, however, was that I rarely referred to Wikipedia's art history pages. Their absence of disciplinary oversight compounded by an entry-level mode of discourse determined my low scholarly opinion of the popular encyclopedia. My bias made sense to me, but not to my students. In the wake of this epiphany, I sensed a missed opportunity.

The second experience coincided with the first. In early February 2014, I participated in the inaugural international Art + Feminism Wikipedia edit-a-thon by attending one of over thirty meetups that took place mostly in the United States. I had learned about the event through a colleague and joined a small group of like-minded citizens (including a student and teaching assistant for a course I taught that term on women in art) at the University of Minnesota in Minneapolis. A local Wikipedia ambassador was on hand to assist us novice Wikipedians in creating user accounts and in learning how to create and edit Wikipedia articles on women in the arts. I made just one edit that evening to an article on a major woman artist. But having attended subsequent edit-a-thons in the Twin Cities, my editing skills and confidence have improved to the point where I am now a regular editor for a variety of pages I feel qualified to annotate.

The umbrella initiative – symbolized by a canny combination of the woman glyph and an upraised hand wielding a paintbrush (Figure 6.1) – originated in New York City with a cohort of art advocates comprising librarians, artists, and educators, and it has since grown in scale and organization. Its aim is "to improve coverage of women and the arts on Wikipedia, and to encourage female editorship" (Wikipedia, 2015a). The impetus for this campaign stems from the revelation in at least two surveys that women editors on Wikipedia constitute only 8.5–16 percent of all editors.[2] This "gender gap" carries significant epistemological implications when you consider the power of Wikipedia, through its popularity and size, to influence public knowledge. Put differently, if a body of knowledge tends to reflect the experience and interests of its contributors, then Wikipedia theoretically

Figure 6.1 Art + Feminism logo. Copyright © Ilotaha13, 2015.

falls short of its encyclopedic mandate. It invites questions like: Why are there so many articles on all manner of submarines and porn actresses and so few on children's book authors (Cowan, 2015)? How this relates to art history is worth considering, as "many articles on notable women in history and art are absent from Wikipedia" (Wikipedia, 2015a). What might it mean to imagine Wikipedia as a new frontier in art history? This is fundamentally a feminist question. The Art + Feminism initiative presents an opportunity to attend to assumptions that distort the field and that could possibly lead to its redefinition. Art historian Linda Nochlin anticipated this opportunity when she asserted the following in 1974: "feminism forces us to be conscious of other questions about our so-called natural assumptions. That is one way in which feminism affects cultural institutions: it sets off a chain reaction" (p. 82). Galvanized by the Art + Feminism Wikipedia edit-a-thon's theory and practice – by its capacity to imagine and effect chain reactions within its community of users – I envisioned integrating the initiative into how I teach students to read art and art history.

In what follows, I offer an integrative strategy that consists of visual analysis, annotated bibliography, and comparative analysis. These sequential components correspond to a scaffolded three-part assignment I developed for the course I teach on women in art, which culminates in an Art + Feminism Wikipedia edit-a-thon I host at my university. Each part of the assignment can function, however, independent of the Art + Feminism enterprise, and I imagine that the Wikipedia assignment as a whole is transferable to a variety of art history course topics. I emphasize the edit-a-thon here because I believe that it is a model for intellectual and civic engagement in today's college and university classrooms. As an alternative to the standard research paper, the edit-a-thon motivates students – both women and men – to participate in the production of public knowledge about art and art history. It empowers them to stake a claim in Wikipedia and to become critical readers of a variety of texts that circulate in our society, from oil paintings to advertisements, scholarly essays to blog posts.

When I conducted a trial run of the edit-a-thon with students in my "Women in Art" class in 2014, I was amazed by how well they took to the project, for which they received no extra credit. Their task was to edit or create a page for the artist about whom they had already researched and written a more conventional term paper. But because I myself had so much angst about the technical side of editing, I feared the experiment would fail. It didn't. Navigating the light html code required on the backend of the editing was second nature to most students, who came of age in the era of MySpace. They had little trouble translating the knowledge they had gained in their research to the language of a Wikipedia page. The instant gratification of seeing their edits immediately go live on the site was a thrill that many of the students from that course have said they have since experienced in their editing. In the spring of 2015, I repeated the experiment using a beta-version of the above-mentioned three-part assignment and experienced similarly encouraging results.

These experiences approach what French philosopher Jacques Rancière calls "intellectual emancipation." In *The Ignorant Schoolmaster* (1991), Rancière tells the story of the early nineteenth-century schoolteacher Joseph Jacotot, who discovered a radical method of teaching in the revelation that he himself – a French teacher, who knew no Flemish – could teach in French to Flemish students, who knew no French. As a radical method, Jacotot's pedagogy is a sort of anti-method insofar as it prescribes neither formulas nor systems, but rather a mutual trust among students and teacher, and a readiness to learn. Indeed, Jacotot's method of "universal teaching" assumes that all human beings possess equal intelligence. He realized that the will to learn can prompt a release from the stultifying hierarchies of conventional pedagogy and lead to intellectual emancipation. Here is a key passage in Rancière's analysis of Jacotot's example:

> one can teach what one doesn't know if the student is emancipated, that is to say, if he is obliged to use his own intelligence. The master is he who encloses an intelligence in the arbitrary circle from which it can only break out by becoming necessary to itself. To emancipate an ignorant person, one must be, and one need only be, emancipated oneself, that is to say, conscious of the true power of the human mind. The ignorant person will learn by himself what the master doesn't know if the master believes he can and obliges him to realize his capacity. (p. 15)

I am neither the first nor the last to admit that Jacotot's radical method, however inspiring, is also both counterintuitive and discomfiting. Our prevailing era of assessment, with its outcomes-based plans, rubrics, and portfolios designed to measure teaching and learning effectiveness within an inch of its life, may well be anathema to the sort of approach that Jacotot advocated. What is more, it is foreign to those of us schooled in the conventional pedagogical practice of explication that assumes a clear distinction between enlightened and ignorant, between the so-called "sage on the stage" and the student. As Rancière might quip: "So goes the world of the explicated explicators" (p. 8). He might also add that Jacotot's approach does not oblige the master to relinquish mastery: "The students had learned without a master explicator, but not, for all that, without a master" (p. 12).

As a theory that radically reimagines the role of the educator, Rancière's interpretation of Jacotot's model is indeed emancipatory. But how might it work in practice?

The three-part Wikipedia assignment I developed represents an attempt to realize Rancière's idea. First, the *visual analysis* helps students to claim their visual acuity through careful looking and vocabulary-building in order to describe and analyze a work of art by the artist whose Wikipedia article they will edit. Part two of the assignment – the *annotated bibliography* – requires students to find and read relevant art-historical texts and craft short summaries of those they will utilize in the edit-a-thon. Third, the *comparative analysis* asks students to evaluate the relative merits and deficiencies of the Wikipedia pages of two historically and/or personally related artists, analysis that provides students with models for their own editing. It is through this tripartite assignment that I attempt, within the prevailing educational system, to approach intellectual emancipation in the reading of art, art history, and Wikipedia.

Reading Art: The Visual Analysis

"LEARN TO READ ART." This imperative tolls reproachfully in the mind of the reader, an impression that has as much to do with the sentence's terse syntax as with its form and context; printed in black and silver ink at a 45-degree angle across the vertical flank of a canvas tote bag I own, the four words are rendered sans serif and demarcated by four black lines that form a narrow rectangle around them (Figure 6.2). The typography does not dominate the tote, but neither is it inscrutable against the raw canvas background; it is both legible and proportioned to the scale of the bag. The words visualize an exhortation in the upward orientation of the capitalized letters – LEARN TO READ ART – and in the frank open-endedness of the sentiment signaled by a lack of punctuation. As the viewer/reader, I am alerted to the imperative's possible meanings by being put on the defensive and thrust into a one-way conversation. "Okay, okay," I think to myself, "I promise I will learn to read art! But how? Where? From or with whom?" The piece is classic Lawrence Weiner, the American conceptual artist known for his typographic interventions into public spaces, including walls, floors, billboards, books, and, yes, tote bags.

A joint gift from a colleague and former student, the bag and its assertion force me to think about what it actually means to read art and to cultivate empathy with my students. Reading art is an act of interpretation, which requires a common vocabulary and a curious mind, along with an

Figure 6.2 Lawrence Weiner, *Learn to Read Art*, 2012. Limited edition tote bag. © Printed Matter Inc. and Lawrence Weiner. Photo: Author.

ability to be both objective and subjective when confronted with the intelligence of art. The defensive position that Weiner's imperative puts me in reminds me of the apprehension my students exhibit in the first days of the semester. This is when we together learn how to read art, a novel exercise for many that can be both intimidating and exhilarating. Students often feel hindered by the assumption that all artworks have "a correct interpretation" and simultaneously emboldened by the assumption that "art is open to interpretation." Both are myths not because they are not true, but because they are only partially true. For example, some interpretations of Maya Lin's *Vietnam Veterans Memorial* are more correct than others, if we agree with Donald Preziosi that the objective of art history is in "the construction of historically grounded explanations for why cultural artefacts – works of art – appear as they do" (1998, p. 577). To Preziosi's definition, I would add that explanations must also be grounded in the visual evidence of the artwork. In the case of Lin's memorial, how does its shape, material, color, and site-specificity invite and preclude certain avenues of inquiry?

Ultimately, so much depends on the interpretive alchemy that transpires when the *what* of the artwork is mingled with *how* students read it.

Essential to this process are a common vocabulary and set of questions. The vocabulary – what I understand as the elements of art and design – includes terms such as *material, technique, form, shape, composition, space, color, line, texture, mass, volume, style, subject matter,* and *content*. Suitable definitions of these terms can be found in most art history survey textbooks; the *Oxford English Dictionary* works just as well, but you must identify the shade of meaning most relevant to the visual arts. Depending on how much time I have at my disposal, I either distribute a ready-made list of terms and definitions or, better yet, give students the terms and require them in pairs to search for and provide the definitions. As for the questions, I have long been partial to those of Sylvan Barnet, who includes a list entitled "Asking Questions to Get Answers" in *A Short Guide to Writing about Art*. I require students to read these questions in advance of class discussion and also in class and in front of artworks on museum and gallery visits. Barnet's suite of questions begins at the level of affect, inviting the student to ask herself: "What is my first response to the work? Amusement? Awe? Bafflement? Erotic interest? Annoyance? Shock? Boredom? Later you may modify or even reject this response, this feeling, but begin by trying to study it" (2015, p. 78). While obliging the student's will to learn, these questions underscore the act of reading as a dynamic process contingent on her own subjectivity, her own ways of knowing.

Moving on from (but not abandoning) the first impression, Barnet is indispensable in his discussion of description versus visual analysis (or what he calls formal analysis). Description, he suggests, "is an impersonal inventory, dealing with the relatively obvious, reporting what any eye might see: 'A woman in a white dress sits at a table, reading a letter. Behind her...'" (p. 49). It is related to, but distinct from, analysis, which involves inference and evaluation. A formal analysis, he states, "is an analysis of the *form* the artist produces; that is, an analysis of the work of art, which is made up of such things as line, shape, color, texture, mass, composition. These things give the stone or canvas its form, its expression, its content, its meaning" (p. 48). I introduce these operations in sequence, beginning with description and graduating to analysis. Students tend to find the former far more difficult than the latter. It is tempting to return to that first subjective impression, to how the work made them feel in that initial encounter. In order to convince them of the utility of description as evidence for a compelling evaluation of the artwork, I offer passages from exemplary visual analyses. Their task is to underline, with their assigned partners, the descriptive observations and circle the inferences. An excerpt I often use comes from art critic Peter Schjeldahl, whose analysis of Gustav Klimt's famous *Portrait of Adele Bloch-Bauer I* never fails to generate discussion. He writes:

> The subject is placed off-center, to the right, on a canvas more than four and a half feet square. Imperious and smart, making her slightly horse-faced features seem a paradigm of feminine perfection, she wears a shoulder-strap gown with a cloak-like, billowing outer layer and broad gold and silver bracelets and a bejewelled silver choker. A storm of patterns – spirals, targets, nested squares, split ovals, checks, dots, short vertical bars, arrowhead triangles, ankh-like eyes – may represent fabric, furniture, and wallpaper, or they may be sheer invention. Most of the ground (not background, because almost everything in the picture that isn't flesh snugs up to the picture plane) is mottled gold. Her asymmetrically upswept hair is painted matte black. Her right hand is oddly raised to her shoulder and, wrist bent at a painful-looking right angle, is grasped by her left, as if to restrain it. (On a Viennese note of that epoch, the pencil-outlined fingers faintly suggest claws.) Her frontal gaze turns inward, registering sensations that can only be sexual. Her dark-shadowed hazel eyes, under tapering black brows, are wells of seduction; someone could fall into them. Her bee-stung red mouth parts to expose two competent teeth. Blue tints along her collarbones, wrists, and hands hint at subcutaneous veins: erogenous zones. She is a lighthouse, or shadehouse, of desire. (2006, p. 76)

Note how Schjeldahl imbricates description and inference to compose an analysis that is both compelling and, at least from the perspective of many of my students, sexist. Once we have parsed the passage, which can take up to an hour, we proceed to a discussion of the assumptions Schjeldahl brings to his understanding of the painting. I hold fast to the conviction, however, that the art critic's analysis is no more or less valid than theirs may be, provided they offer clear descriptive evidence to articulate *what* they see as evidence of *how* they see.

These tasks are easily performed in the dim light of the classroom, but they are also transferable to more site-specific engagements with original works of art. There can be no substitute for such encounters, for which I've developed a drawing exercise that works to further enhance the student's ability to read art. This two-part exercise requires each student to find a work of art in, for example, a selection of rooms in a museum. As a dare, I sometimes challenge them to settle on a work of art that chafes them in some way, a work of art that they could not imagine hanging in their bedroom. I then ask them to temporarily surrender their smartphones to me, so as to prevent any distractions. They are expected to spend ten minutes alone in silence, just looking at the work of art they have chosen. This is no easy task, but it often yields surprises and the occasional revelation. After ten minutes have passed, I distribute to each student a good piece of drawing paper and a pencil. I ask them to take another ten minutes to draw what they see. Despite my assurances that they will not be graded on their drawings, reactions range from surprise to abject anguish and always the declaration that "I am not an artist!" Eventually each settles into the task. This exercise is a heuristic one designed to facilitate their discovery of the artwork for themselves and to sharpen their powers of observation. Students always see things in the artwork that they did not perceive at first glance.

How do these sample tasks fit into the Wikipedia assignment? How do they help the student approach the sort of intellectual emancipation Rancière advocates in his account of Jacotot's "universal teaching"? The answers are related. As part of the Wikipedia assignment, students are required to write their own visual analysis, modeled after the analysis they have practiced in the classroom and (if applicable) in the museum, of an artwork by the artist they have chosen for this semester-long project. I make the written visual analysis a requirement for the Wikipedia assignment so students can wrestle with a discrete example of an artwork by their chosen artist. This serves two purposes. First, it provides the students with the ability to clearly describe in words artworks that they may not – due to copyright restrictions – have permission to reproduce on the artist's Wikipedia page. Second, it brings students closer to the artist, ideally with minimal interference from me. Rancière puts it rather more eloquently: "By leaving his intelligence out of the picture, [the master] had allowed their intelligence to grapple with that of the book" (1991, p. 13). In this case, the object grappled with is the work of art, which brings me to the second part of the Wikipedia assignment.

Reading Art History: The Annotated Bibliography

As a scholar, I believe that the annotated bibliography is a kind of rite of passage into the production of knowledge. Within the context of this three-part assignment, the annotated bibliography provides evidence of the student's capacity to evaluate and select key texts, as well as to read and write critically about those texts that – perhaps even more than works of art – constitute the discipline.

It is a sly paradox of art history that the coin of our realm is words more than artworks. In *Patterns of Intention*, Michael Baxandall once observed, "We do not explain pictures: we explain remarks about pictures – or rather, we explain pictures in so far as we have considered them under some verbal description or specification" (1985, p. 1). Examples of well-written descriptions and specifications are certainly available in art history, texts that are clear and incisive, accessible and rigorous. From the standpoint of "universal teaching," such texts make it easy for me to leave my intelligence out of the student's initial engagement, because in their prose style their authors have graciously acknowledged their reader's will to learn. On the other hand, there are in art history – as in any academic discipline – texts that are clotted with jargon, needlessly dispassionate, and prone to the sort of mystification that John Berger believes "is the process of explaining away what might otherwise be evident" (1972, pp. 15–16). I persist, however, in assigning such texts because the quality of content often overrides the tedious writing, but also because I believe that struggle and friction are essential to effective learning. Some students are not shy to express their exasperation with such texts. A memorable assessment arrived in a response paper in which the student concluded art history to be a "useless field of study contaminated with intellectual masturbators." Another I recall came during a discussion of a particularly dense essay on Picasso, to which a student exclaimed aloud: "This is elitist!" The writing, she meant, not the argument per se. Her remark launched us into a wide-ranging discussion of information privilege, accessibility, and higher education. Both of these reactions provided instructive teaching moments that gave me pause and prompted a solution.

I developed a set of critical reading guidelines that I now include in all of my syllabi. I also regularly issue an assurance that has become a mantra among my majors: "I don't expect mastery, only evidence of engagement." I also freely admit that the essays, chapters, and books I assign hold up well to repeated reading and that it has taken me weeks, months, and (in some cases) years to apprehend the full content and textures of a well-crafted and rigorously researched art-historical argument. This admission has the effect of reassuring students that, again, I do not expect them to master the assigned texts on their first, second, or third readings. The guidelines promote engagement through a battery of questions that accompany the students through the text at several levels. In addition, and apropos the visual nature of my field, I offer a visual hook and a challenge. The banner image on the guidelines is my shelfie, specifically a portrait of my office bookshelves

Figure 6.3 *Professor Hamlin's #shelfie*, 2014. Digital photograph.

(Figure 6.3), that I dare students to emulate by thinking about their own bookshelves as colorful embodiments of their intellectual selves and identities as critical readers.

Guidelines for Critical Reading of Art History

The following guidelines provide some steps and questions that will enable students to read critically and reflect thoughtfully.

Step 1 – Fundamentals
The answers to these seemingly basic questions are essential to critical reading. *Why?* Because they tell you a great deal about the text even before you start reading.

- Who is the author? How is her/his name pronounced?
- What is the title of the text?
- Where was it published? Is it a stand-alone essay from an anthology, one of several chapters in a book by the same author, a newspaper or journal article, an online essay?
- When was it published and when was it written? (These years are not necessarily the same.) You can find this information in the bibliographic citation in the syllabus, on the first page of the text and/or the copyright page at the end of the pdf, or at the beginning of the book. If the text is an online essay, you can typically find the "last modified" date at the bottom of the page or sometimes the date is included at the end of the essay.

Here's an example designed to get you thinking about what this basic information can tell you about the assigned text.

Among other essays this semester, you will read the chapter entitled "Sowo: The Good Made Visible" from Sylvia Ardyn Boone's book *Radiance from the Waters: Ideals of Feminine Beauty in Mende Art* (1986).

- Who? A Google search for "Sylvia Ardyn Boone" yields photos of the author, book covers, as well as several pages hosted by Yale University, where she taught in the art history and Afro-American studies programs. An issue from 2001 of the *Yale Bulletin & Calendar* notes that Boone was "the first African-American woman to receive tenure at Yale" in 1988; she died at the age of 54 in 1993.
- What? Consider the title of her chapter. What are your initial observations and questions? What does the word Sowo mean? What might be the connection between goodness and visibility that her title suggests?
- Where? The book *Radiance from the Waters* was published by Yale University Press. By now, you're noticing a trend. What is Yale University? Go to Yale's website or its Wikipedia page to get a sense of its mission and institutional history. How might this condition the form and content of the book?
- When? This book was published in 1986, probably before you were even born. What was happening in America and in the world in the mid-1980s that places this text in a larger socio-political and cultural milieu? (A hint to get started: the Cold War prevailed!) One way to tackle this question is to scroll through the Wikipedia page for 1986; what were some of the flagship events of that year that might have – consciously or unconsciously – conditioned the form and content of Boone's book?

Step 2 – Skimming

Skim the reading assignment for *general* comprehension. Read the text quickly, focusing on the *overall* structure of the argument. Read only key words and sentences (such as the first sentence of each paragraph). If the author uses sub-headings, extended quotes, illustrations, and/or unusual typefaces, make note of these, too.

Step 2½ – Word Finder

As you skim *and* read carefully, look for unfamiliar words – circle them, highlight them, or write them down. Sometimes, by re-reading the sentence or paragraph in which they appear, you will be able to infer their meanings. More often, it helps to look them up in a dictionary.

Step 3 – Closer Reading

Proceed to a second and closer reading with the following questions in mind. Take notes along the way in either the margins or on a separate sheet of paper.

- How does the author organize the essay? What markers does she or he use, such as subheadings?
- Describe the author's "voice." Does she or he write in the first person, in a passive voice (or both)? How does this affect the argument?
- What sorts of examples (textual as well as visual) support the thesis/main argument? Do these examples effectively support the thesis? Could alternative conclusions have been drawn from these examples?
- What *is* the author's thesis/main argument? Can you underline it? Try to paraphrase it by putting it into your own words.
- Could the author have approached the topic from another perspective? Are some issues neglected?
- What assumptions does the author make about the topic and/or the reader?
- Are there aspects of the essay's structure or substance that remain vague and/or unclear?

These questions are handy in classroom discussion and transferrable to other classes and disciplines.

Once students have become practiced at the sort of critical reading the guidelines promote, I introduce them to the second part of the Wikipedia assignment, which is to annotate the bibliography they are assembling on the artist they have chosen. Most have never been tasked with creating an annotated bibliography, and I offer here an excerpt from the assignment description that students have found helpful. The ultimate objective is to equip them with a selection of reliable sources on their artist. In many cases, I am learning too, and I require a 20-minute meeting with each student to review their sources before they embark on their annotations.

Introducing the Annotated Bibliography

An annotated bibliography requires you to – first – cite the article or book you're annotating. (Please use the bibliographic form you are most comfortable with: Chicago, MLA, etc.) Your bibliography should have between five and ten sources. Second, write five to seven sentences that summarize the main arguments of each article or book and how it relates to your engagement with the artist's Wikipedia article (as it currently exists or how you would like to create it). Think of these annotations as "warm ups" for the editing you will do on the artist's Wikipedia page.

Let's say you were interested in revising the article on the modern American painter **Joan Mitchell**. Here are two annotated sources – a book and an essay in an exhibition catalogue:

[1] Chadwick, Whitney. *Women, Art, and Society*. 5th ed. London: Thames & Hudson, 2012.

One way of thinking about Whitney Chadwick's "seminal" text is as a kind of feminist corrective to Giorgio Vasari's *Lives of the Artists*. Acknowledging the contributions of other feminist art historians to a discipline still very much indebted to Vasari's model, she nonetheless recognizes that "critical issues of women's historical production remain unanswered" (p. 15). In her discussion of Joan Mitchell, Chadwick groups her with other women artists whose work was similarly engaged with Abstract Expressionism. She tells her reader that Mitchell and several in her cohort – including Helen Frankenthaler and Grace Hartigan – were well received by critics and included in major museum and gallery shows. Key to her analysis, however, is the assertion that these *artists* were determined to discuss their work in ways not reducible to their gender (p. 326).

[2] Nochlin, Linda. "Joan Mitchell: A Rage to Paint." In *The Paintings of Joan Mitchell*, by Jane Livingston, 49–59. New York: Whitney Museum of American Art, 2002.

Linda Nochlin's chief objective in this essay is to consider the implications of an interpretive strategy that art historians and critics have used to understand Mitchell's pictures, namely that they are expressions of rage or violence. This strategy, as Nochlin proves, is not entirely fictional; she quotes the artist as having described a group of canvases in the early 1960s as "very violent and angry paintings" (p. 49). In the course of her analysis, Nochlin digs deeper in her account of Mitchell's painting and process by arguing that "meaning and emotional intensity are produced structurally" (p. 55). In particular, she considers two prints – *Bedford I* and *Bedford III*, both in the collection of the Walker Art Center – as visual evidence to support her interpretation.

*

These model annotations are also useful to me inasmuch as they provide benchmarks that make grading easier. Indeed, a challenge that attends "universal teaching" is that of evaluation. How will I know if the student has learned if I am not in charge of explaining the content? For his part,

Rancière offers his own version of assessment with the assertion that: "[*The Ignorant Schoolmaster*] will not verify what the student has found; he will verify that the student has searched" (1991, p. 31). Admittedly, I verify both the evidence of pursuit and the quality of bibliographic quarry, but the responsibility to read and learn squarely rests on students' shoulders.

Reading Wikipedia: The Comparative Analysis

The goal of the Wikipedia edit-a-thon is for each student to contribute to a single article on an individual artist. But since existing articles in need of editing can range from rudimentary to moderately developed, and since some articles do not yet exist, evaluating the student's actual contributions can be slipshod at best. The comparative analysis component of the project, which requires students to analyze and evaluate the relative similarities and differences between the articles on each artist, provides a solution with multiple benefits. On the most pragmatic level, its five categories become the rubric I use to evaluate the student's search. It also enables students to parlay the critical reading skills they are using in their analysis of art-historical texts to an online arena, namely Wikipedia, that is both more familiar and less conventionally scholarly. Similarly, it affords them models of articles that they may wish – or not – to emulate in their own edits. Lastly, and in the spirit of the Art + Feminism initiative, it showcases for the student the constructed nature of biography. What follows is an excerpt from this portion of the assignment.

The Comparative Analysis

For your comparative analysis, choose a pair of historically and/or personally related artists from the list below and write about the noteworthy differences and similarities between their Wikipedia articles. Read carefully – repeatedly and over time – the two articles under consideration. Take notes, highlight key phrases and sections before you start writing. Examine and evaluate the articles' structure, language, content, adherence to the "Rules for Editing," and the "Talk Page." Organize your paper according to these five categories.

- Structure:* How are the articles structured? Is each effective and sufficient to the task of surveying the artist's life and career? Why and/or why not?
- Language:* What sort of language is used in each article? Is it formal and/or informal? Is it primarily descriptive or more metaphorical? What is described? What might metaphorical language recommend to the

viewer? To what extent does it enhance or detract from your understanding of the artist?

- Content:* Is there evidence of substantive research in each article? What aspects of the artists' lives seem sufficiently explored? Are the references from books or articles? When were these articles published? Where are the apparent deficiencies in terms of content? Cross-reference the sources by searching for these artists using the library database; are there numerous *books* on each artist? If so, are any of them referenced?
- Rules for Editing: Do the articles adhere to Wikipedia's "Ten Simple Rules for Editing Wikipedia"? Where and how? And where do they fall short?
- Talk Page: What do the talk pages reveal about the articles? Do you agree with what's there? What is missing? What would you add? Before evaluating, review Wikipedia's Talk Page guidelines.

*With respect to the first three categories of analysis, compare the Wikipedia articles to the entries on these artists in the online resource Oxford Art Online. Consulting this database is intended to serve as a point of departure, not to add more comparisons for analysis. You can access this database via the library website.

Also include introductory and concluding paragraphs that engage your reader by offering a through-line in your thinking. What is at stake in this comparison? Where relevant, utilize what you've learned in the required readings and from discussions in class. Use parenthetical citation. No "Works Cited" or "Bibliography" is necessary; this is not a conventional research paper, but rather an analysis that will leverage your knowledge base and ability to think critically and constructively about the comparison.

*

The exercise yields telling insights. For instance, students have noted that Ana Mendieta's article has been more heavily and carefully edited in recent years than Carl Andre's article, a disparity that may be attributed to the success of the Art + Feminism Wikipedia edit-a-thon. Elsewhere, the tendency to privilege life over art in the biographies of women artists is apparent in a comparison of Frida Kahlo's and Diego Rivera's Wikipedia articles. Several students found that Kahlo's article enumerates the tragedies in her life at the expense of descriptions of her art, while Diego Rivera's article currently dwells almost exclusively on his paintings and murals. Moreover, the intersection of race, class, and gender is evident in a comparison between articles on two nineteenth-century artists. Rosa Bonheur's extensive article elides the social advantages that helped enable her – as an upper-class white woman – to excel in the Parisian art world, whereas Harriet Powers' thinly drawn article is arguably in part a legacy of the racism, elitism, and sexism she must have encountered in her life as a folk artist and quilt-maker in rural Georgia, and in part a product of the restrictive social matrix that her quilt-making resisted. An exercise in cultivating not only historical literacy but also media literacy, the comparative analysis challenges students to be skeptical of the information they consume online by evaluating the quality of the articles under review.

Chain Reactions

When Linda Nochlin used the metaphor of a chain reaction to describe how feminism impacts cultural institutions, she had in mind an interior process of feeling into thinking, whereby strong feelings about injustices spur the interrogation of assumptions. Thinking about injustice, she argues, leads to "doing, writing, publishing." "I don't believe," she continues, "one can separate thought and action: I think thought is action" (1974, p. 88). What does the movement of thought into action have to do with critical reading in art and art history? For Nochlin, the process harbors the potential to disrupt unsustainable models of scholarship and ways of seeing in the field and to (re)consider marginalized artists and their work. Building on her conviction, I believe that by obliging students to use their intelligence in the critical reading of art and art history, such chain reactions are not just possible, they are inevitable. Once the student recognizes that she is implicated in the artwork's intelligence and the discursive realm of scholarship, she understands that – like her – artists, art historians, and works of art are part of a complex social matrix, a common field in which she, too, is obliged to think and act. The Art + Feminism Wikipedia edit-a-thon catalyzes these chain reactions by affording students opportunities to fight injustices in the production and dissemination of shared knowledge. As an enterprise that resembles Joseph Jacotot's radical method of "universal teaching," the edit-a-thon stimulates chain reactions that approach the intellectual emancipation Jacques Rancière imagined.

Notes

1 For readers interested in lesson planning around Wikipedia and knowledge as such, I recommend the Wiki Education Foundation's 2015 brochure *Theories: Wikipedia and the Production of Knowledge*. It includes four models that

address information privilege, authorship, knowledge and neutrality, and ideology on Wikipedia.

2 See Wikimedia's Wikipedia Editor's Study from April 2011 and the United Nations University/UNU-MERIT Collaborative Creativity Group's Wikipedia Survey – Overview of Results from March 2010, respectively.

References

Barnet, S. (2015). *A short guide to writing about art* (11th ed.). Upper Saddle River, NJ: Pearson.

Baxandall, M. (1985). *Patterns of intention: On the historical explanation of pictures*. New Haven, CT: Yale University Press.

Berger, J. (1972). *Ways of seeing*. Harmondsworth: Penguin Books.

Cowan, S. (2015). Art-minded feminists become wikipedians for a weekend. *Hyperallergic* (March 12). http://hyperallergic.com/190185/art-minded-feminists-become-wikipedians-for-a-weekend/ (accessed September 29, 2016).

Garrard, M. (1989). *Artemisia Gentileschi: The image of the female hero in Italian baroque art*. Princeton, NJ: Princeton University Press.

Nochlin, L. (1974). How feminism in the arts can implement cultural change. *Arts in Society: Women and the Arts*, 11, 80–89.

Preziosi, D. (1998). *The art of art history: A critical anthology*. Oxford: Oxford University Press.

Rancière, J. (1991). *The ignorant schoolmaster: Five lessons in intellectual emancipation*. Stanford, CA: Stanford University Press.

Schjeldahl, P. (2006). Golden girl. *The New Yorker* (July 24), 76–77.

Wikipedia. (2015a). Meetup/ArtAndFeminism. https://en.wikipedia.org/wiki/Wikipedia:Meetup/ArtandFeminism (accessed August 2, 2015).

Wikipedia. (2015b). Epistemology. https://en.wikipedia.org/wiki/Epistemology (accessed August 3, 2015).

Wikipedia. (2015c). Wikipedia. https://en.wikipedia.org/wiki/Wikipedia (accessed August 11, 2015).

7

Teaching Critical Reading of Historical Texts
Michael Hogan

Basic Matters

Historians work with and from a framework for whatever history they are doing. This means that they have read a summative history before they have even begun their own research, and before they have begun critically assessing primary sources and other documents. Lord Acton, the well-known British historian, once observed that he had read Macaulay's *History of England* (1849) four times before he even thought about doing research for his own volume. Barbara Tuchman, whose best-selling history *The Guns of August* (1962) brought new light to World War I, had first read dozens of works on that war and attended both undergraduate and graduate lectures on the subject. "Without books," Tuchman reminds us, "history is silent. ... Books are humanity in print" (1980, p. 16).

Reading

Reading history is essential preparation for writing it. We can't teach students historical thinking skills without having them read history. We need to convince students that pre-course completion of a general work of history is a *sine qua non* before taking the actual course. At the American School of Guadalajara we typically assign Howard Zinn's *A People's History of the United States* (1995) the summer before the AP US History class, and Tom Standage's *History of the World in Six Glasses* (2006) to our AP World History students. Any accessible and well-written history will do,

Critical Reading Across the Curriculum, Volume 1: Humanities, First Edition.
Edited by Robert DiYanni and Anton Borst.
© 2017 John Wiley & Sons, Inc. Published 2017 by John Wiley & Sons, Inc.

however. The trick is to get something lively for the students to read that will make them think about history in a broad sense, something that shows them how historical themes are interconnected, but which also allows them to see these ideas illustrated with a wealth of fascinating particulars, and, ideally, couched in a compelling narrative. All of this *before* classes begin. For university courses, students should be advised to do similar preparatory reading before classes start.

Writing

We can deepen students' understanding of history by having them write about their reading and research the way historians do. That writing begins with taking notes. An important aspect of reading like a historian is taking hand-written notes. Research has shown that students who write notes by hand have a higher comprehension of the material they read as well as a more critical understanding than those who use a laptop or other device. This seems to hold true not only for students who take notes from a textbook or document, but also for those who take notes in a lecture hall. For most historians of the previous generation this was a natural activity. However, younger students, and perhaps some teachers, may have grown accustomed to have the computer open when reading or when listening to a lecture. Research shows that this is not a good idea.

In a recent article in *Scientific American*, Cindi May cites a study by Pam Mueller and Daniel Oppenheimer published in *Psychological Science*, which showed that taking notes by hand required an altogether different type of thinking process than that used when notes are typed. Because writing by hand is slower, students tend to think about the material, take time to integrate it into what they have already learned, and then summarize. Students with laptops tend to write more verbatim descriptions of what they have read in the text or what they have heard in the lecture rather than synthesize the material. As a result, they tend to have a weaker grasp of the facts and a more superficial understanding of their implications. In short, succinctly relating major topics and evidence from a reading, or salient discussion points from a lecture, in longhand notes, enhances both comprehension and critical thinking. This is important practical information for those of us who teach history.

Challenges for Teachers

Although we are all aware of the importance of analytical and critical reading skills for academic success, they are seldom taught at the university level because most professors believe that students should have mastered or at least been exposed to these basic competencies during their high school years. What these professors often discover, however, is that many students, especially those in their first year of university, come to them with only a rudimentary grasp of how to engage in textual analysis, and that their reading tends to be hurried and perfunctory, with minimal retention and superficial understanding.

In secondary schools the problem is different. Teachers typically understand that they need to help students develop their reading skills. However, the problem is complicated by departmental fragmentation. Too many history teachers believe that the teaching of critical reading skills is the sole responsibility of the language arts (middle school) or the English (high school) faculty. They think that history teachers should be able to deliver content and provide context for the historical documents that students will discuss or write about. Even many widely touted document-based social studies programs and lesson plans move quickly from the text to ways in which the student can *analyze* and then *write* critically about the text. It is generally assumed that the student already knows how to *read* it. That's an erroneous belief and a dangerous one. And this does not yet address the issue of how to think critically about what students read.

The problem is compounded by the fact that, while many schools have good language arts and English teachers, none can supply either the variety of excerpts or the specific instructions for analysis required for critical reading in history. While some close-reading techniques may be transferable to reading history, there are significant differences. Unless regular meetings take place between departments, most history teachers will remain unaware of the critical reading techniques taught in English class and how they might apply these techniques in their teaching of history.

Three Kinds of Reading

Basic or Surface Reading

This is the initial exposure to a text in which the student skims over the first page of the document, gets a general idea of what the subject is, and then goes on to the next page. There may be vocabulary the student does not know, even some words the student cannot figure out in context. The student has a sketchy idea of the author's point view, a limited awareness of the structure of the argument, and only a superficial understanding of the author's purpose. But a first step, at least, has been taken.

Close or Deep Reading

This is often re-reading and it is generally done with pen or highlighter. The student skims the document quickly to get the general idea, then goes back and reads more carefully, underlining new or complex vocabulary, and circling key words or concepts. The student then analyzes the author's point of view, determines the structure of the piece, what the author's purpose or intention is, what evidence the author gives to support his argument, and how the structure or the rhetorical devices enable the author to accomplish his communicative purpose. Here we may see similarities between general textual analysis – whether of a novel, a religious text, or a page of biology – and analysis of history texts. However, when analyzing a history text, the document alone will seldom tell us all we need to know. And here is where we must break with the standard close reading as pure textual analysis and move on to our third kind of reading.

Critical Reading

This is an extension of close reading. Here the student not only focuses on the author's idea but also looks at the context. How might this work relate to similar things the student has read? How does it diverge from similar concepts of which the student is aware? How does it follow (or not follow) the rules of logic? How might it relate to other social, political, or environmental contexts? What else was going on during the time in which the document was written? How is it similar to or different from other things the author has written? Establishing background is a *sine qua non* of teaching critical reading in history. Thus the teacher plays an integral role, which can be filled by a mini-lecture, a timeline, a PowerPoint presentation, or any combination of contextual framework deliveries, all done with a consideration of students' learning – with attention to what students need to know.

Selecting Historical Documents for Analysis

Choosing texts is also critical. Secondary school administrators encourage teachers to use documents accessible for particular grade levels, or texts that are familiar, or those suggested by a particular history textbook. Invariably, teachers are encouraged to use short passages, since short passages appear in high-stakes exams.

We will suggest another approach here.

The two most common pieces used as models in teacher in-service workshops on teaching students how to write historical analysis are Abraham Lincoln's Gettysburg Address (middle school and high school), and Martin Luther King's "Letter from a Birmingham Jail" (Advanced Placement and first-year college). The College Board's tutorial for teachers on the SOAPSTone technique (described below) uses the former, and College Board president David Coleman's YouTube video on teaching close reading uses the latter. Both would have instructors teach students to read these as almost sacred texts, closely examining the documents in what amounts to scriptural exegesis.

Here we will consider two less-examined works by President Lincoln and Dr. King. In the first we will see Lincoln as an Illinois congressman declaring that the Mexican War of 1846 was begun by the United States based on false information and in violation of the Constitution. It is revealing. It challenges the reader to go beyond the text and see the United States in its posture as an expansionist nation, practicing imperialist policies at the expense of other countries, belying its own democratic claims. It also gives us an opportunity to look at other related texts, such as Thoreau's "Civil Disobedience," which was written in opposition to that war. We will read Lincoln's entire speech, not an excerpt, so that students can see how Lincoln's arguments are developed and extended.

For our second text, we will examine a complex speech by Martin Luther King in which he addresses himself to the US government regarding its perennial military engagements abroad, and continuing income disparity and social injustice at home. King is addressing not segregation or racism, but issues which profoundly affect all races as well all nations. This is a piece that challenges the reader to go beyond the text and understand the other problems of the Vietnam era (interminable conflicts abroad, the grinding poverty of the underclass, and the massive growth of the military at the expense of social welfare programs), problems that continue today.

These profound texts challenge students and teachers alike. If our goal is to help students think critically, they must be allowed to think creatively and independently as well, to see where else the text might lead them, and to question what other works have been inadvertently (or purposely) excluded by the guardians of standard curricula, and where else they might find enlightenment. It is also important that they read entire documents when possible so that they can see how the arguments unfold, how the evidence is presented, how the conclusions are reached. Excerpts seldom show these textual aspects clearly and often have been edited to eliminate contradictory, troublesome, or politically incorrect aspects. Thus they are sometimes misleading.

Document selection therefore forms an integral part of the lesson plan, whether a course is structured chronologically or thematically. Here are some suggestions for selecting documents:

1 The document selected should be firmly rooted in the time period being discussed. Even if it is a thematic lesson, the students should be fully aware of the period in which the piece was written.
2 It should be challenging at several levels: vocabulary, structure, multiplicity of interpretations.
3 It should supply a perspective that allows the students to see nuanced interpretations of the historical events or issue.
4 It should lend itself to connections to other time periods and other themes.

Once a particular document has been chosen, the teacher should spend some time with it. If it is a lengthy document, it might be wise to number the paragraphs so that class discussion of questions regarding the document can be more easily followed. If it is given to the students as a homework assignment, questions should be provided to help them analyze it closely in preparation for class discussion. One useful device is that of SOAPSTone, in which students are asked to write a brief statement about the Speaker, Occasion, Audience, Purpose, Subject, and Tone of the piece.

When class begins, the teacher might read the piece aloud or select a good student reader to do so, pausing from time to time to ask questions, point out key words, and solicit questions from the students. In other words, the teacher should, at least in the initial work on document reading, model what she expects students to do.

Marking and Preparing Historical Documents

Class preparation should include marking up the document to illustrate for students some useful ways to do a close and critical reading. Here are some suggestions:

1 Circle words that repeat themselves, and circle verbs that imply action. Both of these might suggest a theme or intent on the author's part.
2 Number the paragraphs for easy reference.
3 On the left side of the page note any difficult vocabulary, or words capable of multiple meanings. Look these up and be ready to discuss.
4 On the right side of the page write questions relating to your understanding of the work, or the relationship of the work to the historical period or theme.

5   Have a specific purpose in mind as you annotate and prepare your lesson; however, be open to student questions and comments that present different points of view or even different readings of the text as long as they can be justified by textual or other evidence.

6   Have the marked-up document scanned so that you can project it for students, keeping in mind that this is only one way to do analytical reading, and that students may individualize with marker or pen.

7   Avoid dismissing student questions or comments that diverge from the theme or concept you have selected for your lesson. Let the lesson proceed organically. The only reservation should be if a student's question, opinion, or point of view is not supported by evidence from the text or from other historical reading the student has done.

Sometimes a document chosen may come from a student suggestion or question. For example, in a discussion of the Mexican–American War of 1846–1848 in AP US History with a group of high school juniors, one student noted a reference in the text to Lincoln's "spot resolutions" in Congress, after President Polk had decided to declare war against Mexico. The student was unable to figure out exactly what these resolutions were, since not even one specific example in our highly acclaimed textbook was provided. Was Lincoln against the war? Why had we never heard about this before in any history class?

So that evening I did my research and downloaded the spot resolutions. I numbered the paragraphs and underlined the word *whether*, which was repeated frequently. I underlined a recurring statement from President Polk's war message to Congress: "American blood has been shed on American soil," the *casus belli*. I also underlined statements that indicated whose blood was shed and where, as well as statements that reflected who lived in these territories.

I also wrote three questions: (1) What if American blood was NOT shed on American soil? (2) What other documents might help us have a better understanding of Lincoln's work? (3) How does the structure of the work reveal Lincoln's training and worldview?

My students were well prepared for this document. They had read about and had a class discussion on the westward expansion of the republic in the 1840s. They were also familiar with the concept of Manifest Destiny and its roots in the early colonial concept of the City on the Hill. They were aware of the deeply rooted feeling of racial superiority of the Anglo-Saxon in America articulated by some of our finest thinkers and writers from Emerson to Whitman. They had read from Zinn's *People's History of the United States* on this issue. They were also aware that Texas had requested to be, and was, admitted to the United States in 1836, and that since then there had been negotiations to purchase California from the Mexican government, as well as to acquire a route across the southwest United States to the Pacific, i.e. "from sea to shining sea." They knew that the Mexican government had not wished to sell these lands, and that President Polk, a Democrat, had been elected on a platform of western expansion with the intent of acquiring these lands one way or another. Here is the document:

RESOLUTIONS IN THE UNITED STATES HOUSE OF REPRESENTATIVES, Introduced by Abraham Lincoln, Representative from Illinois. DECEMBER 22, 1847

1 Whereas, The President of the United States, in his message of May 11, 1846, has declared that "the Mexican Government not only refused to receive him [the envoy of the United States], or to listen to his propositions, but, after a long-continued series of menaces, **has at last invaded our territory and shed the blood of our fellow-citizens on our own soil**";

2 And again, in his message of December 8, 1846, that "we had ample cause of war against Mexico long before the breaking out of hostilities; but even then we forbore to take redress into our own hands until **Mexico herself became the aggressor, by invading our soil in hostile array, and shedding the blood of our citizens**";

3 And yet again, in his message of December 7, 1847, that "the Mexican Government refused even to hear the terms of adjustment which he [our minister of peace] was authorized to propose, and finally, under wholly unjustifiable pretexts, involved the two countries in war, **by invading the territory of the State of Texas, striking the first blow, and shedding the blood of our citizens on our own soil**";

4 And whereas, This House is desirous to obtain a full knowledge of all the facts which go to **establish whether the particular spot on which the blood of our citizens was so shed was or was not at that time our own soil**: therefore,

5 Resolved, By the House of Representatives, that the President of the United States be respectfully requested to inform this House:

6 First. **Whether** the spot on which the blood of our citizens was shed, as in his message declared, was or was not within the territory of Spain, at least after the treaty of 1819, until the Mexican revolution.

7 Second. **Whether** that spot is or is not within the territory which was wrested from Spain by the revolutionary government of Mexico.

8 Third. **Whether that spot is or is not within a settlement of people, which settlement has existed ever since long before the Texas revolution, and until its inhabitants fled before the approach of the United States army.**

9 Fourth. Whether that settlement is or is not isolated from any and all other settlements by the Gulf and the Rio Grande on the south and west, and by wide uninhabited regions on the north and east.

10 Fifth. **Whether the people of that settlement, or a majority of them, or any of them, have ever submitted themselves to the government or laws of Texas or of the United States, by consent or by compulsion, either by accepting office, or voting at elections, or paying tax, or serving on juries, or having process served upon them, or in any other way.**

11 Sixth. **Whether the people of that settlement did or did not flee from the approach of the United States army, leaving unprotected their homes and their growing crops, before the blood was shed, as in the message stated; and whether the first blood, so shed, was or was not shed within the enclosure of one of the people who had thus fled from it.**

12 Seventh. **Whether our citizens, whose blood was shed, as in his message declared, were or were not, at that time, armed officers and soldiers, sent into that settlement by the military order of the President, through the Secretary of War.**

13 Eighth. **Whether the military force of the United States was or was not so sent into that settlement after General Taylor had more than once intimated to the War Department that, in his opinion, no such movement was necessary to the defense or protection of Texas.**

Reading Abraham Lincoln's House Resolutions December 22, 1847

My students saw the repetition of the "American blood shed on American soil" as intrinsic to Polk's argument that the war was justified and constitutional. If Lincoln could prove that the blood was not shed on American soil, then the war would be unconstitutional, an over-reaching of presidential power, and also unnecessary and unjust.

They saw Lincoln's repetition of the word *whether* not merely as a rhetorical or organizational device, but rather as the lead to a series of practical legal questions. If the answer to any of those questions were affirmative, then the declaration of war would be both justified and constitutional. If the answers to those questions were negative, then the declaration of war would be fatally flawed.

The students noted that it was difficult to actually visualize the area in contention. Where exactly was the original border with Texas? According to all existing maps, it was the Rio Nueces, considerably north of the Rio Grande. What did the map of the area look like in 1836? The students agreed that a map of the region from the specific time period in question would be helpful, so we found one and downloaded it.

When I asked them about the structure of the argument, several students replied that it was "very lawyer-like," "logical," "easy to follow." They also said they would like to see a letter, journal, or memo on the same subject written by Lincoln during this period, so we downloaded one of those as well.

Whenever we have these discussions, I ask the students to have only the document under discussion on their desk. However, I usually choose two students who may also have their laptops open. These students can look up references, find a map or illustration, and, sometimes, an additional document.

I projected one such map so the students could see the area American troops had to cross to reach the Rio Grande. It was apparent that the movement of Taylor's troops across the Rio Nueces to the Rio Grande was a provocation, and that it was intentional. On all the maps of this period, the Rio Nueces was the southern boundary of Texas. Anything below that was Mexican territory, listed as "disputed area" on US-centric maps. It was a disputed region, as one student observed, because when Mexican general Santa Anna was captured after the defeat of his troops in the Texas insurgency of 1836, he agreed to move his army across the Rio Grande. However, in no way did Santa Anna concede this land to Texas; nor did he have the authority to do so since, like the United States, only his Congress in Mexico could approve such a cession of territory. In addition, at no point after Texas became a state did the American Congress seek to expand the territory of that state to the Rio Grande. The southern border of the State of Texas, like the southern border of the Texas Republic, remained the Rio Nueces.

So we went back to the document once again. We saw that the American troops moved into territory occupied by Mexican people. As Lincoln suggests, those people fled from the American army. We also knew that the commander, Zachary Taylor, saw no military necessity to move troops into that territory. Thus the movement of troops into that territory resulted in bloodshed, and then an all-out war, which Lincoln asserted was "unnecessarily and unconstitutionally" incited by the president.

Not everyone agreed with Lincoln at the time, including William H. Herndon, Lincoln's law partner in Illinois. And here is where the second document suggested by the students comes in. What exactly were Lincoln's views about presidential power? As we will see from this additional document, his answer to that question gives rise to further comments about preemptive attacks, abuse of presidential power, and false or misleading intelligence, all of which students will find relevant to later conflicts, such as the second Iraq War.

We might, here, insert an exercise, asking students to read Lincoln's letter of February 15, 1848, to William Herndon.

Exercise

Read the following letter Abraham Lincoln wrote to his law partner William H. Herndon. Find evidence in the letter that confirms Lincoln's views about the abuse of presidential power, preemptive attacks, misleading and false intelligence, and other related issues.

TO WILLIAM H. HERNDON.

WASHINGTON, February 15, 1848.

DEAR WILLIAM,

Your letter of the 29th January was received last night. Being exclusively a constitutional argument, I wish to submit some reflections upon it in the same spirit of kindness that I know actuates you. Let me first state what I understand to be your position. It is that if it shall become necessary to repel invasion, the President may, without violation of the Constitution, cross the line and invade the territory of another country, and that whether such necessity exists in any given case the President is the sole judge.

Before going further consider well whether this is or is not your position. If it is, it is a position that neither the President himself, nor any friend of his, so far as I know, has ever taken. Their only positions are – first, that the soil was ours when the hostilities commenced; and second, that whether it was rightfully ours or not, Congress had annexed it, and the President for that reason was bound to defend it; both of which are as clearly proved to be false in fact as you can prove that your house is mine. The soil was not ours, and Congress did not annex or attempt to annex it. But to return to your position. Allow the President to invade a neighboring nation whenever he shall deem it necessary to repel an invasion, and you allow him to do so whenever he may choose to say he deems it necessary for such purpose, and you allow him to make war at pleasure. Study to see if you can fix any limit to his power in this respect, after having given him so much as you propose.

If today he should choose to say he thinks it necessary to invade Canada to prevent the British from invading us, how could you stop him? You may say to him, – "I see no probability of the British invading us"; but he will say to you, "Be silent: I see it, if you don't."

The provision of the Constitution giving the war making power to Congress was dictated, as I understand it, by the following reasons: kings had always been involving and impoverishing their people in wars, pretending generally, if not always, that the good of the people was the object. This our convention understood to be the most oppressive of all kingly oppressions, and they resolved to so frame the Constitution that no one man should hold the power of bringing this oppression upon us. But your view destroys the whole matter, and places our President where kings have always stood. Write soon again.

Yours truly,
A. Lincoln

Here Lincoln argues with his friend about a related question. If the president had been seriously concerned that there was a threat to the United States, would he have been justified in "crossing the line" and initiating a preemptive invasion of another country? Lincoln says very politely that he is rewording his friend's position here and will respond to him. He adds, however, that this is *not* what happened in the case of Polk. Polk's position was that "American blood had been shed on American soil."

But, as to his friend's question, what do we find? And here a student remarks that Lincoln is equally adamant that such an invasion is neither justified nor constitutional.

"Why? Where is your evidence for this?" the teacher asks. And the student refers to the document and Lincoln's statement that the Constitution was created for the express purpose of limiting that "kingly oppression" of involving the people in a war. "No one man should hold the power of bringing this oppression upon us."

In class we broke up into small groups, with each group discussing how Lincoln's comments were relevant to other wars or other time periods or themes. The discussions (which group leaders were asked to summarize) were wide-ranging: from Hitler's invasion of Poland, to Truman's "police action" in Korea, to Bush's invasion of Iraq to remove the alleged "weapons of mass destruction" based on faulty intelligence.

Other students felt that many of the problems in Mexican–US relations today stemmed from this period and wished that we could explore that issue further. Some felt that a failure to understand the implications of this debate might be responsible for much of the anti-immigrant feeling in the United States, which is based on the understanding that these "illegals" were violating American law and should be punished. What if people understood that the seizure of their territory began with a violation of international law on the part of the Americans? Might this knowledge make Americans more tolerant?

Others made much of the fact that the movie *Lincoln*, which was such a box-office and critical success, was supposedly based on "bold new information on the life of Lincoln" (from a review one of the students found praising the director for his courage in bringing it out). They asked, "Why wasn't there anything about Lincoln's objections to the Mexican War in the movie? This was an example of Lincoln putting his political career on the line. Why wouldn't the director provide his audience with this information about the iconic American president?"

Class discussion and analysis of documents are moving together organically here. This is the ideal. We want students to have certain tools at their disposal, but the horse should pull the cart, not vice versa. In other words, *the tools and techniques of close reading should not be running the class.* The flow of information and the critical analysis of that information should open up new ways of seeing the issue, ways of connecting the topic under discussion with related themes and other periods.

What we model for students in these class discussions, in this analytical give and take with ideas, is the opening up of new paths for research; it is what historians actually do. Historians, in real life, tend to work alone, analyzing documents, seeing how one piece of information fits in with another, and how one document might be better understood by looking at other documents, maps, and statistical data from the period. They also read what other historians have written, analyzing the varying points of view. It is this sense of complexity and interrelatedness we want to share with our students as a way to help them begin doing it on their own. A successful history class should model the heuristics of historical thinking and critical analysis. It is a way of saying to the student: *Go forth and do likewise.*

For those of us who have actually worked as historians, we know that with the exception of an occasional seminar or conference, most of our work is done quietly in the office or at home, not with groups of other historians. And if we truly wish to give our students the gift of "thinking like a historian," we should use these models to help them experience the delights of research – how one thing leads to another, how one question opens up another, how each document can be interpreted and re-interpreted differently by successive generations, how objectivity is often compromised by ideology, and how our best efforts at coming to a final conclusion are often frustrated.

Reading Martin Luther King, Jr.'s Speech Opposing the Vietnam War

To read a Martin Luther King speech as a sacred text, as some close-reading instructors suggest, and ask the student to simply analyze the text without any reaching outside, without examining the context, without even *personally* interacting with the text, is to diminish King's accomplishments.

We know his degree was in theology. His audience was often other clergymen. He was an African American, his audience often other African Americans. What we sometimes forget, however, is that King went beyond the confines of his discipline and the issue of racial equality. He saw social justice as his major cause. He understood civil rights for African Americans as one issue among many to advance that "true revolution of values" which would "look uneasily on the glaring contrast of poverty and wealth." We might remind ourselves and our students that he died while giving a speech supporting black *and white* sanitary workers in Memphis, Tennessee.

The following exercise, which concerns King's speech in opposition to the Vietnam War, can help our students consider the broader contexts and significance of his ideas, and how he communicated them to the public.

Exercise

Read Martin Luther King, Jr.'s speech in opposition to the Vietnam War, which he gave in New York City on April 4, 1967 (the text can be found online at http://www.americanrhetoric.com/speeches/mlkatimetobreak silence.htm). As you read, determine what he is arguing for and why. Identify the evidence King presents in support of his claims. Consider the extent to which you find his speech persuasive and why. You can use the following questions to guide your reading and critical thinking.

1 Do you agree with King that the Civil Rights Movement and the peace movement are somehow related? Why or why not?
2 Why do you think there were cutbacks on Johnson's War on Poverty and the New Society programs as the Vietnam War progressed? What were the effects of these cutbacks?
3 King quotes Kennedy and then says that the United States is on the wrong side of the world revolution. What is his evidence?

4 How does King connect social justice with a revolution in values? Cite specifics from the text.

5 King argues that his dream of a world-wide fellowship is not mere idealism but a practical choice; it is a matter of life or death. Explain and give evidence. Do you agree or disagree? Why?

6 Is King's speech mainly about civil rights for African Americans and the Vietnam War or something more? Explain your thinking.

This is a critical reading history exercise where the students might be permitted to make as many assessments as the time allows. When the discussion has moved along and the students have shared their ideas with each other and in small groups, one might allow the student leaders to present their collective findings and document them on the board. Following that, one might then hand out the short editorial that appeared the following day in the *New York Times* as a response to Martin Luther King's speech. (You can find the editorial, entitled "Dr. King's Error," on the *Times'* website under the date April 7, 1967, or try the link supplied in the reference list below).

After having done the hard work of analyzing Dr. King's speech and seeing its complexity and the interrelatedness of King's ideas, my students were annoyed by the editorial. They observed that, while it was well written, as *Times* editorials usually were, it ignored the basic thesis of King's speech and missed the major points. The students thought that the editorial criticized King for conflating civil rights and the peace movement, but didn't touch at all on his central argument: that all racism, militarism, and drive for excessive profits undermine social justice everywhere and put us on a path to destruction. They also thought that King's speech went beyond a simple argument about racial equality and moved into the area of genuine human brotherhood, true compassion, and international cooperation.

Earlier in the year we had looked at selections from John Henry Newman's *Idea of a University* (1852). This is an important work, particularly the section defining what it means to be a "gentleman," which explains how we should examine and discuss ideas with which we disagree. One common tactic of argument Newman implicitly criticizes is purposely "mistaking the point in argument" as a way of dismissing a view one disagrees with. One of the students remembered Newman's thoughts on this subject and applied them to the *Times* editorial, reading a passage from Newman aloud to the class:

> If [the gentleman] engages in controversy of any kind, his disciplined intellect preserves him from the blundering discourtesy of better, perhaps, but less educated minds; who, like blunt weapons, tear and hack

instead of cutting clean, who mistake the point in argument, waste their strength on trifles, misconceive their adversary, and leave the question more involved than they find it. He may be right or wrong in his opinion, but he is too clear-headed to be unjust. (1996, p. 146)

Conclusion

If our students are to rise above the ordinary, above the limited expectations set out by the advocates of benchmarks and common standards, we must provide them with opportunities to see conflicts of values, and how even "respected, liberal" media outlets may be aligned with a value system that is often questionable, but has little incentive to question itself.

If we are to continue as a free society and if our students are to provide leadership in the world, we must help them discover the interconnectedness among disciplines. We must provide them with opportunities to find the genius in themselves and to make new connections as yet unseen. We must give them the chance to think outside the guidelines of the disciplines, *as* they learn, not after.

Unfortunately, many schools are putting aside what they do well – using inexpensive and workable options to improve the quality of teachers already in place – to follow blindly the least common denominators of public policy, which are leading schools down the path of mediocrity. The search for a packaged curriculum, for the lesson plan that any teacher can follow (even one with no expertise in the discipline), the move away from holistic teaching and a multiplicity of evaluative methods to shallow benchmarks, redundant standards, and incessant testing, are wrongheaded and foolish.

We history teachers are uniquely positioned to make a major contribution to the education of our young people. We have at our fingertips extraordinary resources unavailable to previous generations. We have speedy online access to most of the world's largest archives. We have fascinating narratives written by fine writers. We also have increasingly sophisticated analytical tools, which we can hone ourselves and teach to our students. But more important than the advantages our own historical moment happens to provide is our work ethic and our willingness to challenge ourselves and our students to read more, think more, question more. These qualities, plus mentorship (whether online, at conferences, through books like this one, or in our own academic community), can help us determine the most useful skills and activities to engage our students, and enable them to experience the excitement of reading history critically.

Some Useful Sources for Critical Reading in History

The following sources provide useful material for helping students think critically about historical issues:

1 D. Coleman. (2011, August 19). *Text-dependent analysis in action: Examples from Dr. MLK, Jr.'s Letter from a Birmingham Jail* [video file]. Retrievable from https://www.youtube.com/watch?v=Ho_ntaYbL7o.

   A close-reading lesson by the head of the College Board on Martin Luther King's "Letter from a Birmingham Jail." Teachers might compare this text-dependent analysis with the broader critical analysis of another letter by Dr. King in this chapter. Both have their uses.

2 L. Fisher. (2009). *The Mexican War and Lincoln's spot resolutions.* Damascus, MD: Pennyhill Press.

   This concise monograph supplies the teacher with all the documents, speeches, and resolutions necessary to independently evaluate Lincoln's position in the anti-war debate in the House of Representatives following Polk's Declaration of War.

3 A. F. Greenberg. (2013). *A wicked, wicked war: Polk, Clay, Lincoln and the 1846 U.S. invasion of Mexico.* New York: Knopf.

   This is the first major text by an academic historian that not only analyzes Lincoln's arguments against the war with Mexico, but further shows how contemporary newspapers and politicians reacted at the time and how Lincoln's commitment almost ruined his political career.

4 Queen's College, New York. Evaluating contradictory claims and positions. *Writing on history.* Retrievable from http://qcpages.qc.cuny.edu/Writing/history/critical/contradictory.html

   Evaluating contradictory arguments is an important historical reading skill. This site shows us how to encourage students to not simply choose the evidence that clearly supports their claim, but to acknowledge both sides, thus making one's position even more solid.

5 Stanford Education Group. *Reading like a historian.* Retrievable from https://sheg.stanford.edu/rlh

   This site has a number of useful descriptions of the skills needed to foster historical thinking. In addition there are numerous lesson plans using documents that are helpful to teachers at every level.

6 S. Wineburg. (2012). *Historical thinking and other unnatural acts: Charting the future of teaching the past.* Philadelphia, PA: Temple University Press.

Wineburg disputes the notion that there is a single method to teach history effectively. He encourages teachers to explore the dozens of ways (conversation, reading, reflection, film, debate, document analysis, lecture, research, cartoons, and advertising) in which students can absorb history, participate in the collective memory, and shape their critical thinking skills.

References

Dr. King's Error [editorial]. (1967). *New York Times* (April 7). https://kinginstitute.stanford.edu/king-papers/documents/dr-kings-error (accessed September 29, 2016).

King, Jr., M. L. (1967). Beyond Vietnam – A time to break silence (April 4). *American Rhetoric: Online Speech Bank*. http://www.americanrhetoric.com/speeches/mlkatimetobreaksilence.htm

Lincoln, A. (1847). Resolutions in the United States House of Representatives, Introduced by Abraham Lincoln, Representative from Illinois (December 22). In *The papers and writings of Abraham Lincoln*, vol. 2. Ed. A. B. Lapsley. http://www.classic-literature.co.uk/american-authors/19th-century/abraham-lincoln/the-writings-of-abraham-lincoln-02/ebook-page-18.asp (accessed October 14, 2016).

Lincoln, A. (1848). On the Mexican War: To William H. Herndon (February 15). In *The papers and writings of Abraham Lincoln*, vol. 2. Ed. A. B. Lapsley. Retrieved from www.gutenberg.org.

Macaulay. T. B. (1855). *The history of England*. London: Folio Editions.

May, C. (2014). A learning secret: Don't take notes with a laptop. *Scientific American* (June 3). http://www.scientificamerican.com/article/a-learning-secret-don-t-take-notes-with-a-laptop/ (accessed September 29, 2016).

Mueller, P. A., and Oppenheimer, D. M. (2014). The pen is mightier than the keyboard. *Psychological Science*, 25(6), 1159–1168.

Newman, J. H. (1996). *The idea of a university*. New Haven, CT: Yale University Press.

Standage, T. (2006). *The history of the world in six glasses*. New York: Walker.

Tuchman, B. (1962). *The guns of August*. New York: Macmillan.

Tuchman, B. (1980). The book. *Bulletin of the American Academy of Arts and Sciences*, 34(2), 16–32.

Zinn, H. (1995). *A people's history of the United States, 1492–present*. HarperPerennial.

8

Philosophy and the Practice of Questioning

Matt Statler

Questioning Toward Truth

One party joke that philosophers inevitably endure goes something like this: "Oh, so you don't actually do anything, you just sit around thinking all the time? Gosh, that must really be difficult, ha ha ha ..." And yet, while of course the practice of philosophy does not involve the same sort of physical labor as, say, wildcat mining for sulfur on the side of an active volcano at midday in the South Pacific, it is nevertheless a form of activity. Philosophy can occur concurrently with almost any type of physical movement or posture – some philosophers sit at long wooden desks or lecture from podiums, others huddle in dark carrels amidst the library stacks, and still others walk outside the walls of the city. So, then, exactly what kind of activity is philosophy?

Some would say that philosophy is a mode of action that allows the world to reveal itself truthfully. We could also say in a more contemporary idiom that philosophy involves questioning toward truth, raising the question: What is truth?

Now, the academic discipline of physics involves a search for the truth about the material world, biology the living, anthropology the human, and so on. By contrast, philosophers ask about the truth of truth itself, inquiring, How does truth come into existence? How might it cease to exist or occur? How do we come to recognize or understand it as such? What obligations might it impose upon us? And finally, What value does it have or carry?

Critical Reading Across the Curriculum, Volume 1: Humanities, First Edition.
Edited by Robert DiYanni and Anton Borst.
© 2017 John Wiley & Sons, Inc. Published 2017 by John Wiley & Sons, Inc.

The academic discipline of philosophy has evolved as a long conversation about how to answer questions such as these, and it includes a set of well-established topical themes and rhetorical conventions. Sketched roughly: metaphysics involves raising questions about being or existence; epistemology involves raising questions about knowledge or understanding; ethics involves raising questions about the good, and how to attain it; aesthetics involves raising questions about beauty, and how we perceive it, and so on. Some philosophers understand these topical areas of inquiry as fundamentally related or integrated, and thus develop systematic approaches to them; others understand them as fundamentally distinct, and thus pursue certain questions without regard for others. Longstanding tensions, disagreements, and paradoxes exist within these topical areas of inquiry – some philosophers would reject listing them as a series of topics, claiming, for example, that inquiring into the truth of knowledge and inquiring into the truth of beauty involve very different forms of philosophical investigation.

While some philosophers try to answer these questions or take up these paradoxes through reading and writing and dialogue, other philosophers engage in farming, cooking, sports, the arts, and various other life activities. Since this is a book about critical reading, here I seek to describe and also to perform the practice of reading philosophically. I will focus on the *Meno*, a philosophical dialogue written by Plato in which Socrates speaks with several of his friends about knowledge and virtue. Through this process, I will raise questions such as: How do we know what we think we know? Based on what we think we know, how should we live our lives? How might we think and live differently, and better, than we currently do?

By presenting these questions in written form, I invite readers to view this text not as a model for philosophy in general, nor as a prescription for how philosophers should act in all circumstances at all times, but instead as an opportunity to engage in the practice of philosophical inquiry. The pedagogical motivation is pragmatic, since, as Gilles Deleuze notes, "We learn nothing from those who say: 'Do as I do.' Our only teachers are those who tell us to 'do with me'" (1995, p. 23).

How Do We Come to Know Anything at All?

By most accounts the tradition of western philosophy begins with the figure of Socrates as sketched in a series of dialogues by his student, Plato. In a subsequent section of this essay, we will consider how Socrates' example can animate classroom pedagogy today. But first we perform a philosophical reading to bring the Platonic dialogues into view and ask: What does Socrates do?

Asking Questions

Socrates asks people questions. As recounted in the Platonic *Dialogues,* Socrates grew up as the son of a stonemason and a midwife, fought in a war as an infantryman, and then loitered around the central public square of Athens for many years. During that time, he attended banquets, festivals, and sporting events, took walks, and talked with friends and visiting dignitaries. Eventually he was thrown in jail on charges of corrupting the youth, ultimately dying by execution, a victim of state violence. To the end of his life Socrates asked questions about issues of concern to Athenian citizens, including truth, beauty, pleasure, virtue, justice, and law. Whatever the topic or the occasion, Socrates consistently deployed a dialectical method of questioning, calling commonly held beliefs into question and forcing people who claimed to be experts and authorities to concede the limits of their own understanding. All the while, Socrates claimed to know only that he knew nothing.

Many philosophers have interpreted this posture as ironic – the phrase "Socratic irony" is used commonly today to describe someone who feigns ignorance while posing questions to someone else. Viewed through this lens, Socrates appears as the most cunning man not only in the Athens of his day, but even perhaps in the broad scope of world history. By pretending to lack knowledge, and by using the dialectical method of questioning, he teaches his interlocutors the truth. Through Plato's generous accounts of this activity, Socrates teaches and inspires subsequent generations to the present day. In this interpretation of the *Dialogues,* the truth appears substantively as a body of knowledge about justice, beauty, existence, virtue, and other concerns. Socrates has that knowledge, and he teases it out of his friends rather than explaining it himself, while Plato serves as diligent scribe and author of the *Dialogues.*

Yet other philosophers emphasize the process of Socrates' questioning rather than the substantive content of the knowledge it produces. The truth may be understood not so much in terms of what is revealed by the dialectic, but as the process or event of the revelation itself. The Greek word for truth, *alethei,* can be literally translated as "out-from-darkness," conveying dynamic movement rather than static essence. On this interpretation, the figure of Socrates draws us to consider the relationship between knowing and not-knowing, and to see just how difficult it can be to differentiate these two conditions.

If we think Socrates is ironically playing dumb, then we can find the difference between knowing and not-knowing by watching what his interlocutors learn over the course of the dialogue. At the beginning, they appear to lack knowledge, and after Socrates engages them in dialogue, they appear to have learned something new. Socrates is so skillful that he can teach them what he knows by playing dumb about it.

If we think instead that the truth lies not in what Socrates says, but in the activity of raising questions and engaging in critical reflection through dialogue, then the difference between knowing and not-knowing becomes more difficult to identify. Indeed on this interpretation the signature effect of Socratic irony is that it defers the differentiation of what is known from what is unknown, forcing us to ask again and again: Do we know what we think we know? How indeed do we begin to think that we have ever known anything at all?

We could, of course, try to answer this question by turning to other academic disciplines. We could work, for example, with developmental child psychologists and conduct rigorous empirical tests of early literacy; we could work with neurophysiologists and create models of energy transfer in the nervous system; or we could work with evolutionary anthropologists and dig through the fossil record to pinpoint the historical emergence of representational language and abstract thought among hominids.

Such research activities, fascinating as they may be, are based on certain conceptual and methodological assumptions that must be set forth at the outset of any study, and then taken for granted in order to continue the study and generate knowledge. Following Socrates' example, we could engage instead in philosophical inquiry by calling into question the methods and concepts commonly accepted as legitimate and accurate by our colleagues in the departments of psychology, physiology, and anthropology. How indeed do we come to know anything about language, history, and humanity, about what they are and what they should be? And if we could choose to know anything at all, what would we find most important and relevant for our lives?

The Pedagogy of Paradox

In the *Meno*, Socrates and his eponymous interlocutor choose to consider what it means to be a good person. They discuss a series of virtues commonly attributed to good people – courage, prudence, temperance, and magnanimity among them – and then begin to wonder how we can know what virtue is. Meno asks:

> How will you look for something when you don't in the least know what it is?

> How on earth are you going to set up something you don't know as the object of your search? To put it another way, even if you come right

up against it, how will you know that what you have found is the thing you didn't know? (1989, 80d, p. 363)

With this question, Meno articulates what is known as the "learner's paradox," namely: How can we inquire into anything without already knowing what we inquire about? In the context of a volume on critical reading across the curriculum, we can ask: How can we seek the truth philosophically unless we are already doing it?

Socrates responds to this question in two ways. First, he appeals to "priests and priestesses" who teach that:

> the soul, since it is immortal and has been born many times, and has seen all things both here and in the other world, has learned everything that is. So we need not be surprised if it can recall the knowledge of virtue or anything else, which, as we see, it once possessed. All nature is akin, and the soul has learned everything, so that when a man has recalled a single piece of knowledge – *learned* it, in ordinary language – there is no reason why he should not find out all the rest, if he keeps a stout heart and does not grow weary of the search, for seeking and learning are in fact nothing but recollection. (81c, p. 364)

Again, if we think of Socratic irony in the first sense identified above, this passage appears as one instance in which Socrates is not feigning ignorance, but instead offering his own account of the truth about how we can know anything at all. Going slowly, claim by claim: (1) we have an immortal soul that is reincarnated into different bodies; (2) this process has happened so many times that each soul has, in effect, seen it all and gained knowledge of everything; (3) although that knowledge may at first seem inaccessible to us in our present incarnation, we can recall it with help from friends; and (4) if we try hard enough, we should be able to recall, i.e. learn, everything that can be known. Socrates offers another, similar version of this story in the last book of Plato's *Republic*, where he speaks about how the soul is recycled into a newly born human with personality and past experiences washed free but with some knowledge of eternal truths retained, albeit latent.

These passages could be read as if they provided an account of the metaphysical origins of human knowledge. Socrates appears to invoke religious authority and then postulates the existence of some aspect of humanity – i.e. the soul – that not only transcends but also survives the death of the individual, physical body.[1] But if we think of Socratic irony in the second sense identified above, then this passage from the *Meno* draws attention to the actual and ongoing work of memory in any use of language, including but not limited to philosophical inquiries into the good for human life. From this perspective, when we raise questions about what we think we know, and when we subject this knowledge continuously to critique and doubt, we are forced to draw on our memory of what we have known, or what we previously thought we knew. And as we inquire into the origins of knowledge, Socrates offers us not a grand metaphysical theory, but instead courage ("a stout heart") to continue the search.

In this sense, philosophy begins not with some misty-eyed affirmation of a transcendent world beyond this one, but rather in wonder, with the immanent experience of puzzlement or perplexity that occurs when we try to recall what we think we know to be true. Philosophy continues as we proceed through dialectical questioning to sustain an attitude of doubt or critical skepticism about whether any claim to knowledge is true.

A Numbing Process

At this point in the *Meno*, Socrates claims that we have already known the truth about virtue or the good in human life, but we have not yet recognized it as such. So how could we know if this claim were true? Socrates proposes to engage in dialogue with another person who happens to be nearby, an ignorant slave boy.[2]

Socrates begins this passage by asking whether the slave knows what a square is, and it turns out that he does. Then Socrates proceeds to ask the boy a series of questions about the relationship between sides of the square, gradually inferring from what was originally known about the square as a solid two-dimensional shape of four equal sides and generating additional knowledge about the area of a square with sides of a particular length. Socrates notes that his dialectical questions have the intermediary effect of "numbing the boy like a sting ray" (84b, p. 368), but claims that "the numbing process was good for him" (84c, p. 368). It seems that for the slave boy, as for any student of philosophy who undergoes a similar numbing process, "knowledge will not come from teaching but from questioning. He will recover it for himself" (85d, p. 370).

But what exactly has happened so far in this illustration? Socrates claims that the boy held opinions that he did not recognize as true knowledge, but which when he was subjected to questioning were discovered as such and recognized as true. But just because it is possible to reason by inference about a two-dimensional geometric shape, does that mean we have also discovered true knowledge of the origins and nature of the human soul? Has the human soul "forever been in a state of knowledge," waiting only for a philosopher to come along and awaken it?

In response to this question, Socrates demurs, saying that:

> I shouldn't like to take my oath on the whole story, but one thing I am ready to fight for as long as I can, in word and act – that is, we shall be better, braver and more active men if we believe it right to look for what we don't know than if we believe there is no point in looking because what we don't know we can never discover. (86c, p. 37)

Here then, immediately following his attempt to identify the true origins of knowledge within the human soul, Socrates refuses to take his oath on any knowledge of the truth about the human soul, and insists instead on the value of questioning.

In this light, Socratic irony appears not as a feigned ignorance, but as a problematization of the distinction between words and actions. Following Socrates' example, when we ask philosophically about the truth, are we seeking something that can be identified and represented as such, or instead something that is performed or enacted through the dialectic process? Is the truth something that is known, or something that is done – or both? And, in any case, must we undergo that process in order to understand it?

Knowing and Doing the Good

This problematization intensifies as the dialogue continues with a focus on "what is virtue" (86d, p. 371). Recall the learner's paradox: How do we come to know what virtue is if we don't already know it? Reasoning by analogy to the slave boy's knowledge of the square and its properties, Socrates claims that we must already have some knowledge of what virtue is. But then he asks whether virtue itself might be a form of knowledge (87c, p. 372). In order for us to do the good, must we know how to do it? If it were a form of knowledge, Socrates assumes, then it must be possible to teach and learn it. So, who then are the people who claim to teach and learn virtue?

At this point Anytus enters the scene of the dialogue and is welcomed as a friend both to Meno's family and to Socrates (89e, p. 374). The three men discuss how medicine and flute-playing may manifestly be taught by doctors and musicians, but then agree that the people who claim to have knowledge of virtue – namely the so-called Sophists, the professional teachers of wisdom (*sophia*) common in ancient Athens – are in fact unsuccessful at teaching it (91c, p. 376). Socrates singles out Protagoras, who "took in the whole of Greece, corrupting his pupils and sending them away worse than when they came to him, for more than forty years" (91e, p. 376). Yet as noted above, this charge of corrupting the youth was precisely the grounds for Socrates' own eventual execution. Thus we confront the paradox of using Socrates as a model for philosophical practice; who, exactly, do we think Socrates is, if not someone who has, and can teach, knowledge of virtue?

Socrates and his friends agree that not only are the professional teachers of virtue unable to teach it, but that the people who appear to be virtuous themselves are also unable to teach it, even to their own sons (93e, p. 378). They consider a series of examples and in the end agree that even when sons of virtuous fathers have great natural abilities and undertake the most rigorous education possible, they still do not necessarily become as good or wise as their fathers were (94e, p. 378). So then, if virtue cannot be taught either by the people who claim to know it or by the people who appear to have it, it seems to Socrates, Anytus, and Meno that virtue is not a form of knowledge and therefore cannot be taught (96b, p. 380).

This realization provides an occasion for critical self-reflection. Socrates says that "I have a suspicion, Meno, that you and I are not much good. Our masters Gorgias and Prodicus have not trained us properly" (96d, p. 380). And in turn, this self-doubt also provides a motivation for further inquiry, so "We must take ourselves in hand, and try to find someone who will improve us by hook or by crook" (96d, p. 380). At this point, near the portentous beginning of the philosophical tradition, at the end of the Platonic dialogue on knowledge and virtue, Socrates refuses to accept that we have any knowledge about what virtue is, how it can be known, or how it can be taught.

Truth Is Fleeting

Socrates does acknowledge that there are people in the world who are said to be virtuous or good, and that people are considered good generally when they are useful or profitable to society in some way (97a, p. 380). He further acknowledges that even though people might lack knowledge about virtue, if they have opinions about virtue that happen to be true, then they can still act effectively (97b, p. 380). Yet he complains that such opinions can give you the slip "like a runaway slave," whereas knowledge is "tethered down" (97e, p. 381).

To make matters worse, Socrates says that even if we did have knowledge about virtue, it might not actually be an effective guide for action (99b, p. 383). If only somebody could actually teach people to be virtuous or good, that person would be like "a solid reality among shadows" (100a, p. 383). Socrates briefly considers whether virtue is dispensed to people divinely, by the gods (100b, p. 384), and then concludes the dialogue by saying that "We shall not understand the truth of the matter until, before asking how men get virtue, we try to discover what virtue is in and by itself. Now it is time for me to go …" (100b, p. 384).

Simply put, the *Meno* does not provide a positive account, an affirmative statement of the truth about how we know anything or how we can become good people. It does, however, provide a performative enactment of a process, shared by the reader, in and through which knowledge and virtue might be attained, pending continued questioning and critical reflection in dialogue. The activity undertaken by Socrates, calling into question what appears as knowledge and virtue, has the effect of blurring the distinction between knowledge and its lack. Socrates' explicitly paradoxical claim that he knows that he knows nothing blurs the distinction between thinking and acting and turns our attention toward the performative aspect of philosophy. Phrased positively, philosophers question toward truth – but the truth about what, exactly? About knowledge and virtue, in the case of the *Meno*? But again, what is virtue, and how do we know it?

As we read the *Meno* and reflect on it, the process begins for us yet again …

Toward Practical Wisdom

In the preceding section, I presented a critical reading of a philosophical text in which Socrates raises questions about the origins of knowledge and the foundations of virtue. I did not offer this performance as a model for philosophy in general, or as a set of prescriptions for how philosophy should always be conducted. Instead, I presented it as an occasion for readers to engage in the process of philosophical inquiry, to begin "doing with me" rather than "doing as I say."

In the context of a book for educators about how to teach students to read texts critically, it is necessary to engage in some meta-reflection about how and why the process may have unfolded as it did, or how it may unfold differently in other critical reading applications. In this section, I will retrace my steps and suggest ways to conduct critical inquiry in general, identifying practices that can be applied to reading any philosophical text or to reading other phenomena in the world. Guiding my analysis is a conceptual framework recently proposed by researchers from the Carnegie Foundation for the Advancement of Teaching as a model for critical inquiry.

The Carnegie framework identifies three distinct modes of reasoning: analysis, multiple framing, and reflective exploration of meaning. Analysis involves "abstracting from particular experience in order to produce formal knowledge that is general in nature and independent of any context" (Colby, Ehrlich, Sullivan, and Dolle, 2011, p. 60). Multiple framing involves "the ability to work intellectually with fundamentally different, sometimes mutually incompatible, analytical perspectives" (p. 60). And the reflective exploration of meaning involves raising "questions such as what difference does a particular understanding or approach to things make to who I am, how I engage the world, and what it is reasonable for me to imagine and hope" (p. 60). Educators can use this conceptual framework as a basic script for lesson plans as well as for syllabi. Whether planning a single class or a semester, we can begin by developing a basic understanding of what we are inquiring about; we can then view it from different perspectives, recognizing its complexity; and, finally, we can consider its significance for our lives.

These three distinct modes of reasoning may occur in that sequence, iteratively, recursively, and even simultaneously. Taken together, these three modes of reasoning enable the development of a capability to engage in what the authors of the Carnegie report refer to as "practical reasoning." This notion has its own history within the philosophical tradition, and has been variously referred to in terms of *phronesis*, or practical wisdom, and *prudentia* or prudence. Practical reasoning involves knowledge in and of action, knowledge of how to act well, or to do what is good or beneficial even in uncertain or ambiguous circumstances. We can even think of practical reasoning as the convergence of thought and action for the betterment of humankind. In this sense, the pedagogical goal of reading philosophical texts critically can be framed in terms of attaining a truth that is good for people. This claim merits critical reflection as well – good for whom, exactly, and in what ways? But before we raise these questions, we can first review the reading of the *Meno* through the lens of the Carnegie framework, identifying aspects of the process that can be utilized in a variety of classroom settings.

Analysis

In my critical reading of the *Meno*, I began by describing Socrates' activity in general terms, and then focused on one point of analysis relevant to all the Platonic *Dialogues*, namely the function and significance of irony. By tracing two different conceptualizations of irony, I drew attention to the process of philosophical inquiry in general. At the same time, I began a process of philosophical inquiry into the nature of knowledge, emphasizing the importance of raising critical questions. I then followed Socrates' process of inquiry closely, reading through the dialogue line by line, concentrating on passages that touched most directly on the question of how we can ever come to know anything at all. Finally, I analyzed the *Meno* as an example of philosophical inquiry, while claiming that my analysis of the *Meno* provides another illustration of how philosophical inquiry can be performed.

Following the Carnegie framework, teachers can similarly perform philosophical inquiry themselves and encourage their students to analyze philosophical texts by focusing closely on the meaning of words as well as the logic of arguments. Students can be asked, for example, what they think certain words mean, whether those words mean different things to different people in different contexts, or how the meaning of those words has changed over time. When it comes to knowledge and virtue, students tend to have fairly strong opinions that they may have never analyzed carefully. Teachers can distribute note cards and ask students to write on one side of the card one thing that they know for sure to be true, and on the other side of the card the name of one person who is truly good. These cards can then be collected and presented back to the group in any number of ways so that everybody can see what the others have written, either anonymously or by attribution.

Sometimes this exercise can produce a diversity of responses, and students can proceed with a general discussion of why they answered differently, whether they share underlying assumptions, or whether some answers are better than others, and why. Other times, this exercise yields a convergent or similar set of responses, and in such cases, the class can proceed with a discussion of why the responses were so similar, whether there are any hidden differences or disagreements, or whether the answers have left out or ignored anything interesting or relevant.

Similarly, students analyzing philosophical texts can be asked to summarize the argument, to articulate it in their own words. What's the main claim? What evidence or argument does the author present in support of this claim? Are there any aspects of the text that appear to contradict the claim? Students can be asked to focus specifically on logical premises and conclusions, and also on the rhetorical aspects of the text, including style and structure, as well as its persuasive strategies. If they have been asked to identify something they know to be true, or someone they know to be good, they can reflect critically on the logic as well as the rhetoric they used in their own discussions. What, we might ask our students, did you assume? What did you conclude? How did you seek to persuade others that your conclusion is true?

These analytic questions are phrased generically, here, to illustrate how the process of questioning can unfold in a wide variety of directions and apropos of any number of topics. Any attempt to describe what is going on or to articulate one's own understanding of something can provide an occasion for philosophical inquiry. My analytic claim about the *Meno* is that it presents philosophical inquiry first and foremost as a process of engagement with paradox, uncertainty, and the unknown, that is, with wonder. I chose the *Meno* as the focal point for this essay because it examines topics that philosophers would be commonly assumed to have some understanding of, namely knowledge and virtue, and because it provides an occasion for us to perform philosophy by calling into question our students' unexamined assumptions about knowledge and virtue.

Multiple Framing

The Carnegie report identifies "multiple framing" as a second mode of reasoning that contributes to the development of practical reasoning, and describes it as "the ability to work intellectually with fundamentally different, sometimes mutually incompatible, analytical perspectives" (p. 60). In my critical reading of the *Meno*, I traced out two distinct perspectives on irony – one that suggests Socrates feigned ignorance for pedagogical purposes, and one that suggests Socrates performed philosophy by raising questions about knowledge and virtue. The first of these perspectives focuses on the content or substance of the Platonic dialogues, while the second analytic perspective attends to their form or process. In some passages Socrates appears to articulate a theory of knowledge as a form of memory, while in other passages he curses the limits of his own understanding and restarts the process of inquiry. For students this ground can feel quite slippery at first, and for experienced educators and scholars, it can lead to a recognition that every discovery gives rise to an entirely different and new set of questions that we didn't previously think to ask. The Carnegie report recommends that in order to develop practical reasoning we should become familiar and comfortable with this experience of discovery leading to further questioning. And rather than avoiding or rejecting it, we should affirm and embrace it.

In one sense, multiple framing is extremely easy to perform in a classroom with students. In the example described above, by soliciting answers to questions about what is known or who is good, we can demonstrate the range and variety of analytic perspectives. If we were reading the *Meno* in a course focused entirely on Plato, then we could identify passages in the *Republic* that deal with knowledge and virtue, asking students to analyze them carefully and consider whether they are consistent with each other or not. If we were reading the *Meno* in a course focused on ancient Greek philosophy, we could ask students to compare and contrast Plato's conceptualization of *phronesis* (practical wisdom) with Aristotle's. In a course focused more broadly on great ideas or world civilizations, we could compare and contrast the Greek approach with the approach articulated in the *Tao Te Ching*, or the *Bhagavad Gita*, or even Google's "Code of Conduct."[3]

Yet in another sense, students can find multiple framing difficult to sustain. Sometimes after considering multiple perspectives on a topic such as virtue, if it appears that there is no agreement or grounds for reconciliation, students can feel that the inquiry is pointless – if ultimately there's no single right answer, then why are we asking the question? Even bright students who engage in multiple framing can find themselves clinging dogmatically to a particular perspective and believing that they are right while everyone who thinks differently is either ignorant or mistaken. Thus it is important to choose perspectives that are already somewhat familiar to students, or perspectives that inspire exploration and motivate deeper understanding.

For example, several years ago I found that the Occupy Wall Street movement provided a powerful set of perspectives that challenged my undergraduate business school students to think differently about virtue in their own lives. One prominent financial services firm that many of my students dream about working for was described at that time as a "a great vampire squid wrapped around the face of humanity, relentlessly jamming its blood funnel into anything that smells like money" (Taibbi, 2010). My students reacted strongly against this characterization, but they were forced to recognize that their own assumptions about the value of such firms for society were not widely shared among their peers.

Similarly, global climate change presents us all with an occasion to reflect on our basic assumptions about knowledge and virtue. Indeed, what if it turns out that modern, industrial society – widely considered to have enabled unprecedented population growth as well as an increase in standards of living and life expectancies for many – has had effects on the planetary ecosystem that will in the years to come bring terrible consequences not only for humanity, but for thousands of other living species as well? As we live and work, contributing productively to society and consuming the fruits of contemporary civilization, what if at the same time we are actively hastening the demise of that same civilization and the irreversible disruption of the natural systems on which it depends? Such questions can animate intense debate among students, requiring them to consider carefully the variety of disciplines and approaches that are required in order to understand these challenges and address them appropriately.

Reflective Exploration of Meaning

The Carnegie report identifies the reflective exploration of meaning as a third mode of reasoning that involves raising "questions such as what difference does a particular understanding or approach to things make to who I am, how I engage the world, and what it is reasonable for me to imagine and hope" (p. 60). In my critical reading of the *Meno*, I focused on the difference that a particular understanding of Socrates' practice of questioning can make for me, and for readers of this book, as educators. The most basic and direct implication is that if we want to teach students how to read philosophy texts critically, then we cannot merely describe that practice in general or abstract terms, as a method or a set of principles that exists apart from practice. Neither can we simply choose a topic commonly addressed by philosophers such as knowledge or virtue, and then inventory the various philosophical positions on those topics, remaining exclusively focused on the content or substance of those positions. Instead, we must perform philosophy by engaging in a practice of questioning, and we must invite students to take up those questions for themselves, responding and articulating new questions of their own. I noted above that Socrates' mother was a midwife; in a dialogue called the *Theaetetus* Socrates refers to himself as an intellectual midwife who assists with the birth of ideas. The ancient Greek word for this health-care practice is *maieusis*, and in this sense Socrates' example provides us with a maieutic method of engagement with students. When we teach critical reading of philosophy, we assist them as they develop not only ideas of their own, but additionally the capability to reason practically about their world.

Reflective exploration of meaning can precede the analysis and reframing, it can be woven into them both, and/or it can follow them in sequence. In the classroom exercises outlined above, the analysis of knowledge and virtue can begin with reflection on students' own identity and aspirations. Indeed, by identifying someone else who is good, students implicitly articulate their own values. Teachers can prompt further reflection by looking backward, asking students to recall the people or experiences who helped shape those values. In today's climate of identity politics and sensitivity to micro-aggressions and the perpetuation of systems of oppression or exclusion, teachers can facilitate reflection precisely by continuing to raise questions rather than affirming or denying the reality or value of any particular subjective experience. By asking about how students' own values have taken shape, teachers can bring into view historical trends, institutional structures, cultural identities and differences, and even political beliefs and affiliations.

My sense from teaching in the context of a highly diverse and multicultural urban university is that students actually crave the opportunity to discuss thorny and contentious questions with people who have different backgrounds and experiences. Rather than issue trigger warnings so that students can opt out of potentially uncomfortable discussions, I invite them to collaborate on the development and maintenance of a safe space within which they can challenge and learn from each other. There are many ways to do this. For example, in the first session of my professional ethics course this fall, I asked all students to write down the principles or guidelines they thought the class needed to follow. I collated and typed up these responses, put them on a slide, and at the beginning of the next class displayed the slide so they could all see each other's responses. I asked them to review these responses, identify shared as well as divergent interests, and flag any principles that they thought would inhibit their own learning process.

It was clear from the responses that many of the students feared being judged negatively by their peers or, conversely, that they craved each other's recognition and respect. The sticking point for that particular group of students had to do with whether they should have the freedom to speak openly about their own authentically felt experiences, or whether they should exercise a margin of restraint, considering how what they might say would be heard or felt by others in the room. The group was not able to articulate a principle or rule that would guide all students in all cases as they struggled to strike this balance. They were, however, able to agree that this balance is crucial across the entire field of higher education today. They were also able to agree that the list of their responses could function as a charter, enabling them to hold each other mutually accountable for the maintenance of a safe space for productive dialogue. Finally, they were able to accept that the classroom charter would remain subject to critical reflection and review on an ongoing basis throughout the semester, allowing anyone who felt uncomfortable or discriminated against to raise the objection as a reflection on the process rather than as a direct reaction to a fellow student or to me. Emboldened (and I would say, emancipated) by this meta-reflection on their own sense of knowledge and virtue, the students were able to engage in deep personal reflection, discussing their upbringing, their family and friends, their position as undergraduate business students, and their future professional trajectory.

So What? The Effects of Reading Philosophy Critically

In this essay I have demonstrated and described philosophy as a practice of questioning, and of reading philosophical texts in terms of analyzing the questions they raise. This practice of questioning can be undertaken in almost any context and in view of almost any aspect of human experience. It begins in wonder, and continues by sustaining an attitude of doubt or critical skepticism about what is known and the value it has for life. The immediate effects of this practice include the disruption or destabilization of other practices of generating knowledge or attaining the good. Yet as the Carnegie report suggests, the longer-term effects of the practice can include the development of a capability to reason practically, that is, to respond to uncertainty and ambiguity in ways that contribute to the well-being of society. By teaching our students how to engage in the practice of questioning using different modes of reasoning, we can help them to become more practically wise. The critical reading of philosophical texts offers an ideal way to help students develop these essential skills while also gaining practical wisdom.

To be sure, some professional philosophers will remain in library carrels, seminar rooms, and coffee shops, and I would claim that their teachings and writings can benefit society even in cases where they would resolutely resist or deny it. Most of the students we teach will, however, not go on with further study of the history of philosophy, and few if any of them will become professional philosophers. Our students will focus their education on other disciplines, and go on to work in other fields. Many of them will work in multiple different fields over the course of their careers. By teaching them how to engage in philosophical inquiry and to read philosophical and other texts critically, we make it more likely that they will seek the truth and attain the good in whatever field they choose. How exactly will they know what is true or good in a particular context? The process begins anew …

Notes

1 It is interesting to note in passing that Plato uses the phrase "all of nature is akin" here, suggesting that the soul's transcendence of the body does not necessarily involve a transcendence of the physical realm of nature in which human and other bodies exist. Yes, he does refer to "things both here and in the other world," but the "other world" exists in a way that is also natural rather than supernatural. This notion contrasts with certain monotheistic religious doctrines that emerged after Plato's time and remain widely embraced today, and which locate the origins of the soul (as well as the divinity that created it) in a metaphysical realm that exists outside of and apart from the physical realm of nature.

2 The political, ethical, and aesthetic dimensions of this character, his relationship to Meno and to Socrates, and the resonance of this passage throughout the subsequent history of philosophy, merit philosophical critique that extends beyond the scope of this chapter. Suffice it to say in passing that philosophers are greatly at risk of hubris…

3 abc.xyz/investor/other/code-of-conduct.html

References

Colby, A., Ehrlich, T., Sullivan, W. M., Jr., and Dolle, R. (2011). *Rethinking undergraduate business education: Liberal learning for the profession*, vol. 20. San Francisco: Jossey-Bass.

Deleuze, G. (1994). *Difference and repetition*. Trans. P. Patton. New York: Columbia University Press.

Plato. (1989). *The collected dialogues of Plato*. Ed. E. Hamilton and H. Cairns. Princeton, NJ: Princeton University Press.

Taibbi, M. (2010). The great American bubble machine. *Rolling Stone* (April 5). Retrieved from http://www.rollingstone.com/politics/news/the-great-american-bubble-machine-20100405 (accessed September 30, 2016).

9

Engaging Religious Texts

Thomas Petriano

"Pay Attention!"

According to a well-known Zen story, a young disciple once asked a respected Zen master for a single word of wisdom. With a quick stroke of a brush, the master drew the character for the word "attention." "Is that all?" asked the disappointed student in response. The master then wrote the word twice: "attention, attention." Becoming angry the student scoffed, "What's the wisdom in that?" Silently, the master wrote the word three more times: "attention, attention, attention." Finally, at the end of his patience, the student implored his master, "What does the word 'attention' mean?" "Attention means attention," was all he replied (adapted from Beck, 1993, p. 168).

Lack of intentionality and the inability to be attentive, illustrated in this story, present major obstacles to any kind of meaningful critical reading, and therefore constitute a challenge to those of us who teach theology or religious studies. However, in this essay I argue that the study of the world's religions can help overcome these obstacles, because such study fosters an approach to reading that is embodied, engaged, mindful, and transformational.

One of my earliest recollections of my own education is as a first grader at Ss. Joachim and Anne School in Queens Village, New York. My first-grade teacher was Sr. Catherine Anne. I can remember, as clearly as if it were yesterday, her frequently repeated words to me: "Thomas, pay attention." This mantra was sometimes slightly expanded to: "Thomas, sit up

Critical Reading Across the Curriculum, Volume 1: Humanities, First Edition.
Edited by Robert DiYanni and Anton Borst.
© 2017 John Wiley & Sons, Inc. Published 2017 by John Wiley & Sons, Inc.

straight and pay attention." Little did I know then how profoundly meaningful those words were to become and how much they are at the core of
a meaningful experience of reading. As we are aware, our fast-paced and
consumer-oriented culture makes the habit of paying attention – what Buddhism calls "mindfulness" – a fading practice. Perhaps one of the greatest contributions we, as teachers of religion and theology, can offer our
students is the practice of mindfulness urged in the admonitions of Sr.
Catherine.

Our classes contain students of varying beliefs, ranging from those who
are intensely devoted to a particular religious tradition to those who are
skeptical of or even hostile to religious beliefs, as well as those who are spiritual but not religious. Can religious texts from a variety of religious traditions evoke, among such a broad range of believers and nonbelievers, a
response that Jack Miles, in his preface to the *Norton Anthology of World
Regions*, calls "intelligent delight" (2015, p. xlvi)? It is an intriguing phrase.
We teachers of religious studies undoubtedly have found just such delight
in these texts, but how do we invite and enable our students to make the
same discovery? I believe that it is possible, and, in the pages that follow,
offer some strategies toward reaching that goal.

The wisdom of Zen Buddhism is but one example of how the world's religions can be a resource to help students read more attentively. Before mining those traditions for effective strategies to engage with religious texts, we
should remind ourselves of some basic principles of effective reading.

Reading as an Embodied and Dialogic Act

Reading is an embodied and dialogic act. Long before the Cartesian split
between mind and body, medieval monks were deeply engaged in and committed to a mode of reading that emphasized its physical and emotional
nature. In *Religious Reading*, Paul Griffiths reminds us that religious readers have a distinctive attitude toward what they read: "To read religiously
is to read as a lover, wanting to savor the experience" (1999, p. 45). Peter of
Celle, a twelfth-century monk, captured the physical and embodied dimension of reading well when he referred to the spiritual reading practiced by
medieval monks as "the soul's food, light, lamp, refuge, consolation, and
the spice of every spiritual savor" (1987, p. 35). Hugh of St. Victor, another
monk of the twelfth century, even more directly characterized reading as
a carnal and not just an intellectual activity. Ivan Illich points out that for
this reason medieval monasteries were often referred to as dwellings for
"mumblers and munchers of the text" (1993, p. 54).

In addition to being an embodied activity, and despite appearing solitary, reading is a dialogic practice, a form of social encounter. An author writes to initiate a conversation, to begin an exchange of ideas with readers. The attention we give to a book ought to be akin to the attention we give to a partner in conversation. To read carefully and deliberately is to interrogate a text *and* to allow ourselves to be interrogated by the text. Questioning a text and being questioned by it are both essential. This requires putting aside preconceptions and being open to the thoughts and ideas expressed in the manner of a true, authentic dialogue.

In "Learning to Stop, Stopping to Learn: Discovering the Contemplative Dimension in Education," Richard Brady (2007) shares his practice of asking students to formulate four questions in response to every reading, three that they can answer and one that they cannot answer. The class then shares the questions they cannot answer. In a sense, the activity turns reading into something like a dinner conversation, where the author is a guest together with a group of people working to share their insights and responses. It provides students with the kind of rapid validation they receive when posting on Facebook. Most of us are usually anxious to see how many, if anyone, "liked" our post. How much better do we feel when someone has taken the time and interest to "comment" on our post! Not only are students commenting on the text in this exercise, but also on each other's comments. A conversation has been initiated, the goal of any author.

As a complex, embodied, dialogic activity, reading demands *practice*. I am thinking here of practice as used in eastern traditions of yoga and, especially, martial arts. Developing skill in martial arts requires commitment to a practice. The movie *Karate Kid* illustrates this point. When young Daniel wants to learn karate from Mr. Miyagi in order to defend himself against bullies in the schoolyard, one of the first things he is asked to do is wax Mr. Miyagi's car. The famous "wax on, wax off" scene from that movie has become iconic: through the repetition of those seemingly pointless arm motions, Daniel refines his fighting technique, eventually becoming a competitive martial artist. Successful engagement with religious and theological texts, like success in playing an instrument, or excelling in a sport, dance, or even religious devotion, demands commitment to a practice, and we know from experience that such commitment is ultimately transformative. The same holds true for the practice of reading.

Paolo Freire's insights into the goal of education are helpful here. The Brazilian educator and philosopher, in his now classic *Pedagogy of the Oppressed* (1970/2000), argues for a liberating model of education that results in what he calls "conscientization," the developing of consciousness directed toward changing the world. In this model, students are not mere containers for information, but rather become agents of their own liberation (Browning, 2014, p. 23). Though Freire's critique of traditional education has a distinctly political orientation, his essential observations apply equally well to the reading of religious texts. Religious texts are meant to transform as much as inform. They are meant to liberate by leading to action to better oneself and the world.

Should not the goal of reading ultimately be personal transformation? Asking students either of the following questions may bring home this truth: "Is there any book that you have ever read or has been read to you that changed you or your outlook on life?" Or: "Is there any book or text that you have ever read that has led you to action?" A sharing of student responses could be most interesting, especially if students are asked to bring in their readings. Reading exists for more than just theoretical purposes. It should be oriented toward action. To awaken students to this potential, at the end of any reading we can ask them, "What difference does this text make?" Or: "How might it actually affect your life?"

Keeping in mind these general approaches to reading, we are ready to look at some more specific critical reading strategies inspired by the world's great religious traditions.

Insights from the Religions

Our English word "religion" may not derive, as is most commonly asserted, from the Latin *religare*, meaning "to reconnect," but rather from *relegere*, meaning to "reread." Paul Griffiths (1999) points out that this was in fact the view of Cicero. While this issue is still debated among scholars, it is an intriguing proposition. Because reading sacred texts has long been understood as a religious activity, the religions have much to teach us about developing reading skills. We can begin by considering what Christianity might teach us about reading.

Christianity

In the book of Ezekiel, we find a metaphor for reading that was a favorite of medieval monks, and one that provides insight into how they approached reading sacred texts:

> Moreover he said unto me, Son of man, eat that thou findest; eat this roll, and go speak unto the house of Israel. So I opened my mouth, and he caused me to eat that roll. And he said unto me, Son of man, cause

thy belly to eat, and fill thy bowels with this roll that I give thee. Then did I eat *it*; and it was in my mouth as honey for sweetness. (Ezekiel 3:1–3, Authorized Version [AV])

Understanding texts as food provided a basis for a number of alimentary metaphors for reading, such as "mastication," "rumination," and "digestion," and was central to the monastic practice known as *lectio divina*, or sacred reading (Robertson, 2011, p. 205). The food metaphor was sometimes complemented by the metaphor of the vineyard or garden. In the twelfth-century treatise known as the *Didascalicon*, Hugh of St. Victor has written a guide for monastic reading worth the consideration of any of us who seek to help our students develop better critical reading skills. The subtitle of Hugh's book is *De studio legendi*. Ivan Illich, in his commentary on the *Didascalicon*, points out that while this could be translated as "on the study of reading," it is truer to the original meaning of *studium* to call it the "affection" or "pleasure" of reading. In a medieval cloister, reading was meant to engage the student's heart and senses as well as his mind. According to Illich, Hugh strove to develop in students, in this case young monks, "a commitment to engage in an activity by which the reader's own 'self' will be kindled and brought to sparkle" (1993, p. 17). We might well ask if this is an impractical if not impossible goal that may have worked for twelfth-century monks, but would never work for twenty-first-century college students. Exploring a little further the methodology of the *lectio divina* may help answer this question.

In monasteries the purpose of *lectio divina* was none other than transformation. A classic example in Christian literature is the story of St. Augustine's conversion, as told in Book VIII of his *Confessions*. There we read Augustine's account of observing St. Ambrose reading aloud, as was common in those days. Later, walking in a garden, Augustine hears a voice instructing him to *tolle et lege*, take and read. In response to that voice Augustine picks up a copy of the New Testament and reads from St. Paul's letter to the Romans, chapter 12, which occasions his religious conversion. Of course it doesn't have to be a religious text that occasions conversion. The important point is the medieval recognition of the transformative power of words, or even of a single word. Students can be encouraged to consider this power by inviting them to choose a word or phrase from a text they have read and spend some time ruminating on it. Having students write about what they choose and share those reflections with each other can be a useful way to adapt the practice of *lectio divina* to our own classes.

By becoming acquainted with the medieval tradition of *lectio*, students can discover that effort and intentionality are central to the successful reading of religious texts. The term most commonly used for this is the Latin word *assiduitas*, usually translated as "assiduity." Michael Casey, in his book *Sacred Reading* (1996), identifies four characteristics of assiduity, as understood in medieval monasticism. First it requires time. Making time is different than finding time; it involves actively prioritizing reading. The second and third characteristics are regularity and repetition: good reading depends on reading a text as many times as necessary and consistently finding opportunities to do so. Lastly, assiduity requires perseverance. Extracting meaning from a text does not usually come instantly. Read me once, read me twice, read me once again. Developing the practice of assiduity is essential to engaging religious texts in a way that is meaningful and ultimately transformational.

Judaism

Judaism also offers valuable insight into how students can engage a text effectively. In the book of Joshua we read: "This book of the law shall not depart out of thy mouth; but thou shalt meditate therein day and night" (Joshua 1:8, AV). As this verse exemplifies, the reading of Torah has always been a central component of Jewish practice. Accordingly, Raymond Studzinski points out:

> The religious reader approaches texts with reverence and treasures them, not like a voracious consumer who uses and then discards what provided satisfaction. Religious readers pursue their reading with a firm conviction that "everything is in the text," that wonders are waiting to be discovered in works that are endless sources of delight. (2009)

Though not all of our students will necessarily be "religious readers," an instructive example of religious reading can be found in Chaim Potok's novel *The Chosen*. The two main characters, Danny Saunders and Reuven Malter, both grow up in Orthodox Jewish households. Both study the Torah assiduously, but although they live only a short distance from each other, their understanding of the Torah differs significantly. An example of this difference can be seen in how Reuven is permitted by his family to read Charles Darwin, while Danny is not. Though Reuven considers himself an Orthodox Jew, Danny, who was raised with a much stricter view of the Torah, does not. This difference forms the central plot of this powerful story, which offers readers many valuable lessons, including how the consequences of reading a text differ according to the reader's intentions, experiences, and perspectives (Studzinski, 2009).

The third-century Jewish text known as the *Pirke Avot* (Ethics of the Fathers) offers a fascinating glimpse of the importance the Torah came to have in Jewish life after the destruction of the Temple. It shows the importance of meditation on the word in a way that anticipated the role of *lectio divina* in medieval monasticism:

> Torah is [acquired]: through study, attentive listening, careful repetition [out loud], perceptivity; awe, reverence, humility, joy, purity; apprenticeship to sages, association with colleagues, debates with students, serenity, [knowledge of] Scripture and Mishnah; a minimum of business dealings, a minimum of labor, a minimum of gratification, a minimum of sleep, a minimum of idle chatter, a minimum of partying; patience, a kind heart, trust in sages, and acceptance of one's own sufferings. (Quoted in Studzinski, 2009)

Notice the emphasis on oral recitation and attentive listening in this prescription for reading Torah. One can only surmise what advice third-century rabbis would give to students who live in an age filled with the numerous distractions wrought by social media.

Islam

An emphasis on listening and recitation appears even more prominently in the etiquette for reading the Qur'an as it developed in Islam. Within this religious tradition, an actual physical connection with a religious text is given central place. The word *qur'an* is derived from the Arabic word *iqra*, which can be translated as either "recite" or "read." When applied to the Qur'an, which translation is the correct one? Scholarly consensus asserts that both are needed for full understanding. There is an intrinsic connection between reading and reciting, and it is precisely for this reason that the recitation (as well as memorization) of the Qur'an is such a widespread and recommended practice (McAuliffe, 2004, p. 369). The auditory dimension of reading the text contributes to its becoming ever more a part of the life of devout readers.

The medieval Islamic philosopher Al-Ghazali, in *On the Etiquettes of Qur'an Recitation*, lists "Ten External Rules for Approaching the Qur'an." The first of these rules is that the reciter of the Qur'an must be in a state of ritual cleanliness (*wudu*), politeness, and quietness, facing the Kaaba (a large, cube-shaped building sacred to Islam), neither sitting cross-legged nor leaning against anything. Another rule has to do with each reader determining the appropriate amount of the Qur'an to read in one sitting, depending on how much has been understood. Each of the ten rules reflects a strong awareness in the Islamic tradition of engaging the text as a whole person (Al-Ghazali, 2011). In his masterful commentary on the Qur'an, *The Jewels of the Qur'an*, Al-Ghazali writes:

> When the Qur'an reader enters into the fields of the Qur'an, plucks different types of fruits from its gardens, enters into its closets, views the brides, wears the brocades, is relieved of cares, and dwells in the khans, then all these absorb him wholly and keep him from things other than these; consequently his mind cannot be inattentive, nor can his thought be separate. (1977, p. 62)

Regardless of one's personal beliefs about the nature of the Qur'an as a revealed text, we and our students can benefit from being reminded of the prescriptions about posture and recitation in reading the Qur'an in order to derive the greatest benefit from it. As the prescriptions of Al-Ghazali make clear, reading the Qur'an is an embodied act, one that must be entered into with proper mental and physical dispositions, as well as intentionality. These prescriptions represent wise guidance that can be applied to any religious or theological text.

Hinduism

Hinduism offers analogous advice for developing the art of attentiveness. As we have seen thus far, concentration, attention, and intentionality are key elements for fully and effectively engaging texts. Concentration, however, can be especially difficult for students who are constantly bombarded by an endless flow of distractions. Masters of meditation and yoga in India show us that concentration, the ability to stay focused and attuned, can be developed. The Sanskrit word *ekagrata*, used by Hindu yogis, can be translated as "one-pointedness." Concentration is an acquired ability in which we learn to notice when the mind becomes distracted; once aware, we can bring it back to its focus. As Mark Muesse points out in his series of lectures, *Practicing Mindfulness*, the most important part of learning one-pointedness is being aware of when the mind drifts. Because our "default" position, as he calls it, is mindlessness, we are not always aware of losing focus (2011, p. 9). We need to help our students understand that concentration can be developed and improved. It is a key element of meaningful engagement with a text.

Buddhism

Building on Hindu insights into practices that still the mind and facilitate concentration, the Buddhist tradition has a rich body of teaching on living mindfully that can be effectively applied to mindful reading. "Do not just look for what you want to see, that would be futile. Do not look for anything, but allow the insight to have a chance to come by itself. That insight will help liberate you." With these words, Vietnamese Buddhist monk Thich Nhat Hanh (2010) offers sage advice on how to approach a text. Key to the practice of mindfulness is this relinquishing of all expectations – of letting insight happen. As the Buddhist word *bhavana* suggests, mindfulness is not a kind of thinking, but a "cultivation" of awareness and discipline. Mark Muesse explains, "Bhavana is less about thinking intensely than creating the kind of mind that provides fertile ground from which skillful thinking arises" (p. 45). Indeed, what we might call "mindful reading," or, reading with attentiveness, can be of real value in teaching students to fully engage the texts they read. Students can be invited to spend an interval of time in contemplative quiet before approaching a text, one that focuses on breathing and posture. Helping students acquire contemplative skills for more mindful reading can enable them not only to better engage with texts, but also to better engage with life as a whole.

The Three Worlds of Religious Texts

Being mindful, intentional readers also requires students to develop an awareness of the hermeneutical questions brought to the fore in the study of ancient scriptural texts. While each religious tradition has its own hermeneutical methods, certain general principles can help students engage texts more meaningfully. As Paul Ricoeur suggests, every text offers the reader new possibilities for living and acting in the world: "If reading is possible, it is indeed because the text is not closed in on itself but opens out onto other things" (1981, p. 158). Accordingly, in analyzing religious texts, students must keep in mind three intersecting worlds: the world behind the text, the world within the text, and the world in front of the text. Although some schools of criticism would isolate these worlds from each other, they are better navigated in conversation with one another. Helping our students recognize these three worlds and their place as readers in them is essential for successful critical reading.

The world behind a text focuses on the historical context of the author, the *Sitz im Leben*, as biblical scholars call it. It involves understanding the world of the author, the purposes of the author, and the influences on the author. To enter as much as possible into this world, the tools of the historical-critical method are generally employed. The findings of archeology, linguistic studies, source criticism, form criticism, canonical criticism, and redaction criticism are all important tools for understanding the world behind a text. To illustrate the significance of this approach, an instructor could have students read the account of the Beatitudes in the Gospel of Matthew (Matt. 5:1–9), and compare and contrast it with the account of the Beatitudes in the Gospel of Luke (Luke 6:20–26). What does each account tell us about each evangelist and his world? Can we surmise anything about the different time periods when each text was composed?

Discovering the world within a text is an approach that focuses on the autonomy of a text, apart from its historical setting. Advocates of this approach argue that the author's intention is not relevant to analysis and interpretation. For them, identifying and understanding the literary genres and conventions operative in religious scriptures is of primary importance (Tate, 2008). Here are some examples of how to help students engage questions of literary form:

1 Read the prayer of Habakkuk in 3:1–19 and identify at least one occurrence of each of the following: (a) metaphor, (b) simile, (c) personification, (d) irony (Tate, 2008, p. 100).
2 Read the Gospel of John and do a word search of all the times the word "world" is used. What are the different meanings the word has and what are their implications?
3 How does water function as a symbol in the *Tao Te Ching*?
4 What are various ways to interpret the Zen proverb, "If you see the Buddha on the road, kill him"? Which one do you think is correct?
5 Read the *Chandogya* Upanishad. What literary forms do you notice? How do they work to support the teaching of the father to his son, "Thou Art that"?

Finally, besides the world behind the text and the world within the text, we must be mindful of the world in front of the text. Readers interpret texts differently because each reader brings his or her own worldview to the text. Different readers bring their own presuppositions, interests, and experiences to their reading. In this view, meaning is more the creation of the reader than of the author. As W. Randolph Tate (2008) points out, central to hermeneutics is a recognition that both the reader and the author bring to a text issues of social class, ideology, gender, culture, and myriad other internalized orientations.

Knowing one's own presuppositions and preconceptions is vitally important for meaningful textual encounters. For reading specifically religious texts, it's important for students to recognize what faith or lack of faith, what theological perspective, what social location they bring to the text. Such self-awareness can be cultivated by making the classroom a neutral space where all religious and social identities are welcome. Tate's definition of social location is helpful here. He defines it as "a matrix of contexts (ideological, cultural, literary, religious, etc.) within which individuals understand, make judgments, value, and think" (p. 219). This is similar to the insight of liberation theology that what we see is determined by where we stand. Inviting students to recognize and identify their own social location, where they stand, is an important component of helping them to become better critical readers. One way of doing this is by showing them a work of art, perhaps Rembrandt's *Prodigal Son* or *Six Persimmons* by Zen monk Mu Qi, and without providing any background information asking them to interpret what they see. For example, what feelings does *The Prodigal Son* evoke? Which character does each viewer identify with? What feeling does looking at *Six Persimmons* evoke? Writing on a blackboard the different reactions to these and similar questions can allow students to identify the various social locations they bring to these visual texts.

Paul Ricoeur (1981) provides another tripartite method to approach religious texts and experience their transformative power. In place of the perspective of three worlds, he identifies three stages of reading religious texts. The first involves a *naive grasping* of the text as a whole (*1st naiveté*). Secondly, the reader delves into a *historical, critical*, and *literary analysis* of the text. Finally, in the stage Ricoeur calls *2nd naiveté*, the reader returns to the text with openness, but an openness now informed by the deeper insights afforded by the previous stage, allowing the reader to challenge what he or she first assumed (1976, p. 74). When engaging in this process, the reader is thus changed. Speaking of New Testament hermeneutics, but in a way that could apply equally to any religious text, Sandra Schneiders writes, "To really enter the world before the text is to be changed, to 'come back different'" (1999, p. 168).

Practices for Engaging Religious and Theological Texts

I recommend a number of specific practices for engaging with religious and theological texts. Each of the following approaches reflects a religious mode of reading and is anchored in spiritual practices of long tradition.

Reading Mindfully through Allowing Space

Although the monastic method of *lectio divina* was most often applied to scriptural texts, it can also be a useful tool in engaging any theological text, or indeed any text. The practices of *lectio* (reading), *oratio* (prayer), *meditatio* (meditation), and *contemplatio* (contemplation) require us to do the following: *listen* for a word or phrase that most strikes us; *reflect* upon and savor the word and allow it to unfold; *respond* to what this word is saying to us; and, finally, *rest* (be still) with that word (Painter, 2013). Creating space and being patient are central to engaged reading. Encouraging students to appreciate the need for paced and patient reading, and to create a contemplative space after reflecting on a word, phrase, or theme, is essential for successful meditative reading practice.

The Three Rs

In her book *Field of Compassion* (2010), Judy Canato offers a meaningful strategy to engage theological texts. It revolves around the three words "resonance," "resistance," and "realignment." *Resonance* asks students to consider what in the text rings most true with their own experience. What is it that most resonates with them? *Resistance* encourages students to consider whether there is any contradiction between what they have read and their own beliefs or point of view. Is there something in the reading that creates dissonance or raises vigorous disagreement? It's important to pay attention to that reaction. The third R, *realignment,* invites readers to ask whether the text has caused any kind of change or shift in the way they understand the world or themselves. For resonance, resistance, and realignment the key is to approach the process without judgment. Indeed, the heart of good meditative practice requires nonjudgmental thoughts and reactions, which is precisely the approach Canato recommends. I often have students read Thomas Aquinas' Five Arguments for the Existence of God in Question 2 of the First Part of the *Summa Theologica*; applying the three Rs to this text and discussing among students their responses helps them discover the significance of Aquinas' arguments and how the arguments impact them personally.

Shared Inquiry – Learning from Each Other

Shared discussion, as defined in the *Shared Inquiry Handbook* of the Great Books Foundation (2007), is an "intellectually rigorous group activity that focuses on the interpretation of meaning in written texts." This type of text-oriented learning is rooted in the Socratic style. The heart of the method involves engaged student reading in which students pose their questions and then listen and respond to the questions of their classmates. The instructor, as facilitator, has the role of posing questions that are *factual*, *interpretive*, and *evaluative*.

An example would be having students read the Islamic text known as "The Hadith of Gabriel." A factual question might be: "What are the three questions posed to Muhammad by the angel Gabriel?" After students have been grounded in the facts of the text, interpretive and evaluative questions can follow. An interpretive question might be: "What is the significance of each of the questions posed to Muhammad?" An evaluative question might be: "Is Muhammad's description of *ihsan* (excellence) relevant today?" Asking the group to discuss their positive and negative responses could follow. Challenging students to enter ever deeper into a text through penetrating questions is key to this method. A very important part of this method is close reading of texts, even to the point of going through a passage line by line, using the questions "What?" "So what?" and "Now what?"

What, So What, Now What?

The questioning process should always center on ways to achieve deeper engagement and even transformative impact. Like the levels of questioning in Shared Inquiry, the three questions "What?" "So what?" and "Now what?" are designed to draw students more deeply into a text, ultimately asking them to consider what kind of change the text inspires. One text I have often used in a course on liberation theology and another course on peace and justice is Martin Luther King, Jr.'s "Letter from a Birmingham Jail." A "what" question might look something like this: What position is Martin Luther King defending in this letter? So what: What are the wider implications of this position? Now what: How does his explanation of extremism affect me and the choices I make? Asking students to respond to their reading with these simple but potentially profound questions provides material for valuable discussion. These questions have also proven useful for effective journal writing, and I have found them to be a good rubric for students to follow in writing about service learning projects.

Wordle and Word Searches

Yet another approach takes advantage of current technologies. Technology can be a two-edged sword in the classroom. It can be a distraction, which prevents attentive and mindful engagement with texts; when used judiciously, however, it can provide ways for students to enter more deeply into conversation with an author. For instance, using word cloud programs such as Wordle or using a word search function can provide effective access to a text. We might ask students to take a section of the *Tao Te Ching* and create a word cloud, a type of word collage that identifies dominant themes and most frequently used words. These words and themes provide a point of entry into a text and its implications. Word clouds provide students with key words that they in turn can, as the medieval monastics recommended, chew over and ruminate on. Using a word search function, students can access an online version of a text, search for a specific word, and note the different ways that word is used. For example, students might search through the Gospel of John for how often and where a particular word – "world" or "life" or "glory" – is used. Noticing the different usages and possible nuances of meaning helps students enter into a text on a deeper level.

Less Can Be More

How much students should be asked to read is always a quandary for us teachers. In teaching students to read intentionally, mindfully, and attentively, we need to choose texts judiciously. The adage attributed to Lao Tzu, "If you seek knowledge, add something every day; if you seek wisdom, take something away," applies here. Most of the time, greater benefits can come from a close, paced reading of a short selection than from a long, less disciplined reading of a text of many pages. In helping students read intentionally, mindfully, and attentively, we will be helping them develop a skill that will serve them well in many facets of their lives. Learning to live mindfully can be transformative; we can contribute to that process by helping them to read mindfully. An important insight for reading sacred and theological texts that students can carry into every facet of their lives is that less can be more. The task may seem daunting because we are going against a strong cultural current, but making the effort is something our mission as teachers requires, and involves being highly disciplined, careful, and discriminating in the amount of reading we assign.

Conclusion

In an essay honoring Richard R. Niebuhr entitled "Attending to Attention" (1995), Carol Zaleski addresses the issue of *attention* as a key to cognitive and moral life, as well as being a religious category that is paramount in all the great religious traditions. For a long time the centrality of attention as a religious practice has been absent from academia. Zaleski's essay credits Richard R. Niebuhr with helping to restore this concept to its proper place in religious discourse. This insight, learned by Zaleski at first hand from her mentor, has been a central theme of this essay.

As many of the sacred stories of the great religious traditions remind us, it is easy to become distracted and forgetful. Stories of amnesia, sleep, exile, boredom with life, and unawareness of our true nature abound. Gilgamesh cannot stay awake for seven days and nights in order to be worthy of everlasting life; Jesus' disciples are unable to stay awake with him in the Garden of Gethsemane. In the monastic tradition, boredom is called *akedia*, the tendency to submit to the so-called noonday devil. Today researchers call it "attentional inertia," a lowered activity of the brain in processing complex information (Zaleski, 1995).

Also drawing on the monastic tradition of *lectio divina*, Zaleski points out that in classical Latin *meditatio* refers to an intentional act of thinking something over carefully. For medieval monks it was an effort to listen deeply to religious texts, which of course required sustained thoughtful attention. Inattention, on the other hand, is our shared tendency to be carried away by distraction. As we have had occasion to point out, the Asian religions place a similarly high value on attention and thus emphasize techniques for developing and enhancing awareness, especially through various meditation practices.

The world's great religious traditions provide us with an invaluable resource for developing effective practices of attention, and that attentiveness is ultimately the key to deep reading, the goal of which is human transformation. We read to live; indeed we read to live better, and religious and theological texts at their best are written with that goal in mind. We engage them more effectively when we enter them with an attentive mind and open heart, something I first learned from Sr. Catherine Anne in first grade.

References

Al-Ghazali, A. H. (1977). *The jewels of the Qur'an: Al-Ghazali's theory*. Trans. M. A. Quasem. London: Kegan Paul.

Al-Ghazali, I. (2011). *On the etiquettes of Qur'an recitation*. Imam Al-Ghazali Institute.

Beck, C. J. (1993). *Nothing special: Living Zen*. New York: HarperCollins.

Brady, R. (2007). Learning to stop, stopping to learn: Discovering the contemplative dimension in education. *Journal of Transformative Education*, 5(4), 372–394. doi: 10.1177/1541344607313250.

Browning, M. (2014). Reading basically. In E. Barreto (ed.), *Reading theologically* (pp. 15–30). Minneapolis, MN: Fortress Press.

Canato, J. (2010). *Field of compassion*. Notre Dame, IN: Sorin Books.

Casey, M. (1996). *Sacred reading: The art of lectio divina*. Ligouri, MO: Ligouri Press.

Freire, P. (1970/2000). *Pedagogy of the oppressed*. New York: Bloomsbury Academic.

Great Books Foundation. (2007). *Shared inquiry handbook*. Chicago: Great Books Foundation.

Griffiths, P. (1999). *Religious reading: The place of reading in the practice of religion*. New York: Oxford University Press.

Hanh, T. N. (2010). Dharma talk – Bat Nha: A koan. *The Mindfulness Bell*, 54. http://www.mindfulnessbell.org/archive/2014/12/dharma-talk-bat-nha-a-koan-2 (accessed October 1, 2016).

Illich, I. (1993). *In the vineyard of the text*. Chicago: University of Chicago Press.

McAuliffe, J. D. (Ed.). (2004). *Encyclopedia of the Qur'an*, vol. 4. Leiden: Brill.

Miles, J. (2015). Introduction. In J. Miles (ed.), *The Norton anthology of world religions* (pp. xli–l). New York: W. W. Norton.

Muesse, M. (2011). *Practicing mindfulness: An introduction to meditation*. Chantilly, VA: The Teaching Company.

Painter, C. V. (2013). *Eyes of the heart: Photography as a Christian contemplative practice*. Notre Dame, IN: Sorin.

Peter of Celle. (1987). *Selected works*. Trans. H. Feiss. Kalamazoo, MI: Cistercian Publications.

Ricoeur, P. (1976). *Interpretation theory: Discourse and the surplus of meaning*. Fort Worth: Texas Christian University Press.

Ricoeur, P. (1981). *Hermeneutics and the human sciences*. Ed. and trans. J. Thompson. Cambridge: Cambridge University Press.

Robertson, D. (2011). *Lectio divina: The medieval experience of reading*. Collegeville, MN: Liturgical Press.

Schneiders, S. (1999). *The revelatory text: Interpreting the New Testament as sacred scripture*. Collegeville, MN: Liturgical Press.

Studzinski, R. (2009). *Reading to live: The evolving practice of lectio divina*. Kindle ed. Collegeville, MN: Liturgical Press.

Tate, W. R. (2008). *Biblical interpretation: An integrated approach*. Grand Rapids, MI: Baker Academic.

Zaleski, C. (1995). Attending to attention. In S. Lee, W. Proudfoot, and A. Blackwell (eds.), *Faithful imagining: Essays in honor of Richard R. Niebuhr* (pp. 127–149). Atlanta, GA: Scholars Press.

10

Gender Studies as a Model for Critical Reading

Pamela Burger

What exactly constitutes the "critical" component in critical reading? How do we as educators differentiate between the various levels of analytic sophistication involved in what we imagine critical reading to be? Although we might define critical reading as any form of interpretation or active engagement with the text, there are certainly different types of active reading, which vary considerably in complexity and nuance. Yet pedagogical discussions of critical reading often begin and end with the same basic formula: students should be able to understand text and subtext, examine both denotation and connotation, and, as a result, come to independent conclusions regarding a text's meaning(s). This is of course an admirable, and difficult, goal, but it should not be the final stage in teaching students engaged reading. For scholars, critical inquiry entails an active examination of a text that can account for multiple interpretations, one that often requires critical or aesthetic distance, attends to a range of contexts, and decodes several levels of textual signification. As students develop their analytic ability, it is imperative that they move beyond the initial stages of critical reading, and that instructors model the various levels of critical analysis.

This essay presents two assignments meant to guide students through the process of becoming more adept critical readers. The first assignment assists students in developing preliminary critical reading skills; the second pushes them to understand precisely how texts operate on multiple levels of interpretation, with reference to multiple contexts, and – as sites of cultural subversion and resistance – in self-contradictory ways. Drawing attention to and differentiating between these "levels" might help us consider how to

Critical Reading Across the Curriculum, Volume 1: Humanities, First Edition.
Edited by Robert DiYanni and Anton Borst.
© 2017 John Wiley & Sons, Inc. Published 2017 by John Wiley & Sons, Inc.

design effective assignments that lead students through increasingly rigorous modes of critical reading. These assignments do not originate in gender studies courses, but they do take the study of gender as their site of critical inquiry. As we will see, the deconstruction of gender provides a strong model for critical reading, in part because it is widely applicable across disciplines.

As an academic field, gender studies is quintessentially interdisciplinary, taking as its analytic focus the operations of gender ideologies throughout the spectrum of human endeavors, from artistic creation to social interaction to scientific inquiry. The term "gender" in this context broadly refers to the categories of femininity and masculinity as well as cultural conceptions of sexuality and sex. Gender studies courses are designed around the premise that gender is a social construction and that, through scholarly investigation, categories of sexual difference can be deconstructed and thus demystified. Yet too often the study of gender is banished to a handful of cross-listed course offerings scattered throughout an undergraduate catalogue. Even though issues pertaining to the classification and social parameters of sex and gender are constantly in play in nearly every high school and college class – from introductory biology to American history – students are rarely asked to consider how or why these categories have come into being. Instead, such questions are reserved for highly specialized "women's studies" or "queer theory" classes (usually electives) that focus entirely on gender and sexuality as categories of study. As the title of this essay suggests, I propose that the field of gender studies need not be isolated as a distinct area of teaching: classroom activities and assignments that teach students how to critically read gender establish a template for active analysis of the world.

Gender Studies and Critical Reading

Before we look at particular assignments and classroom practices for teaching critical reading of gender, we need to consider what we mean by both "gender studies" and "critical reading." It is only over the past five decades that women's and gender studies departments have come into existence, arising out of the feminist movement of the 1970s. Historically, the rhetorical move from "women's studies" to "gender studies" emerged after the shift from second- to third-wave feminism. Third-wave feminists sought to create a more inclusive movement, one that considers the differing experiences women have based on respective categories of race, class, and sexuality. Part of this shift included a move away from the binary thinking of

1970s women's studies classes, in which the idea of "patriarchy" was presented as categorically privileging all men over all women through gender oppression. At the end of the twentieth century, colleges began to include the words "gender and sexuality" in departmental fields, as "women's studies" often morphed into "women's and gender studies," or as separate programs focusing on sexuality and gender were created. This small shift was meant to open up the field of inquiry, to provide further study of how gender oppression affects everybody, including men, and how it operates in conjunction with other forms of marginalization. The inclusion of queer theory and masculinity studies under the umbrella term "gender studies" thus significantly broadened the field's scope. By taking into consideration how gender operates at all levels of society, critics have developed a more thorough understanding of how the categories of male and female are constructed. Yet the purpose of this field remains consistent with its second-wave origins: to end forms of oppression based on gender identity and sexual orientation.

To accomplish this goal, the study of gender involves observing, analyzing, and deconstructing representations of gender, a methodology consistent, perhaps even synonymous, with critical reading. One of the primary goals of teaching critical reading as a general skill is to inspire students to engage actively with ideas rather than passively accept information as it is presented. Such "active reading" requires a clear understanding of what is being said in a text (or depicted in an image), but it also requires further analysis of who is speaking and from what perspective or position. Two questions central to critical reading remain consistent across disciplines: *why* and *how*? Why has the author of a text – and "author" here can be broadly understood as anyone who speaks or represents – chosen to convey information in this manner, and how has the author gone about creating the desired effect? What is the effect, both intentional and unintentional, of this text on its audience? Approaching a text critically requires a certain degree of readerly distance, an interpretive stance that is not necessarily skeptical, but rather considers how the text has been constructed as a meaning-making apparatus within the culture of its origin.

The aims of gender studies as a field are perfectly aligned with such goals: when we critically read gender, we do not accept that gender is an essential, naturally occurring phenomenon, but rather a collection of socially constructed assumptions, behaviors, and taxonomies, which we can refer to as the matrices of gender. These culturally specific matrices shape our conceptions of what it means to be male or female, but they are seamlessly woven into the fabric of our society: in examining how traditional categories like "masculine" and "feminine" have come into being, and how they serve a given culture, a gender critic must reconsider the most basic assumptions upon which that society is built. Because gender and sexuality are naturalized categories of daily life, their operations are rarely obvious, and deconstructing representations of gender requires that gender critics – as well as their students – refuse to take information at face value, and instead query how a text is constructed and why it has been constructed in the way that it has.

Deconstructing Gender

Professors of gender studies often encounter the same obstacles as any teacher attempting to guide students through the process of critical reading. Chief among these obstacles is moving beyond the initial step in critical reading, which, at its core, is an act of observation. This first step answers the question: What does the text state outright? A much more challenging question must follow: What does this text imply? What does it communicate without explicitly stating? When deconstructing gender, as we will see in the activities below, the initial stage can be easy for students to engage in, as it requires simply identifying the gender roles operative in a given representation or social situation. Gender inquiry begins with an analysis of the normative roles pervading a culture, and identifying where such binaries can be located. Gender roles are often easily identified as "stereotypes" – a fairly accessible idea for first-year college students. However, to develop a critical reading process, students must make a leap from simply repeating gender stereotypes to drawing original conclusions about those same stereotypes. The first level of gender deconstruction asks students to parse the well-known gender binaries: women are passive, nurturing, and emotional, whereas men are strong, virile, and rational. It is usually easy for students to identify the flaws in a system that claims all women want to stay at home and take care of their families, whereas all men want to go out and conquer the world. Yet the work of critical reading is not merely to state the existence of such constructions, but rather to look at where exactly these binaries come from, and how they manifest in more diffuse and nuanced ways.

This leap from identifying stereotypes to critically reading those stereotypes is perhaps subtle, and it requires that students understand the difference between observation and analysis. Or, phrased another way, it asks students to move beyond summarizing a text to analyzing that text. When engaging with traditional academic texts, many students are more comfortable explaining what they have read than probing a text's meaning and implications; the same is true when students deconstruct gender. For the "critical" process to take place, readers of gender must begin to look at *why* and *how* these constructions have come into being, and in what other, less obvious, ways they influence our thinking. This next level of analysis can be difficult for students to achieve, as well as for teachers to explain. The following assignments can provide teachers with a means for helping their students make this critical leap.

Documentary Project

Although the term paper is the hallmark of humanities seminars, it has its limitations. Traditional academic papers follow conventions that students have spent years being trained to understand, and although sustained, evidence-based written analyses are perhaps the most important pedagogical tools for critical reading, they can at times limit the creativity that allows students to consider texts in fresh and innovative ways. Assigning a video documentary project alongside a more traditional paper helps restore creativity and freshness to the research process, as digital storytelling that combines interviews, images, and reflective analysis offers students a more immediate medium for exploring culture. As an interactive activity, the documentary project allows students to physically and intellectually confront their immediate surroundings, as well as more richly develop their ideas and questions in response to the feedback of collaborators and interview subjects. Additionally, the project turns familiar, daily situations into sites of inquiry, and therefore forces students to reconsider how and why gender is constantly in the process of being constructed all around them, in even the seemingly least noteworthy circumstances.

In the spring of 2015, I worked as an instructional technology consultant with history professor Daniel Hurewitz to develop this type of video project for students in The Peopling of New York, a required first-year seminar for Macaulay Honors College at Hunter College. The philosophy behind using digital technology in this seminar is to provide a fresh dynamic in student thought, while simultaneously equipping students with the technological skills required for twenty-first-century careers. This course is organized around the study of the different populations of the city; Professor Hurewitz designed his section around the history of sex and gender in New York, and subtitled the course "Sex and Gender in the Twentieth Century." As described in the syllabus, the learning goals included understanding "how notions of masculinity and femininity have evolved" and "how ideas about heterosexuality and marriage have developed." By placing the history of sex and gender in the context of the populations of New York City, the course invited students to reexamine how the city itself reflects constantly shifting ideas of gender and sexuality in the culture at large.

For the documentary project, students worked in pairs to create 5- to 8-minute "documentaries" that examined how gender operates in their own peer groups in relation to a particular social or cultural practice or norm. They were required to conduct peer interviews and to compose original voiceover and/or onscreen text. Crucially, their videos had to project a specific point of view: students had to digest and distill the material of their interviews, arrive at synthesizing conclusions, and edit and frame the raw footage accordingly.

Each pair chose topics they found personally interesting, examining activities and subcultures they themselves took part in, such as video gaming or bodybuilding, as well as bodily or social practices they felt pressured to conform to, including leg-shaving, wearing make-up, and "hooking up." Through the process of recording interviews, in which they questioned peers about these topics, students became active observers in dialogue with their community. By examining manifestations of gendered thinking in their own peer community, students directly applied the difficult concepts being taught in class to their daily lives. Yet this type of assignment is not an exercise in the kinds of "personal experience learning" often associated with gender studies. In other words, it does not privilege the feelings of students based on their private experiences. Rather, it asks students to step back and look at how their community talks about gender, to ask their peers how they experience gender, and to draw analytic conclusions based on the investigative process. As we will see, the process of making the video draws out critical reading skills as they are applied both to the community and to the students themselves.

Including a video documentary project in a humanities course can seem like a daunting task for professors who are not steeped in video production or filmmaking. It is important, then, to stress that, although this project focuses on digital storytelling and the production of a cohesive video, it is not an assignment in the art of filmmaking. Rather, the medium of digital video is a means for students to collect data – by recording interviews as audio or audiovisual documents – and, subsequently, to demonstrate their findings and represent their conclusions. To ease students through the process, the assignment requires staging, or scaffolding, and should be started at least six weeks in advance of the due date. The students do not need to become filmmakers in six weeks; they simply need to collect interviews, develop an analysis of the data, and arrange its presentation in a coherent way.

Staging the Documentary Project

The first stage of the project for students is simply identifying a specific topic and creating research questions. At the outset, it is useful to give sample topics and explain the types of analysis you expect. In addition to the topics mentioned above, sample student topics included video game culture, educational choices (such as how students choose their major), and the gender coding of masturbation. Once students have identified topics, the class should, as a group, discuss interview strategies and potential questions. Having students perform practice interviews during class time, either in front of the class or in small groups, helps them become more comfortable with their role as interviewer, while also providing an opportunity to discuss interviewing tactics, such as asking follow-up questions and avoiding leading questions. Practice sessions also provide the opportunity to show students that interviewing is an important scholarly tool employed across the social sciences and humanities. Scholars follow ethical guidelines when working with human subjects; any discussion of interview strategies with students should highlight the ethics of research that involves people. In The Peopling of New York, students were given consent forms that all interviewees had to sign. The forms explained how the footage would be used and offered privacy options. As an added step in similar projects, students can work together as a class to create such a form. Thinking through the role of the interviewer in this process, and considering the ethical issues related to creating a documentary, help foster critical understanding by allowing students to reflect upon their effect on the investigation, even as observers: how do they, as questioners, influence responses? What are their responsibilities as documentarians and scholars?

In the assignment's second stage, students were given several weeks to find and interview their peers. Using their phones as recording devices, most students conducted interviews in their dorms, or found friends willing to act as subjects. This stage entails more than mere data collection, however, as the interviews themselves enact the process of critical engagement. An example of this process can be seen in one student team's video, which featured interview subjects discussing the gendering of cosmetics. Unsurprisingly, the students who were interviewed noted that cosmetics are generally meant for female use, and men who wear make-up are considered effeminate. However, in the process of interviewing, both the documentarians and the subjects were forced to discuss the issue at length, because a two-minute interview simply stating the obvious would not have rendered sufficient footage. The medium itself thus inspired a more prolonged discussion. In the course of the recorded sessions, interviewees eventually elaborated on specific elements of gendering, including what constitutes a feminine look and what a more masculine approach to the wearing of cosmetics might be. In addition, the subjects had to reflect on their own feelings about the pressure to engage in certain conformist behaviors regarding the use of cosmetics. Many seemed to express conflicting views, admitting that, although they did not care at all whether individuals of either sex chose to wear make-up, they did perceive make-up to be for either straight women or queer men. One young man who was interviewed claimed that he enjoyed wearing make-up in theater productions, and he knew that, in seventeenth-century France, both men and women powdered their faces. He thus understood there is nothing inherently "feminine" about putting powder on one's face.

In this investigation, mass-produced cosmetics become a text, and in the footage the interviewees enact the process of interpreting this text. Calling upon knowledge of the history of powdering in the seventeenth century and applying that knowledge to the present-day circumstances of women who wear foundation, all in the service of constructing an original argument regarding the arbitrariness of contemporary gendered associations, created a clear moment of critical engagement. In discussions like these, students came to the conclusion not only that the labeling of behaviors as masculine and feminine is culturally contingent, but also that, despite our awareness of the arbitrary nature of gender norms, many of us are complicit in their cultural reproduction. Although we know there is nothing biologically female about wearing make-up, men and women continue to associate rouged cheeks and painted lips with the ideal of feminine beauty. As one interviewee explained, "Make-up's for girls, and I don't think that's right, but that's the way it is."

After students had collected interviews, they began editing their footage together on basic software like iMovie, and one class session was devoted to workshopping a selection of videos. During this workshop, we discussed not only the footage students had collected, but also what the following, third stage would entail: creating a narrative out of their interviews. At this point it had become clear to the groups what conclusions they wanted to draw from their videos. The movement from gathering material to organizing a coherent video is perhaps the most significant part of the project. Turning the video from a collection of spliced interviews into a digital narrative is the point at which students apply what they have learned in the course. This is also the moment at which students make that all-important leap from summary, or observation, to analysis, or critical reading.

The workshop itself provides a key moment of intervention, during which the methods of critical reading are reproduced as students engage with one another's work. One pair of students who created a documentary on weight-lifting initially found only male subjects to interview, and their footage consisted entirely of men discussing their desire to "gain inches" of muscle in order to look good. During the workshop phase, their classmates expressed a desire to see women interviewed, and to get the added perspective of men who have no interest in working out. They also offered potential questions that could lead interview subjects to provide more details regarding their associations between masculinity and bodybuilding. Although these seem like fairly simple suggestions, they are in fact key indicators that the students are, as a group, thinking critically about both the material at hand and the methodologies employed to gather and convey that material. Such feedback encouraged the student documentarians to investigate the subject further and with more attention to questions of gender. Ultimately, this group found a female classmate whose hobby was bodybuilding, and she spoke frankly about her frustrations with the lack of resources and support for women in this sport.

Following the workshops, students began the third and final stage of the project. They followed up on workshop suggestions and wrote scripts for either voiceover narration or title cards that oriented viewers while simultaneously presenting the documentarians' conclusions. This final stage allowed students to synthesize all the information they had collected alongside the input of their peers. On the final day of class, we held a screening for all the videos. When I interviewed several students after this final screening, they all noted how much they had learned from their peers' work, in large part because the videos exposed various subcultures that were unfamiliar to other students. For example, most students were unfamiliar with the subculture around online video gaming, and so the video that detailed what it means to be a girl in the gaming community highlighted a new arena of gender discrimination. And yet the same stereotypes about what is "masculine" – playing aggressive shooter games, going on imaginary quests – remained consistent in this video and many others. Thus the documentaries as a collective whole exposed how gender construction is always operating in myriad, interconnected ways.

One student, who had created a documentary on the gendering of masturbation, noted, "This project exposed me to so much more than the paper did. I began to notice that all the stuff we've been talking about in class is constantly happening in my life. It made me pay closer attention to gender in my normal life." Her partner agreed, "I had never thought about any of this stuff before. We never talked about it in high school, but I noticed that even my mother, who's a feminist and a liberal, sometimes says things that affirm gender roles." For these students, the documentary project provided a fresh model for application of newly acquired knowledge, and shifted the purview of their critical reading from historical New York to their own, contemporary city.

The video project thus helped students begin to examine the subtexts of gendered codes in the world around them, and it offered opportunities to deconstruct products and activities that may have once seemed to contain very little subtextual meaning. It is a useful tool for teaching students how to recognize gender constructions and explore *how* and *why* those constructions play out; in other words, it is a strong exercise in critical reading. Yet this project remains somewhat limited in the scope of its critical reading; the documentarians identified gender constructions and attempted to engage with those constructions, but they were unable to analyze complex representations of gender that moved beyond binaries and stereotypes. For students to move beyond this first-level critical reading to more nuanced forms of analysis, they require exposure to complex representations of gender, including texts that attempt to resist gender construction. Such texts encourage audiences to query the idea of resistance: what does it mean to resist gender, why do we want to resist, and how do we do so? In other words, to deepen the nuance and complexity of the critical reading process, we must model how to interpret texts more complex than those that merely affirm gender roles. If the first level of critical reading, as practiced in this documentary project, identifies and analyzes text and subtext, the next level considers how some texts might produce multiple possible meanings, some of which work in opposition to one another. The following activity was designed to help students develop such higher-order critical reading skills.

Aesthetic Distance and Ironic Images of Gender

This activity consists of a series of exercises developed for an interdisciplinary first-year writing course, the purpose of which was to equip college students with the critical reading and thinking skills they would need throughout their academic careers. The activity centers on an examination of the photographs of feminist artists Melanie Pullen and Cindy Sherman, viewed in the context of advertisements and editorial photography from fashion magazines. Through in-class discussion and reflective writing, students consider how these photographs offer simultaneous and conflicting meanings that are not easily resolvable. The assignment leads to a possible formal paper, in which students can discuss the images' use of "irony" and "resistance" in further detail. Its ultimate goal is to introduce students to the concept of irony, an essential component of the kind of complex critical reading I have been describing.

The course itself was divided into four sections that emphasized different critical approaches to reading pop-culture texts. In the "Reading Gender" section in which this activity was used, I dedicated several weeks to analyzing gendered images in photography, film, and television to model how to read such texts critically. (The activity is thus applicable to a variety of fields, including art, media studies, and, of course, women's studies.) In this activity, students come to understand how artists employ irony to achieve a certain effect. Here "ironic images" indicates photographs in which visual signification is not meant to be taken literally, at face value; rather, the image serves as a commentary on its own representation. I use such images to help students understand that texts don't always offer a clear "message" or an insidious stereotype, but, instead, can operate on multiple levels to produce conflicting, and conflicted, meanings.

In the first step in the activity, I ask students to look through print or online magazines and identify advertisements and editorial photographs they think contain gendered content. I begin with advertising and magazine imagery because it is an accessible site for gender analysis. Ask students to find a piece of advertising that reifies gender norms, and they will quickly be able to find pervasive stereotypes: cleaning product ads aimed at women or car commercials that sell men on the idea that a certain brand is "strong," "powerful," and "smooth." Identifying mass media images that rely on, and cater to, gender norms is useful in starting a discussion of the prevalence of such norms. However, if the goal is to teach critical reading, activities like this, common enough in first-year writing courses, are limited in their efficacy, and need to be followed up with more complex images. One particular sticking point I have found in looking at images reproduced in mass media is that students are readily able to identify, and eager to discuss, the "messages" carried by such images. These "messages," many are quick to point out, are often limiting or even harmful for men and women; for example, my students are often unsettled by the unrealistic idealization of certain kinds of women's bodies in fashion magazines, and further bothered by the advertisements for weight loss products that appear alongside such images. That these "messages" exist is significant, but it is a concept already familiar to most students by the time they have graduated high school. Decoding such messages does not necessarily require thoughtful analysis, as it often lingers on the images at face value. A woman raving about how much she loves cleaning products clearly plays into the stereotype of the happy housewife; reading into the gendered message is a good initial step in critical analysis, but it does not move much farther than the surface of the image.

I recommend pairing this activity with reading an essay like Brian Moeran's "The Portrayal of Beauty in Women's Fashion Magazines" (2010), an accessible but thorough article that describes how advertising and editorial content create a "technology of enchantment" that persuades skeptical women to buy into the "beauty myth." Moeran identifies one of the difficulties in analyzing mass media images: consumers are aware of the inconsistencies inherent in advertising, and in a sense understand that they are being manipulated by "messages." And yet such imagery continues to shape our conceptions of how the female body should be publicly presented. To grapple with this inherently conflicted and even paradoxical facet of gender ideology – so clearly articulated by the student in the above-mentioned documentary, who claimed, "Make-up's for girls, and I don't think that's right, but that's the way it is." – I present students with images that, through irony, can accommodate multiple sentiments.

This more demanding stage of critical thinking requires students to stretch their analytic skills, to problematize images and understand that a text can contain multiple levels of meaning, some of which might be contradictory. To push students to a deeper level of critical awareness, it is necessary to work with images that do not merely represent gender norms, but rather actively engage with such norms, images that present complex sites of simultaneous capitulation and resistance. Such material requires awareness not only of what is represented and the various semiotic codes at play, but also how the author is playing with those codes to create a site of resistance. Such texts require that the viewer also maintain an aesthetic distance to fully comprehend what is being articulated. The ads or photo spreads from magazines present an easy starting place, which can then be followed up with an examination of images that challenge viewers to reconsider their own spectatorship.

Melanie Pullen's *High Fashion Crime Scenes* and Cindy Sherman's *Centerfolds, 1981*

Melanie Pullen's series *High Fashion Crime Scenes* is a collection of large-scale photographs taken between 1995 and 2005. (Some of these photos are viewable on highfashioncrimescenes.com.) The crime scenes are elaborately staged, elegantly crafted, and are intended to resemble the haute couture fashion spreads found in magazines like *Vogue* or *Vanity Fair*. The models are dressed in designer brands that remain recognizable even as the body is splayed across a subway platform or dangles from a noose. Pullen's intent is to comment on the persistence within our media landscape of images featuring violence against women. As she told the *Los Angeles Times*: "We have become apathetic to these images. ... I took this horrific subject and turned it into something aesthetic" (2004). The effect is unsettling, at once disturbing and alluring. The reference to high-fashion imagery is instantly recognizable in the clothes, lighting, and dramatically stylized backdrops. Viewers, accustomed to consuming such images as aesthetically pleasurable, are placed in the uncomfortable position of being repulsed and pleased at the same time.

The complexity of the image renders it difficult to align with simplistic gender binaries or stereotypes. Unlike a straightforward high-fashion spread – in which waifish, airbrushed women wear impossibly expensive clothes and set unrealistic expectations of feminine beauty – the gender norms on display here cannot easily be identified. Rather, the image demands viewers adopt a distanced perspective from which to look, so that they can perceive how the image comments on its own representation. The photograph is at once beautiful and dreadful, but part of its beauty stems from the horrifying scene, as the ostensibly murdered female body, the focal point of the photo, is an aesthetically pleasing object. Despite its appeal, however, the image is too grotesque to be described as uncompromisingly "beautiful." On the other hand, it cannot be written off as simply exploitative of the female body, or as promoting violence against women. Taken as a complete series, the photos comment on the media saturation of such violent images, and provoke the viewer to reflect upon the sheer familiarity of both the violence and the high-fashion aesthetic. In addition, the juxtaposition of the murdered female form and high fashion satirizes fashion photography's objectification of the female body.

These interpretations of the photos, however, are not necessarily obvious upon first glance, and they require thoughtful analysis and discussion to be drawn out for students. For this assignment, I show these photos as a counterpoint to the mainstream ads and fashion spreads, in which the "messages" are decoded with relative ease. In Pullen's photos, the codes are familiar but put to very different use, and the motivation behind the images is not easily interpretable. We could not argue that Mullen is clearly projecting an idealization of feminine passivity, as her photos hyperbolize the typically passive poses of fashion models. Such exaggeration – rather than reclining alluringly, the women are splayed in mock-victim poses – indicates the photos are treating such idealization ironically, and are inviting viewers to reconsider how they respond to the passive female body as an object of desire. In Pullen's photographs, unlike fashion photos or ads that want viewers to take aesthetic pleasure in the object on display, there is no singular message of "this is desirable" or "this is undesirable." Instead, it is up to each viewer to peel back the layers of the image and construct an independent interpretation of what constitutes "desirability."

For many of my first-year students, this activity marks their first encounter with a text where the "message," or meaning, works in opposition to what is being represented. Although the photos depict aestheticized violence, they do not endorse such violence; rather, they are intended to resist the same types of exploitation in which they are engaged. By combining multiple genres, including art performance, crime fiction, and fashion photography, Pullen blurs the viewer's sense of exactly what the representation intends to signify. If we take pleasure in their beauty, are we also participating in the bodily violation on display? This implication of the viewer disturbs the clear-cut construction of meaning present in mass media images: rather than representing an idea of beauty for the viewer to emulate, these photos suggest that beauty is horrifying. And yet, because the photos are themselves alluring, they require readers to acknowledge a paradox in signification: the photo presents both an act of exploitation and a critique of its own exploitative intentions.

I follow our discussion of Melanie Pullen by presenting students with Cindy Sherman's series of photographs titled *Centerfolds, 1981* (currently available as a slideshow on the MOMA website). Perhaps the most famous feminist photographer to employ irony, Sherman offers a plethora of texts that demonstrate how an image can self-consciously play with the concept of objectification. *Centerfolds, 1981* is in many ways a precursor to Pullen's *High Fashion Crime Scenes*. The staged images, which feature Sherman herself in different guises as the subject, are modeled on a classic centerfold format. Framed horizontally and posed in various reclining positions, Sherman performs a range of personae, none of which conforms to the conventions of pornographic or pin-up femininity. The photographs combine self-portraiture with art performance, and subvert the notion of revelation or authenticity in self-presentation. Sherman is less interested in revealing herself than in demonstrating how a woman might slip into – and out of – various roles assigned to femininity, particularly the role of passive, victimized object.

Writing for the *New York Times* in 2003, Grace Glueck recalled Sherman's series: "More than simple spoofs of the stereotypes promulgated by various magazines, these photographs manage to convey the ambiguities of women playing gender cliché roles and even Ms. Sherman's own unease at casting herself in them." As both the object of the gaze and the photographer who controls the image, Sherman destabilizes the binary of objectifier/objectified. It is therefore difficult to dismiss the images as merely reifying cultural attitudes toward feminine glamour and beauty. However, a woman who objectifies herself is not necessarily engaging in an act of resistance. Both Pullen and Sherman walk a thin line. Representing the female body in poses that mimic bodily exploitation, they could be accused of consenting to their own objectification.

For the viewer to understand these images as ironic or resistant, he or she needs to look not only at text and subtext, but also at context. Both *High Fashion Crime Scenes* and *Centerfolds, 1981* exist in dialogue with photographic genres (fashion and pornographic/pin-up photography, respectively), as well as with the cultural conventions surrounding those genres. It would be impossible to understand fully either woman's work independent of their intertexts. Moreover, taken as a whole, the photographs in each series interact with one another to create a cohesive critique of the photographic genres to which they refer. These intertextual links provide a further layer of nuance to the viewer's interpretation: all of these photos must be read in conjunction with images which are only referred to, and thereby place an additional burden on the viewer to call upon extra-textual cultural knowledge.

To point this out, I close this activity by asking students to reflect on the significance of context for their own interpretive processes. I return to a few images from the start of our discussion – that is, an image from a magazine spread that features a particular idealization of femininity – and ask them how they might interpret this image differently in light of the subsequent photos we examined. At this point in the discussion I return to the idea of "resistance" as it pertains to feminist critique. Have Pullen and Sherman's photos successfully reoriented the students' relation to these pop-culture images, and if so, does that qualify them as successful sites of resistance? Or, conversely, have these photographs merely reinvented these stereotypical images? Do they simply highlight the same problems students were already able to recognize on their own?

At the close of class, I present the above questions in the form of a writing prompt: *These photo series refer to popular magazine photo spreads featuring the female body. How do Sherman and Pullen's photographs differ from those they emulate, and how are they the same? Given these differences and similarities, do you consider these series subversive, or do you think they recreate the same gender constructions as their source materials?* This in-class writing exercise may form the basis for possible future papers discussing the concept of aesthetic distance and irony. But its most immediate benefit is to provide students the opportunity to write reflectively, to synthesize the preceding discussion, and to begin to perform their own analysis of multivalent, ironic images. As skillfully wrought works of art, such images continue to challenge the most seasoned of critical readers, and create the possibility of genuine cultural understanding and change.

References

Glueck, G. (2003). Cindy Sherman – "Centerfolds, 1981." *New York Times* (May 23). http://www.nytimes.com/2003/05/23/arts/art-in-review-cindy-sherman-centerfolds-1981.html?_r = 0 (accessed October 2, 2016).

Hundley, J. (2004). Fashion victims. *Los Angeles Times* (June 17). http://articles.latimes.com/2004/jun/17/news/wk-gallery17 (accessed October 2, 2016).

Moeran, B. (2010). The portrayal of beauty in women's fashion magazines. *Fashion Theory*, 14(4), 491–510.

Pullen, M. (2005). *High fashion crime scenes*. Paso Robles, CA: Nazraeli Press.

11

Reading and Teaching Films

William V. Costanzo

The French film theorist Christian Metz once wrote, "A film is difficult to explain because it is easy to understand" (1974, p. 69). His words highlight a paradox at the heart of all film studies. The seeming simplicity of watching movies may pose the biggest challenge to reading them with a critical eye. To read anything critically, of course, requires certain transferable skills. The ability to analyze a text – to interpret its meanings with searching questions, understand its inner logic, or evaluate its worth – depends on faculties of higher-order thinking that may be applied across disciplines. But when the text is a movie, the act of watching it may seem so natural, so effortless, we easily forget that any film depends on a system of significance, actually several systems, which must be learned. Movies communicate their meanings largely through codes and conventions that have evolved over time, the various "languages" of sound, image, and editing. Learning to read these languages and to understand them within wider contexts is the focus of this essay.

For teachers who include films in their classes, the deceptive ease of watching them is abetted by another fact. Movies famously foster an illusion, the willing suspension of disbelief. They hide the seams of their construction so that we, the audience, can lose ourselves in fabricated worlds. Students understandably may resist our efforts to subject these worlds to scrutiny. After all, it's just entertainment. Why ruin a pleasurable experience by taking it apart? Teachers need to move their students past the point of resistance, to pursue a more productive path of engaged, critical inquiry. It's a path where curiosity about the movie world can lead to a more

Critical Reading Across the Curriculum, Volume 1: Humanities, First Edition.
Edited by Robert DiYanni and Anton Borst.
© 2017 John Wiley & Sons, Inc. Published 2017 by John Wiley & Sons, Inc.

informed appreciation of film and where greater fluency in the languages of cinema brings pleasures of its own. For a generation immersed in media, as likely to connect through moving images as through spoken or written words, we can build on our students' media-mindedness to shape more critical habits of mind.

Beyond the films themselves are the frameworks built around them. Every community has its favored topics of conversation, the questions and concerns that members talk about with one another. Within the discipline of film studies, students need to know how to analyze a film in formal terms (to identify and interpret its meanings and motifs, evaluate the acting, understand what camerawork and set design contribute, for example). They also require an acquaintance with the historical developments that shape the movies, their reception, and the literature on film. In other words, they need some familiarity with the issues (such as changes in technology, feminism, multiculturalism, globalism) that preoccupy film scholars, reviewers, critics, and theorists, as well as filmmakers, in order to understand and actively engage in the conversation.

In a book about reading across the curriculum, it's worth noting that filmmaking is by nature multidisciplinary. Film is an art with many parallels to other arts, but it is also a business, a technology, and a cultural force. It can be overtly political or covertly ideological. It can reflect the fashions of the day, comment on history, and predict future possibilities. Whatever aspect you emphasize in your classes – whether you use films in a high school social studies class, a college course in literature, or a new curriculum in global citizenship – this chapter is intended as a practical guide. It begins with a survey of critical approaches to film, applies them to selected films, and concludes with a set of classroom-tested student exercises.

Personal Response

The starting point for any critical inquiry often is a personal response. Whatever the filmmakers' intentions might be, whatever talent and resources went into its creation, a film is little more than a blueprint without a viewer to complete it. Reader-response theorists like Norman Holland, Wolfgang Iser, and Louise Rosenblatt emphasize the primacy of readers. It is readers, they argue, who bring literary works to life, imparting meaning through individual acts of interpretation. Viewed this way, the reader is part of a collaborative triangle that includes the author and the text. The triangle of cinema may be more complex, since the author of a film typically includes more people (director, cinematographer, actors, producers); the text is multisensory (words, images, sounds, motion); and the viewer often watches a film interactively with others. In a sense, there are as many versions of a movie as there are viewers, or even viewings, since the reception of a film may differ from time to time and place to place, from person to person, and even from one stage of a person's life to another.

If your goal is to develop your students' critical thinking, consider ways to redirect their attention from subjective experience to more objective sources. Help them to discover the roots of their impressions in the particularities of the film itself, to connect those cinematic moments with events in their personal lives and in the world around them.

In its initial form, the reaction to a film may come as a simple expression of approval or dislike, a thumbs up or a thumbs down. But a general pronouncement is not as interesting, or valuable, as understanding what's behind the personal response of individual viewers. Since individuals respond differently, a closer look at specific trigger points can reveal a lot about those individuals as well as the about film itself. A few pointed questions can guide students to clarify their reactions and the reasons for them.

- What words best describe your overall response?
- What were the film's most memorable moments? What feelings or ideas did they evoke?
- Where were the highs and lows in your engagement? What caught or held your attention? At what points did your interest fade?
- Did some settings seem familiar? What made them so?
- Which characters remind you of people you know from other films, from literature, or from life?
- What other associations (music, stories, images) might help to clarify the thoughts and feelings you experienced during the film?
- How did your personal responses compare to those of other viewers? How might the differences and similarities be explained?

Analyzing Story

Movies that tell stories, what might be called cinematic fiction, have much in common with novels, plays, epic poems, and other forms of literary fiction. Their narratives can be analyzed in terms of setting, character, plot, point of view, and theme – the basic elements of any story. Every story takes place at a particular time and place, often several times and places. This setting may provide a simple backdrop to the story, contribute to its tone, and reveal things about the characters. The harsh conditions at sea in *Mutiny on the Bounty* (1962), for example, bring out the best and worst in the sailors and their captain, providing contrasts between the idyllic moments on Pitcairn Island and the courtroom scenes in England, when they face the legal consequences of their actions.

What sustains our interest is usually some kind of conflict: a struggle between protagonist and antagonist, a battle between larger forces (a feud, a war), or an internal struggle taking place within a character. In classical narratives, the conflict generates a series of related actions that lead to a dramatic climax. It is this causal chain of events – one action leading to another – that students of literature call plot. One way to analyze a movie's narrative is to identify key features of the plot: the main conflict, complication, exposition, climax (sometimes called crisis), denouement, or resolution of the conflict, and recognition scene, if indeed a protagonist comes to understand the true nature of his or her condition.

A distinction can be made between a movie's plot and its structure, since sometimes events unfold out of order. *Double Indemnity* (1944) has the structure of a flashback: it opens with the protagonist speaking his story into a Dictaphone. *Citizen Kane* (1941) and *Rashomon* (1950) use the structure of multiple perspectives: different characters recount the same events from their own subjective points of view. The non-linear structure of *Memento* (2002) mirrors the confusion of the protagonist, who suffers from a defective memory. In well-told stories, such variations in the order in which events are related may serve a writer's purpose to complicate the narrative, raising questions about a narrator's reliability or the trustworthiness of narration itself.

Most stories, though, unfold chronologically and sustain a consistent point of view. They may be more or less limited to the perceptions of a single character, like *One Flew Over the Cuckoo's Nest* (1975), in which the camera rarely leaves its protagonist, the con artist Randle Patrick McMurphy. More often, though, the camera assumes a more objective stance, like the omniscient narrator in a Dickens novel, with the ability to go anywhere and observe anything, even the unspoken thoughts of characters. Movies seem to favor this detached perspective, as if the camera lens naturally captures the objective truth. But of course we know that this perspective is always mediated by decisions about framing, lighting, even the choice of lens, decisions that limit and distort what we see on the screen. Learning to notice these decisions and account for the distortions is one way to develop a critical eye.

Students who have tried this kind of story analysis in English classes may resist it as a tedious exercise, and they have a point. Breaking down a story into its component parts is not an end in itself. The payoff is understanding how these parts work together, appreciating the dynamic interaction of character, setting, action, and perspective – and grasping why this is important. The why of any film, its underlying purpose, may be hard to state definitively. A movie may entertain us with emotional appeals – make us laugh, bring tears to our eyes, frighten us out of our seats – but it may also work in other ways. It may present important issues, directly or indirectly exploring themes like gender roles (*Victor Victoria*, 1982), drug addiction (*Trainspotting*, 1996), or the place of humans in the natural environment (*Avatar*, 2009). It may cause us to question certain deeply held beliefs. One of our tasks as teachers is to help students look behind the structure of a story, to understand how it was constructed and consider reasons why it was made one way and not another.

The following questions can help students analyze these aspects of films:

- Who are the main characters? What are their goals in the story? What obstacles must they overcome to achieve these goals?
- Where and when is the story set? How does the setting affect the action, influence character, or contribute to the story's tone?
- What basic conflict drives the action? What are the key features of the plot?
- Does the film favor a particular point of view? Are events shown from the perspective of one or more characters? Does the camera cross barriers of time, place, and subjectivity? What is left out, and what difference does this make in our understanding of events?
- How is the story structured? Why are events presented in this particular order?
- What themes or larger ideas emerge as the story progresses? Where are they most apparent? Does the film itself seem to take sides on certain issues? How can you tell?

Basic Film Terms

All films have in common a large pool of techniques to draw from. The filmmaker's tool box includes options for camerawork (close-ups, tracking shots, zooms), sound (dialogue, music, Foley sound effects), and editing (flashbacks, crosscutting, montage), all of which have evolved through more than a century of film history into a kind of cinematic lexicon, a vocabulary of interpretable conventions.

How do we know that a scene represents a flashback to the past? How do we recognize when the enlarged view of an insect on the screen is meant to show a close-up, not a giant spider? When do we understand that the music on the soundtrack is coming from an off-screen orchestra, not the actor's mind? Finding answers to such questions reminds us of how much we've already learned (or have yet to learn) about the signifying systems of cinema – its multiple overlapping codes.

A good way to survey the variety of film forms is to review the film terms that describe them. Consider what a brief selection of these terms reveals about the way movies work.

Camerawork generally refers to options available to the **cinematographer**, who is responsible for the **camera setup** and its operations on the set. This includes various kinds of camera **movements**: along a horizontal plane (**tracking** shot, **dolly** shot), through vertical space (**boom** shot, **crane** shot), pivoting left or right (**panning**), **tilting** up or down. It takes into account a camera's position (a **low-angle shot** from below the subject, a **high-angle shot** from above) and its distance to the subject: a **medium shot** (which usually shows an actor from the knees up), **long shot** (showing the entire figure and some background), **close-up** (which might show an actor's hand or facial features), and variations (**extreme long shot, aerial view**).

Lighting is part of the cinematographer's responsibilities. The chief light illuminating the subject is called the **key light**. In **high-key lighting**, the scene is flooded with bright illumination, giving it a joyful, buoyant feeling. In **low-key lighting**, illumination is low and soaked with shadows, creating an ominous or melancholy mood. **Spotlights** focus strong beams on the subject. **Floodlights** wash the scene in a more diffuse form of illumination. A halo effect might be created with a **backlight**, or an **eyelight** might add sparkle to the subject's eyes.

Sound has always been an essential part of film experience. Even in the silent period, theaters employed musicians to add **background music** and occasionally create **sound effects**. Today, music usually is part of a film's recorded **soundtrack**, and sound effects are added digitally or synthesized by special **Foley artists**, who may simulate a horse's gallop with coconut shells or the punches of a fistfight by striking watermelons with a hammer. A typical soundtrack may also include the actors' **spoken dialogue, voiceover** to represent a character's unspoken thoughts or an unseen narrator, and **ambient sound** to add a sense of realism to the scene.

Color became a staple of the movie industry in the 1930s, but even earlier it was common practice to tint black and white film stock for emotional effects: blue for a romantic night scene, red for a battle, green for peaceful moments. Today, color-conscious directors may deliberately choose a color scheme, or **color palette**, for similar reasons, as Mira Nair does with the masala hues of *Monsoon Wedding*. Some directors, like Michelangelo Antonioni in *Red Desert* (1964), have been known to paint the landscape

Table 11.1 Shot-by-shot analysis: Six consecutive screengrabs from *Crouching Tiger, Hidden Dragon*

Transition: cut (23 sec.) Framing: long shot Action: a caravan moves slowly through the desert Angle: camera cranes down from slight high angle to road level as caravan passes left to right Movement: camera cranes down slightly while panning left to right Lighting: outdoors near noon Sound: slow music on sound track, SFX of camel bells	Transition: cut (10 sec.) Framing: close-up Action: Jen and mother jostling along in carriage; mother tells Jen to stop playing with her comb Angle: eye-line Movement: none Lighting: low-key, faces in shadow Sound: music and SFX continue, Mother: "Stop playing with it" Jen: "I won't break it"	Transition: cut (4 sec.) Framing: extreme long shot Action: caravan continues its slow progress left to right (as in shot 1) Angle: high-angle Movement: none Lighting: same as shot 1 Sound: same as shot 1

Transition: cut (8 sec.) Framing: Medium to long shot Action: Lo watches the caravan with his mounted brigands from atop a cliff Angle: from low to high angle	Transition: cut (5 sec.) Framing: Reverse-angle shot of caravan from behind Lo, still mounted on horseback Action: Lo waits as caravan approaches the cliff	Transition: cut (2 sec.) Framing: close-up Action: Lo's face tightens, his hair blowing in the wind, as he raises his sword and shouts for the charge

Table 11.1 (*Continued*)

Movement: camera rises (crane shot) from below cliff to reveal Lo and his men Lighting: Lo (Dark Cloud) silhouetted against bright blue sky Sound: two ominous chimes interrupt caravan music	Angle: high angle Movement: none Lighting: caravan in sunlight, Lo in silhouette Sound: music rises	Angle: eye-line Movement: none Lighting: normal Sound: Lo: "Charge!"

Source: *Crouching Tiger, Hidden Dragon* (*Wo hu cang long*), dir. Ang Lee, released 12 January 2001 (USA), produced by Asia Union Film & Entertainment Ltd, China Film Co-Production Corporation (as China Film Co-Production Corp.), Columbia Pictures Film Production Asia, Edko Films (as EDKO Films), Good Machine (as Good Machine International), Sony Pictures Classics, United China Vision and Zoom Hunt International Productions (as Zoom Hunt International Productions Company Ltd).

for tonal consistency. Others make use of color contrasts, as with the little girl's red coat that stands out strikingly against the black and white photography of Steven Spielberg's *Schindler's List* (1993).

Editing, or cutting, is the process of composing a film from its constituent parts. Individual **shots**, produced by a non-interrupted running of the camera, are joined together to form **scenes**, which represent the same general action at a particular place and time. Scenes from different places or times might be combined into a **sequence**, unified by a common idea or theme. When Michael Corleone attends a baptism near the end of *The Godfather* (1972), his henchmen carry out a series of murders all across the country. The baptism scene and the murder scenes are cut together to create a powerful sequence of deception and revenge. A sequence that shows the passage of time or illustrates a single idea, like the linked scenes of a couple falling in love, is known as a **montage**. The marriage montage in *Citizen Kane* (1941) demonstrates the disintegration of a marriage over time. In each successive shot, Kane and his wife appear a little older, less communicative, and seated farther apart at the breakfast table. It's a classic example of how good movies show, rather than tell, a story.

Formal Analysis

To analyze a film in formal terms is to study how it's made, to notice how the technical elements work together to show the story in cinematic form.

By paying close attention to decisions about costume, set design, performance, camera placement, sound, or editing, we come to understand how
the film communicates its meanings. We're in a better position to explain
our personal responses in concrete terms, to appreciate the film's aesthetic
qualities, and to evaluate its overall effectiveness.

Let's take a scene from Ang Lee's *Crouching Tiger, Hidden Dragon* (2000;
see Table 11.1 above). Jen, the film's protagonist, is traveling through a
hostile desert region in a caravan. Lee establishes the scene with a lengthy
shot (23 seconds) of the carriages and pack animals viewed from above. As
they move forward slowly, left to right, the camera moves down, craning
slightly, and pans across the caravan, revealing its large size and desultory
progress, punctuated by the occasional ring of camel bells. Dark shadows
on the sandy road tell the time, near noon. The next shot is a 10-second
close-up of Jen and her mother in one of the carriages. The camera views
them head on, at eye level, as the older woman tells her daughter to stop
playing with her comb. In contrast to the bright colors and remoteness of
the previous shot, this shot is darker, more subtly lit, giving us an intimate
glimpse of character and focusing attention on an object, the comb, which
will play a significant role later on. The camera then cuts to the caravan
again, this time in an extreme long shot from a higher angle, suggesting a
new point of view. The new perspective is soon clarified, 4 seconds later,
with a low-angle shot of a lone horseman against the sky. This is Lo, the
leader of an outlaw gang, whose figure is impressively revealed as the
camera cranes upward from the cliff on which he stands and rises steadily
until we see the band of mounted men behind him. Two chimes ring out
over the camel bells – a warning sound of imminent danger.

At this point, the camera shifts to a reverse-angle shot from behind Lo.
We see him from behind now, a dark shadow to the right of the frame, surveying the caravan far below. As he waits for his prey to approach the cliff,
we watch with him, and the music rises. It continues to rise as the camera cuts to a close-up of his face, just enough time (two seconds) to make
him human, a romantic figure with long, dark hair blowing across his determined gaze as he cries, "Charge!" These six shots are prelude to the dramatic
action sequence that soon fills the screen. Lo's men swoop down, engaging
the caravan in fierce combat. Defying her mother, Jen opens the carriage
window, confronting the attackers, and when Lo taunts her, snatching her
comb, she leaps onto a horse and chases after him.

There is nothing extraordinary about these shots, but they do show how
a well-made film tells its story through careful lighting, camerawork, and
editing. After a leisurely establishing shot of the status quo (23 seconds of

the caravan's progress through the desert), the pacing picks up (shot length decreases to 8, 5, and 2 seconds) and the music intensifies to signal the coming conflict. The scene's two principal characters are shown in close-up – Jen in the shadowy interior of the carriage, Lo in stark silhouette against the sky – suggesting a thematic link. Jen, who feels hemmed in by her traditional role as a Chinese woman, will find in Lo a chance to realize her youthful notions of freedom and romance.

Even if we've entered in the middle of the movie, we can probably tell from these six shots that we're watching some kind of action film. In this case, what we're seeing is a particular form of action movie, a Chinese genre known as *wuxia*, which features the martial arts, including highly choreographed combat, acrobatic stunts, and even flying, often with women in the most aggressive roles. To appreciate this aspect of cinema, we need to pay more attention to the role of genre.

Genre Analysis

The labels under which distributors market films are partly meant to help audiences find the kinds of movies they are looking for. Broad categories like drama, comedy, and action identify a particular kind of film experience. More specific labels, such as Western, romantic comedy, or techno-horror, classify films into subgenres that can be studied like branches of a family tree. A genre and its offspring may evolve over time, changing forms, developing new traits, but still displaying certain family resemblances that are recognizable to audiences.

In *Film/Genre* (1999) Rick Altman offers evidence that genres develop organically before they become recognized as such. Terms like "musical" and "Western" were used as descriptive adjectives ("a musical version of *The Three Musketeers*," "Western Romance and Adventure at its Best") before they were used as nouns denoting categories (a musical, a Western). In other words, film promoters considered music and Western settings as add-ons before they recognized that music and the Wild West could be the generic substance of a new kind of film. A process of **genrification** develops when features of a cycle of popular films are deliberately copied to cash in on their success. So the box-office triumph of *My Big Fat Greek Wedding* (2002) was followed by a succession of wedding films, including *Bride and Prejudice* (2004), *Wedding Crashers* (2005), *27 Dresses* (2008), *Bride Wars* (2009), and *Bridesmaids* (2011), all variations on the theme of wedding-centered comedy dramas marketed to similar audiences. Some scholars, like Thomas Schatz (1981), have found predictable patterns in the way genres evolve, arguing that a genre might begin in an *experimental* stage, when the genre's codes and conventions are tentatively formulated; then pass through a *classic* stage, when they become established and widely understood; continue through a period of *refinement*, when new films add formal details and stylistic flourishes; and finally enter a period of *baroque* embellishment, when self-conscious preoccupation with the genre's codes shifts attention from the substance of the genre to its style.

The concept of genre can be an important component of film study, especially for movies made for the popular market. Horror films or gangster movies are often best understood in relation to other movies of their kind. So Francis Ford Coppola's *Godfather* series (1972, 1974, 1990) draws on earlier crime movies like *Little Caesar* (1931) and *Scarface* (1932) for its characters, plots, settings, scenes, and themes – influencing, in turn, later films like *Goodfellas* (1990) and *Casino* (1995). This kind of analysis also helps us understand how movie audiences, their interests, and their attitudes change over time. A brief comparison of early Westerns like *Stagecoach* (1939) and *The Searchers* (1956) with more recent examples, such as *Dances With Wolves* (1990), *Unforgiven* (1992), and *The Quick and the Dead* (1995), tells a good deal about how women and Native Americans are represented at different moments of American history.

To analyze *Crouching Tiger, Hidden Dragon* in terms of genre is to explore the defining elements and history of *wuxia*, a form of storytelling that dates back some 2000 years. The heroes in these stories emerge from the lower classes and marginalized peoples of China, including the poor and the disenfranchised, as well as women. These *wuxia* heroes fought singly or collectively against government corruption and oppressive power, much like Robin Hood and his band of outlaws, making disciplined use of the martial arts, magic weapons, and sometimes occult knowledge. Although considered criminals by the authorities, they followed a strict code of behavior in the interests of justice and righteousness. Knowing this adds a historical dimension to the desert bandit Lo, who belongs to a minority group that has long been mistreated by mainstream Chinese society. It helps to explain his special appeal to Jen, a rebellious young woman who feels constrained by rigid gender roles and who turns out to belong to a minority group herself. Knowing about the genre and its evolution in Chinese cinema also helps to explain why Ang Lee's film was a bigger hit in the West than in the East, largely because Chinese audiences had seen it all before – female warriors gliding over rooftops, single-handedly taking on an army of armed men in the local inn, crossing swords with a master in the bamboo forest – in countless Chinese movies since the days of silent film.

Here are some questions about genre to consider with your students:

- Choose a genre like the Western, horror, or fantasy. What explains the genre's special appeal to its fans?
- List some of the genre's characteristics: iconography, character types, common settings, recurring scenes, plots, and underlying themes.
- What must a film have to belong to the genre? Where, for example, do you draw the line between horror and science fiction, a musical and a movie with music?
- How has the genre developed over time? Has it gone through identifiable phases, split into subgenres, or come in and out of favor? How do these changes reflect changes in our history and audience tastes?
- What do generic heroes, such as western gunmen, Japanese Samurai, Chinese martial arts practitioners, and their weapons (Figure 11.1), tell us about the cultures that produced them?

Cultural Analysis

Movies, then, can serve as windows onto other cultures. An Indian wedding film like *Monsoon Wedding* (2001), for example, or a wedding movie from the Middle East (*Wedding in Galilee*, 1987; *The Syrian Bride*, 2004) can introduce our students to the rituals and customs of societies quite different from their own. Watching them together and noticing where common practices diverge, noting which observances seem puzzling or strange, offers opportunities to learn about alternative belief systems and to interrogate our own assumptions.

A good subject for this kind of cultural analysis is the genre known as foodie films. Most movies have scenes involving food since eating is a basic human need. Filmmakers also focus on the way people eat, what they eat, and how they dine together in order to explore character, create dramatic moments, and develop a story's themes. In foodie films like *Soul Food* (1997) and *Tortilla Soup* (2001), food is at the center of the story. Human relationships are defined in relation to food. The fact that *Soul Food* is about an African American family and *Tortilla Soup* is about Mexican Americans offers insights into the way these cultures are represented on the screen. Foodie films set in other countries – in Japan (*Tampopo*, 1985), Denmark (*Babette's Feast*, 1988), Mexico (*Like Water for Chocolate*, 1992), Taiwan (*Eat Drink Man Woman*, 1994), Germany (*Mostly Martha*, 2001), or France (*Le Chef*, 2014) – tell us much about their cultural traditions and beliefs. Each country has its national cuisine, its stereotypes, its particular ways of

The Magnificent Seven (1960)

Seven Samurai (1954)

The Way of the Dragon (1972)

Figure 11.1 Screengrabs from *The Magnificent Seven*, *Seven Samurai*, and *The Way of the Dragon*. *The Magnificent Seven*: dir. John Sturges, prod. Walter Mirisch, Lou Morheim, and John Sturges (released 1960; production by The Mirisch Company, (as The Mirisch Company), Alpha Productions (as A Mirisch-Alpha Production), and Alpha (as A Mirisch-Alpha Production)). *Seven Samurai* (*Shichinin no samurai*): dir. Akira Kurosawa, prod. Sojiro Motoki (1954; released in the USA 1956; production by Toho Company). *The Way of the Dragon* (*Meng long guo jiang*), dir. Bruce Lee, prod. Raymond Chow and Bruce Lee (released in the USA 1972; production by Concord Productions and Golden Harvest Company).

procuring, preparing, presenting, and consuming meals. Examining these cultural aspects of cinema is a good way to nourish critical thinking.

Returning to *Crouching Tiger, Hidden Dragon* with this critical eye for insights into culture, we might look closely at the costumes, settings, social customs, and body language. What features of daily life appear different from ours, and what do these tell us about Qing Dynasty China? As the daughter of a ranking Chinese bureaucrat, Jen lives in a household adorned with beautiful, expensive furnishings. She wears fine clothes, is educated in the high art of calligraphy, and knows how to speak with the refinement of her class. But her clothing is constrictive, her polite speech feels unnatural, and her home seems like a prison to her. Moreover, her father has arranged a marriage of convenience, his convenience, to someone she doesn't love. It is in stark contrast to this assigned role that she has been secretly studying the darker arts of magic and swordsmanship with Jade Fox, the evil mother figure who appeals to her rebellious side, which later finds another object of desire in the romanticized figure of Lo. At the same time, she must come to terms with Shu Lien and Li Mu Bai, who represent alternative female and male role models, less tediously traditional than her real parents but more principled than Jade Fox or even Lo. Like any cinematic hero or heroine, Jen must define herself and choose her future within the limits of her cultural milieu.

Use questions like these to explore the cultural dimensions of movies with your students:

1 What seems unusual or puzzling about the movie's cultural environment? What seems universal or more similar to your own milieu?
2 Notice the characters' body language. How do they greet one another? How close are they when they speak? How do they express feelings and ideas beyond the use of speech?
3 Describe their speech patterns. Are they more or less formal than your own? Do any of their set phrases offer clues about their culture's ways of thinking?
4 Observe the way they dress. What can you tell from their clothing about their lifestyle or position within society?
5 How do the film's settings and set design reflect the culture's values and beliefs?
6 Consider what the characters want and what gets in the way. To what extent are their motives and obstacles shaped by the society in which they live?

Historical Analysis

Another way to explore movies is to study them as historical artifacts, as mirrors of the time that produced them. Consider the evolution of horror films as an example. Writing at the end of the last millennium, Paul Wells, a scholar of the genre, observed that "the history of horror film is essentially a history of anxiety in the twentieth century" (2000). The silent horror films, especially those from Germany (*The Cabinet of Dr. Caligari*, 1920; *Nosferatu*, 1922), are filled with imagery evoking the horrors of World War I. In the United States, the classic monsters of Universal Studios, drawn from English Gothic novels, embodied fears about contamination from abroad (Bela Lugosi in *Dracula*, 1931) or the misuses of science (Boris Karloff in

Frankenstein, 1932). In the 1940s, with another bestial war raging in Europe, a spate of noirish films like *Dr. Jekyll and Mr. Hyde* (1941) and *Cat People* (1942) reminded Americans of the beast lurking in man – or woman – despite our civilized appearance.

The 1950s brought another kind of conflict, the Cold War. America's paranoia, its fear of communist infiltration, took the form of alien pod creatures in *Invasion of the Body Snatchers* (1956) and other invasion narratives during the height of McCarthyism. In the 1960s, these creatures became the mindless zombies in George Romero's *Night of the Living Dead* (1968), which has also been linked to the Civil Rights Movement and the war in Vietnam. By the 1970s, the American family became a focal point for deep concerns about traditional values and the basic social unit that was supposed to harbor them. These anxieties were projected onto the screen in films like *The Hills Have Eyes* (1977) and *The Texas Chain Saw Massacre* (1974), where middle-class families come under grotesque attack, not from aliens but from disenfranchised Americans.

The next decade witnessed a political reversal. Ronald Reagan's presidency, spanning most of the 1980s, ushered in a new spirit of conservatism. New monsters, like Jason Voorhees in *Friday the 13th* (1980) and Freddy Krueger in *A Nightmare on Elm Street* (1984), were now punishing teenagers for pot-smoking and sexual promiscuity, creating a lucrative franchise of slasher films in the process. This kind of exploration could be continued decade by decade, country by country, connecting horror and history for each era and every region of the globe.

A particularly creative form of historical analysis is comparing remakes or sequels. Compare the 1991 remake of *Father of the Bride*, starring Steve Martin, to the original 1950 version, featuring Spencer Tracy in the title role. The differences will reveal a lot about changes in performance styles, the role of father figures, American weddings, and audience expectations over a forty-year period of the nation's history. Or compare the first Freddy Krueger movie to its latest sequel and note how times and tastes have changed in quite specific ways.

Students can use the following questions for comparing remakes and sequels:

- Compare the actors who play major roles. What changes do you find in their clothing, body language, and the roles themselves that might signal historical change?
- Note any differences in the use of language, kind of comedy, or level of violence. What can you infer from these differences about shifts in audience tastes over time?

- Pay attention to matters of film style, like the use of color, computer-generated imagery, pacing, sound, and camerawork. How do these reflect changes in technology and expectations?

Representation in Film

When we look into the mirror of the movies, what images look back at us? Do we see an accurate reflection of ourselves? Are the characters with whom we most identify true to our realities? Do the groups that we belong to – ethnic, racial, gendered, religious, generational – appear on screen as realistic, multidimensional communities, or as simplistic stereotypes?

Courses can be organized around issues of cinematic representation. They might take the form of historical surveys, tracing the images of African Americans, Asians, Latinos, or other identity groups over more than a hundred years of motion pictures. Or they might examine the way different groups are portrayed in various genres: women in Westerns, gay men in comedies, teenagers in road movies or slasher films.

Here are some questions on representation for students to consider:

- How do we fit ourselves into the movies? With whom do we identify, and why?
- Who gets to write the scripts, and whose stories get told?
- What roles are available?
- How do movies define us?
- When are stereotypes damaging and when are they benign?
- Who benefits from these images, who loses, and what can or should be done about the social inequalities sometimes reinforced by films and the filmmaking industry?

Film Theory

Every discipline has its leading theorists and camps, which have their moments of ascendancy and decline. Some familiarity with film theory is useful in analyzing films, but particularly in navigating the published work in cinema studies. Much of the earlier interest in semiotics (the study of signs and codes, applied to film most notably by Christian Metz in his *Film Language*, 1974), psychoanalysis (Sigmund Freud, Jacques Lacan), and deconstruction (Jacques Derrida, helpfully interpreted by Peter Brunette and David Wills in *Screen/Play*, 2014) has given way to newer methodologies like cognitive studies, an effort to understand how movies affect the human mind independently of ideology. The cognitive approach, based largely on empirical research, has been explained by Joseph Anderson in *The Reality of Illusion* (1996). Feminist studies, highly influential in the 1970s and 1980s (thanks to Laura Mulvey, Christine Gledhill, Claire Johnson, Linda Williams, and many others) has become less uniform, focusing more on the diverse perspectives of, for example, queer women and women of color, and also on historical research about reception (see the work of Jackie Stacey and Diane Negra). Meanwhile, the Marxist view of film as an instrument for social change, one of the oldest approaches to cinema, continues to be explored by those who draw on the insights of Walter Benjamin, Antonio Gramsci, Theodor Adorno, Louis Althusser, and Fredric Jameson. These approaches are collected in a number of useful anthologies, including those by Toby Miller and Robert Stam (2004) and by Leo Braudy and Marshal Cohen (2009).

Exercises

Making movies is a team effort, so group work can be an appropriate pedagogical technique in any class. Working in groups gives students more interactive time on task than they usually get in full class discussions. Group assignments can also help to build confidence in their individual ideas before contributing them to the class at large.

Viewing Profile

Ask each student to answer a short questionnaire before class. How many movies do they watch in an average month? What portion of these is viewed in theaters, on television, on DVDs, or via streaming video? What are their favorite movies or movie genres? What do they notice about their personal preferences or viewing habits? Do they watch films alone or with others, on large screens or small? Then give them a chance to pool their findings in small groups. Each group prepares a group profile, an opportunity to compare individual patterns, account for similarities and differences, and report their findings to the class.

Shot-by-Shot Analysis

Few exercises do more to focus attention on cinematic style than a careful, shot-by-shot analysis of a selected scene. A good way to prepare for this assignment is to divide a class into teams, each group concentrating on a particular aspect of the film: camerawork, acting, sound, lighting, set design, and so on. These teams might mirror actual job descriptions within the industry, one team focusing on the editor's role (shot length, pacing, transitions, use of cutaways, reverse-angle shots, and point of view editing), another on the cinematographer's responsibilities (framing, camera movement, lighting), etc. Project the scene several times, allowing each team to record and discuss its observations, then combine all perspectives into a composite analysis using a grid like the one for *Crouching Tiger, Hidden Dragon* in Table 11.1. Encourage students to practice using the film terms they have learned.

Music Minus One

Watch a scene with the sound turned off. Or listen to the soundtrack without the picture. Experiencing part of a movie with one missing element can give your students a vivid appreciation of that element's importance. For example, they might listen to the dialogue and sound effects from the seduction scene in *The Graduate* (1967) and imagine what decisions they would make if they directed it. What would be shown on the set? Where would they place the actors? How would they be dressed? What would the camera be doing as the scene progressed?

Plot Segmentation

For a better understanding of the story's narrative arc and the script's construction, have your students break down the film, or part of it, into its component parts. What are the key scenes, and where do they take place? What does each scene contribute to the film's action, characterization, or tone? In terms of plot development, which scenes serve the purposes of exposition, conflict, rising action, climax, recognition, or denouement? Here are a few examples from *To Kill a Mockingbird* (1962):

1 Credit Sequence. Close-ups of objects create a nostalgic mood and introduce thematic symbols.
2 Maycomb, Alabama: Daybreak. Sets story in rural South of 1930s. Introduces Scout, Atticus, Jem, and Dill. Atticus is "too old to play football for the Methodists." Dill learns about the mysterious Boo Radley next door.
3 Finch Yard. Atticus and the children greet the ornery Mrs. Dubose.
4 Scout's Room. She reads aloud to Atticus and asks about her dead mother.
5 Front Porch. Judge Taylor asks Atticus to take the case of Tom Robinson, a Negro accused of raping a white woman, Mayella Ewell.

Character Wheel. Casting Chart

Using a circle to represent a major character, divide the circle into slices that signify personality traits. What portions of Michael Corleone's character in *The Godfather* (1972) could be attributed to family loyalty, discipline, or a thirst for power? How does Al Pacino display these traits, and what changes do they undergo? To track the interaction of several characters, create a chart of the principal roles and add annotated arrows that describe their relationships.

How Films Are Made

This is a competitive activity. Groups compete with each other in the class to identify the steps involved in filmmaking and the specialists who perform each task. Each group lists as many steps – in order – as its members can think of, from the original conception to the final screening. For each step, the groups are encouraged to give the professional title of the person or people responsible for that phase of film production (director, cinematographer, script supervisor, editor). The group that can prepare the most complete, accurate list wins the competition, a reminder that the industry itself is largely based on competition.

Evolution of a Genre

Students select several clips from films that illustrate changes in a film genre over time. For example, they might choose combat films from the time of World War II, the Korean War, Vietnam, and other recent conflicts. Or they might choose films from a single war (*The Green Berets*, 1968; *Apocalypse Now*, 1979; *Platoon*, 1986). Explore with them the changes reflected in these clips. How do these films reflect historical attitudes toward combat? How do they show changes in film technique and popular taste? Other genres to consider include science fiction, Westerns, romance, comedy, adventure, and film noir.

Compare Classic and Remake

Select comparable scenes from two versions of the same story and screen them in succession. You might show scenes from J. Lee Thompson's *Cape Fear* (1962) and Martin Scorsese's 1991 remake in order to explore the evolution of film noir. You might compare the original *King Kong* (1933) with one of its more recent incarnations (1968, 1976, 1986, 2005) to trace changes in special effects. Or you might show *The Searchers* (1956) and *Star Wars* (1977) to see how Lucas borrowed from Ford to refashion the sci-fi genre in the image of the Western.

References

Altman, R. (1999). *Film/genre*. London: Palgrave Macmillan.

Anderson, J. (1996). *The reality of illusion: An ecological approach to cognitive film theory*. Carbondale: Southern Illinois University Press.

Braudy, L., and Cohen, M. (eds.). (2009). *Film theory and criticism: Introductory readings* (6th ed.). New York: Oxford University Press.

Brunette, P., and Wills, D. (2014). *Screen/Play*. Princeton, NJ: Princeton University Press.

Metz, C. (1974). *Film language: A semiotics of the cinema*. Chicago: University of Chicago Press.

Miller, T., and Stam, R. (eds.). (2004). *A companion to film theory: An introduction*. Oxford: Blackwell.

Schatz, T. (1981). *Hollywood genres: Formulas, filmmaking, and the studio system*. New York: Random House.

Wells, P. (2000). *The horror genre: From Beelzebub to Blair Witch*. London: Wallflower Press.

12

Thinking Through Drama

Louis Scheeder

Lee Strasberg, the iconic acting teacher and creator of "method acting," and later the leader and chief proponent of The Actors Studio, is renowned for his legendary elevation of emotion to the apogee of the actor's craft. Several years ago, however, I discovered that he had also once stated, "To really think on stage may very well be the most important thing" (Rice, 1957). Strasberg, as ever, was on to something. He was referring to the actor's ability to create spontaneity and establish truth on stage, a goal of a majority of acting approaches in the nineteenth and twentieth centuries. Theorists constantly ask: "What is the best way to achieve the Holy Grail of 'truthfulness' and 'spontaneity'?" Many contemporary playwrights, for example, seek to establish their pursuit of truth through behavior, while postmodernists, such as Anne Bogart and her SITI Company, often attempt to create a distinct version of truth through the body's relation to space. An answer well might lie in a devotion to argument and an attendant emphasis on action. These emphases can create the thinking that Strasberg sought. I use the word "argument" here to refer to the attempt to persuade a scene partner to adopt the point of view of the speaker, while "action" is the basic tool of the actor, the internal process by which the actor plays a role.

Drama and Argument

In my encounters with Shakespeare and other dramatists, I have come to believe in the primacy of argument, for argument, it seems, lies at the heart of Western drama. This emphasis on argument stems from ancient Greek

Critical Reading Across the Curriculum, Volume 1: Humanities, First Edition.
Edited by Robert DiYanni and Anton Borst.
© 2017 John Wiley & Sons, Inc. Published 2017 by John Wiley & Sons, Inc.

drama and is fully realized, for instance, in the debate between Antigone and Creon over the burial of Polyneices, her brother. What is missing from our contemporary world of production is the interplay of debate, the thrust and parry of competing visions of the world. What is also frequently absent is an actor's ability to articulate a character's particular vision of the world persuasively. This is our ongoing challenge in putting on a play. We should continue to probe ideas through focusing on argument in drama and drama as argument – whether in Shakespeare or George Bernard Shaw, himself a fabled arguer. We may analyze argument in the plays of a host of dramatists, including Henrik Ibsen and August Strindberg, as well as Eugene O'Neill, Arthur Miller, and Tennessee Williams.

Shaw, an early champion of Ibsen, created plays such as *Major Barbara* and *Heartbreak House* in which ideas clashed. O'Neill studied those damaged by war, modern fables, and pipe dreams, in plays such as *Mourning Becomes Electra* (his revision of the House of Atreus saga of ancient Greece), *Strange Interlude*, and *The Iceman Cometh*. Ibsen's work in *Ghosts* and *A Doll's House* unshackled women from a Victorian conception of marriage. Strindberg, in *Dance of Death* and *The Father*, wrote of a world in which men and women had been forced into adversarial roles. Miller, currently undergoing a reassessment in line with the hundredth anniversary of his birth, was also a social critic, his work depicting dreamers trapped in a capitalist nightmare in *Death of a Salesman*, and immigrants bound by society's dictates struggling to attain the right to work in *A View from the Bridge*. And in *A Streetcar Named Desire* and *Cat on a Hot Tin Roof*, Williams dramatically explored the problems of those whose sexual behavior deviated from the heteronormative practices of the mid-twentieth century.

Eric Bentley's book *The Playwright as Thinker* (1946) aptly sums up the role of many of these dramatists. They were not writing entertainment; they were thinking through the problems of their times. When transferred to the mass media, their ideas were inevitably watered down, revealing the inadequacies of the motion picture and the studio system's reluctance to contend with the problems of modern life. The rise of movies with sound as the primary mode of popular entertainment placed an emphasis on the primacy of emotion. But in my view, genuine feelings, feelings with human and social significance, and feelings possessing dramatic power, derive from an argument either explicit or implied. And just as feeling is most compelling when buttressed by argument, argument is most persuasive when allied and entangled with feeling. The question becomes how to recognize and access a character's emotion in relationship to the language and formal structure of the play. And the best way, I believe, to arrive at this emotional component is to understand the dramatic argument at its root.

Sophocles' *Antigone* has incited argument and debate from its premiere, circa 442/41 BCE. The play still has the power to ignite passions that inflame the young and the old, the religious and the secular, women and men, and those who subscribe to a law presumed to be natural versus those who favor the laws of the state. Some view the debate between Creon and Antigone, uncle and niece, brother-in-law and daughter of Oedipus respectively, as a mere repetition of fixed positions, seeing their clash as an irresolvable conflict. As with many plays touched on in this essay, there is no final resolution to the arguments presented – which is why we turn to them again and again. Analyzing their debates will continue to engage and teach us about dramatic art and the complexity of thought.

Instruction in argument and debate is instrumental in the creation of a more articulate actor and, perhaps more importantly, the creation of a more intelligent citizenry. New York University's Tisch School of the Arts has always attempted to produce thinking artists. Our approach to undergraduate education, combining a liberal arts emphasis with rigorous conservatory training, supports this effort. Our emphasis on argument creates more nuanced actors who are better able to embody characters and to convey the thinking and ideas inherent in a play's script. Through their studio work in drama, and through their intellectual and emotional engagement with the arguments plays embody, students become more adept thinkers, readers, and communicators.

One way to think about argument is to consider how it emerges in the thoughts of characters who soliloquize, who engage us in conversation. A useful example is the following soliloquy, which opens Shakespeare's *Richard III* (I. i. 1–40):

> RICHARD. **Now is** the winter of our discontent
> Made glorious summer by this son of York;
> And all the clouds that lowered upon our house
> In the deep bosom of the ocean buried.
> Now are our brows bound with victorious wreaths,   5
> Our bruisèd arms hung up for monuments,
> Our stern alarums changed to merry meetings,
> Our dreadful marches to delightful measures.
> Grim-visaged war hath smooth'd his wrinkled front;
> And now, instead of mounting barbèd steeds   10
> To fright the souls of fearful adversaries,
> He capers nimbly in a lady's chamber
> To the lascivious pleasing of a lute.
> **But I**, that am not shaped for sportive tricks,
> Nor made to court an amorous looking-glass;   15

I, that am rudely stamped, and want love's majesty
To strut before a wanton ambling nymph;
I, that am curtailed of this fair proportion,
Cheated of feature by dissembling Nature,
Deformed, unfinished, sent before my time   20
Into this breathing world, scarce half made up,
And that so lamely and unfashionable
That dogs bark at me as I halt by them –
Why, I, in this weak piping time of peace,
Have no delight to pass away the time,   25
Unless to spy my shadow in the sun
And descant on mine own deformity.
And therefore, since I cannot prove a lover,
To entertain these fair well-spoken days,
I am determinèd to prove a villain   30
And hate the idle pleasures of these days.
Plots have I laid, inductions dangerous,
By drunken prophecies, libels, and dreams,
To set my brother Clarence and the king
In deadly hate the one against the other;   35
And if King Edward be as true and just
As I am subtle, false, and treacherous,
This day should Clarence closely be mewed up
About a prophecy, which says that G
Of Edward's heirs the murderer shall be.   40

How can we help students find the argument embedded in the language of this soliloquy? By analyzing its overall structure, and especially by attending to Shakespeare's use of the iambic pentameter verse line.

We can break the soliloquy down into three parts: lines 1–13, 14–27, and 28–40. Notice how those parts begin "Now is"; "But I"; "And therefore," which form the skeleton of an argument. We might summarize that argument like this: (1) The bad times are over for our family. We now are enjoying the pleasures of victory and my brother is indulging his taste for the sybaritic lifestyle that he adores. (2) But I am not well suited to the pleasures of peace. I am ugly, malformed, and discontented. (3) And so, if I can't be a lover, like Edward, I'll be a villain.

Notice how, as is usual in Shakespeare, the main thoughts incorporate the present tense. Also, Richard, like many of Shakespeare's villains, is improvising as he goes along. He changes constantly, like the "camelion" to which he compares himself in *3 Henry VI* (III. ii. 191). Richard specifically absolves Edward of engineering Clarence's imprisonment. He blames Queen

Elizabeth for doing so. Nonetheless, audiences over the last four hundred years have been enchanted with Richard's quickness and rapidity of thought.

A second way to help students understand how argument and verse go together is to consider the use of antitheses to develop thought. Let's look at the first four lines of Richard's soliloquy from this standpoint.

> Now is the winter of our discontent
> Made glorious summer by this son of York.
> And all the clouds that lowered upon our house
> In the deep bosom of the ocean buried.

These four lines comprise one unit of sense by means of two images, one for each pair of lines linked together by "And." In the first pair of lines, the speaker contrasts the "winter of our discontent" (and uses the formal, royal plural "our") with the "glorious summer." That immediate transformation has been brought into being by Edward IV, the "son," who also serves as a "sun" to disperse winter's clouds, which have given way to sunny, summer days. Those clouds, which threatened the royal house of York, are now buried in the ocean's deep. Only in Shakespeare does summer follow winter while clouds lie buried in the ocean's bosom. Notice the sexual implications of "bosom" and Edward's profligate reputation.

Shakespeare begins his next set of four lines with "Now" (as previously) to emphasize a contrast between "Now" and "Then." The sequence of "Our" lines lets us know that the world has changed: weapons have become ornamental, the noise of battle has been transformed into polite social discourse, and ominous marching has given way to dizzying displays of dance.

We need to help students see the illogic of Shakespeare's use of antithesis. The way to do that is to divide and conquer by identifying the parts that make up the soliloquy's overall structure and then to dig in to the smaller units of language to reveal how the verse works its wonders. We will consider the verse line in greater detail a bit later in our discussion of the iambic pentameter line.

The Classical Studio

The Classical Studio is an advanced training program for undergraduates, the smallest of the studios that make up the NYU Department of Drama. We enroll eighteen students for a rigorous year during which they explore the multiplicities of Shakespeare's dramatic art. We start with the basic dramatic structure of antithesis, first by examining it on a micro level, as in the lines "To be or not to be," and "Now is the winter of our discontent / Made glorious summer by this son of York." We then move rapidly into more complex issues, such as how the plays are structured antithetically on a macro level. For every Prince Hal, there is an attendant Hotspur, as in Shakespeare's *1 Henry IV*. In that play, a pair of fathers (or father figures) provides another example of structural antithesis: the spiritual father in Falstaff and the biological one in King Henry. Additionally, we cover a number of figures of speech that affect the syntax of verse, including hendiadys, or the use of two thoughts, as in "Oh, what a rogue and peasant slave am I," in which "rogue" is immediately intensified by "peasant slave." In The Classical Studio, we have come to understand that the argument is often encased in the structure of verse.

The Structure of Verse

What is verse structure? The answer to this question begins with an examination of iambic pentameter, in which unstressed beats alternate with stressed beats. Iambic pentameter has often been referred to as the "heartbeat" of English verse. Indeed, when we learn lines "by heart" we are generally referring to this "heartbeat." I am not advocating a slavish adherence to the rhythm "dee-DUM, dee-DUM, dee-DUM, dee-DUM, dee-DUM," in which the iambs are pounded out. There are, of course, recognizable trochaic elements to the verse. (A trochee is the antithesis of an iamb, DUM-dee rather than dee-DUM.) One of the most famous trochees occurs at the start of Juliet's "Gallop apace, you fiery footed steeds." In The Classical Studio, however, we ask students to default to the iambic rhythm in order to both discover argument and recognize patterns of thought that might not be readily apparent without that attention to verse structure.

We urge students to not only default to the iambic, but to make the verse line iambic – even if it does not at first glance appear to fit that pattern. In doing so, they create slurs, squashes, extensions, and other rhythmic elements that express and enforce the argument, with the result that the thinking inhabiting the verse is clarified. Each stress in an iambic pentameter line is usually more important than the stress that precedes it. The second stress is more important than the first, the third more important than the second, the fourth more important than the third, until we reach the fifth stress, where the argument of the verse line is clearly encapsulated. This sense of relative stress can be most clearly realized in a simple exercise in which the instructor asks students to list the first word of a series of verse lines, and then the last word of those same lines. In Hamlet's "To be or not to be" soliloquy the first words are: *To, Whether, The, Or, And, No, The,* and *That.* These are then set against the final words of the same lines: *question, suffer, fortune, troubles, sleep, end, shocks,* and *consummation.*

> To be, or not to be – that is the question:
> Whether 'tis nobler in the mind to suffer
> The slings and arrows of outrageous fortune
> Or to take arms against a sea of troubles
> And by opposing end them? To die, to sleep –
> No more – and by a sleep to say we end
> The heartache, and the thousand natural shocks
> That flesh is heir to. 'Tis a consummation
> Devoutly to be wished.
>
> (III. i. 56-64)

The last words, and their attendant stresses, consolidate the idea of each line (e.g. "question," "suffer," "sleep"), and the major terms of the soliloquy's argument, which concerns the existential doubt prompted by the unavoidable experience of pain and uncertainty. Furthermore, a trajectory can be traced across these terminal stresses, from the repeatedly hit notes of questioning and suffering to the concluding desire for the closure and "consummation" death provides.

Relevant to my argument is the current contention that because Shakespeare's language differs significantly from the language of today, his plays should be translated into contemporary English. This is a grave error because modern English translations destroy the iambic rhythm of Shakespeare's verse and with it the cumulative emphasis of the iambic line. The sense of a word is influenced not by imposing contemporary readings on a text but by rigorously following the scansion of the verse itself.

The proper use of line endings enhances the simulation of thought and can create the illusion of real speech. Paradoxically, in order to achieve Strasberg's goal of creating real thought on stage, we seek refuge in the formal properties of the verse. We educate students not only to be aware of line endings, but also to actively use them in order to present the simulation of thought. We encourage students to use their line endings to breathe, to mirror human thought, to think. If we allow the speaker of verse to pause, however briefly, at the end of the verse line, we create the possibility of Strasberg's desire for thought. How often do people pause in order to capture the absolutely correct phrase? How often do we get lost in what we are trying to say? Or gallop so far ahead of ourselves that our words need to catch up with our thoughts, or our thoughts with our feelings?

Yet what students often do is to find what they consider to be the most important word in a line, the "operative word." In doing this, they run roughshod over the verse. The practice of finding and emphasizing the "operative word" is akin to the principle of encouraging feeling over thinking, with outbursts of emotion substituting for reason. To put the emphasis back where it belongs – on thought and argument – we need to listen more carefully and pay even greater attention to the intricacies of speech and language. Pausing – taking a breath – helps us in these situations, particularly when verse structure and meter provide us with clues to do so.

Following the Verse

Students often ask, "What exactly is the difference between verse and prose?" A short answer is that while prose follows the rules of grammar, verse observes not only grammatical structure but also metrical pattern. In English, the most familiar pattern is iambic pentameter. Let us begin with the verse line itself: those ten syllables that typically make up a single printed line of iambic pentameter verse.

In the theater, we are in the business of creating illusion. We set out to create that illusion of thought through the creation of real speech. And the best way to create the illusion of thought in classical texts is by adhering to the structure of the verse line (in contrast to some who advocate focusing only on the unit of the sentence). For the verse line holds both the essence of argument and the pattern of thought that produces argument. Strict adherence to the verse line enables actors to decipher clues to patterns of thought and argument, which leads to a lively, thoughtful presentation of the dramatic scene.

A case in point occurs in the opening scene of *Hamlet*, in which Francisco challenges Bernardo with the line, "Nay, answer me, stand and unfold yourself." ("Unfold" here indicates "disclosing" or "identifying" oneself.) The stress on "me" clarifies the question of who is actually on guard. (Students often think it is Bernardo, as he begins the play with the famous "Who's there?") Many editions cloud the issue further by adopting either the second Quarto's or the Folio's "Enter two Centinels" as opposed to the first Quarto's "Francisco upon his Post; Enter, to him, Bernardo." With "and" in the stressed position, the young actor will think about the difference between "standing" and "unfolding" oneself, two decidedly different physical acts.

The first and most common variant of the iambic pentameter line is the inclusion of the "feminine" or "unstressed" line ending. The most famous Shakespearean line has a feminine ending: "To be, or not to be – that is the question," in which the presence of the "chun" in "ques-chun" is not stressed. As we saw in the exercise described above, the line begins Hamlet's soliloquy, the unstressed ending evoking a sense of his initial doubt, perhaps weakness, and the subsequent stressed line endings communicating Hamlet's increasingly concrete awareness of – and frustration with – his misfortunes.

Another way Shakespeare varies the rhythm of the iambic line is with the caesura, or mid-line break, which may indicate a shift in thought or realization on the part of the speaker, as in "To be, or not to be – that is the question." In the great tragedies, such as *Macbeth, Othello, Antony and Cleopatra,* and *Coriolanus,* Shakespeare experiments with epic caesuras, lines in which an extra metrical beat is needed to regularize the verse, and which may well be intuited rather than mandated.

While punctuation, as with the dash in the aforementioned line, can be a help, it can at other times be a hindrance to understanding the verse. Punctuation, we should remember, helps readers navigate the written script, and in Shakespeare's plays has often been added later by editors and scholars. However, when actors pause at commas, take full stops and breaths at periods, and embrace semi-colons for their own sake in violation of the iambic pentameter, or when they avoid pausing simply because such punctuation is absent, they may end up abandoning the spirit and emotion of the text's argument.

We advocate that teachers of acting employ an exercise that allows students to pause or take a breath even where punctuation is absent. This breathing allows for the thoughts to be replicated in real speech with its attendant hesitations, attempts at accuracy, stumbles toward correct phrasing, and general vagaries. Although I teach at a university where many of the faculty are capable of speaking in fully formed paragraphs, let alone fully formed sentences, passionate discourse, when presented on stage, can and must be messy, though easy to follow, precise yet human.

Consequently, contradiction – and phrasing that reflects contradiction – play an essential role in effective acting. That speakers in Shakespeare's plays can be contradictory, however, is often difficult for students to grasp. We have become imbued with the notion that *Hamlet,* in the words of Laurence Olivier's Academy Award-winning film of 1948, might well be "the tragedy of a man who could not make up his mind," as opposed to a more nuanced and sympathetic portrayal of a character who constantly changes his mind. The shifts and turns of contradictory thought make Shakespeare's characters human and, thereby, interesting.

As James Shapiro (2015) has noted, even the best directors often stumble when confronting the contradictions of classical texts. Elia Kazan, perhaps the greatest of mid-twentieth-century film directors, who made his reputation directing screen versions of classic American plays such as *A Streetcar Named Desire*, found himself caught short when confronted for the first time with a classic text. Writing long after the fact, he probed and questioned his reliance on the Stanislavski system in his work on Middleton and Rowley's *The Changeling*, which he had directed in the 1960s. He wrote:

> The play became a series of progressions, each of which consisted of the fact that a person did a certain thing that responded to a certain want. ... But today, when I observe life, I see it takes much less direct paths, circuitous paths, subtle and subterranean. ... In life people are uncertain ultimately as to what they want. They oscillate, wander, drift in relation to their aim – or they change their aim. In short, they want this, then that ... it is there that the poetry of life dwells, these contradictions, these sudden deflections, these aspirations that spring up and disconcert. In short, while I once had a unilinear approach to life, I now interest myself more and more in the complexity of things. (2009, pp. 273–275)

Even though they themselves experience similar "complexity" in their daily lives, students trained in the rigorous logic of the contemporary theater are often flummoxed by the seeming illogic of contradiction. An example from *Much Ado About Nothing* is helpful in this regard: the constant movement of change is what makes a character such as Beatrice so appealing to us. In one famous scene, after Hero's aborted marriage to Claudio, she contradicts herself while attempting to explain her feelings to Benedick. He declares his love for her, then questions her about his own feelings in the following exchange:

BENEDICK. I do love nothing in the world so well as you. Is not that strange?
BEATRICE. As strange as the thing I know not. It were as possible for me to say I loved nothing so well as you. But believe me not; and yet I lie not. I confess nothing, nor I deny nothing. I am sorry for my cousin.

(IV. i. 264–269)

Young actors often experience difficulty with this scene due to a misapprehension of Stanislavski's (and later Strasberg's) famed sense of logic and coherence. In The Classical Studio we make sure that this scene is always among those we work on during the fall semester precisely because of this rapid shift of thought. The apparent contradictoriness of Beatrice is why great actors regularly test themselves on these plays. The challenge to the actor is to accurately create and believe the moment represented, to commit to that moment, and then to embrace a contradictory moment and, in turn, commit fully to that moment.

Exercises

Acting is an embodied art. While it may seem that much of our work in The Classical Studio centers on the mental approach to acting, we also incorporate the physical into our training in order to help students better understand antithesis, meter, and dramatic argument. We "read" the bodies of our students in order to get a sense of what they are doing. As Martha Graham famously taught us, "The body does not lie" (1991, p. 122). It has become apparent to me over the years that the body instinctually knows more than the brain. A close reading of the body can reveal unconscious patterns of thought that inhibit and constrict both argument and spontaneity.

In The Classical Studio, we have borrowed an exercise from The Factory UK, an experimental theater company with which I am professionally affiliated, that allows faculty to monitor a student actor's unconscious. We use the "To be, or not to be" soliloquy in an exercise that requires students to use their brains and their bodies simultaneously. As they recite the lines, students throw a tennis ball while making eye contact with a fellow member of their class. They throw the ball on the last stressed syllable of the verse line, and another student (with whom they have made eye contact) catches the ball on the first stressed syllable of his or her own line. After numerous false starts, groups of actors are able to whip the ball around the circle and embody both the verse and the thinking that remains our grail. Through the use of this exercise, the students literally embody the argument of this touchstone of Western dramatic thought.

Another exercise through which students have the opportunity to embody the thinking embedded in verse involves representing antitheses through physical gestures. Students are urged to make as full use of their bodies as possible – arms and legs as well as hands. We start with a simple passage, such as "Now is the winter of our discontent / Made glorious summer by this son of York," from *Richard III*. Students grasp immediately the difference between "summer" and "winter," and as they think through the passage rapidly discover that "discontent" and "glorious" are also antitheses. Some are able to then identify the chiastic structure of the two lines, which they physically represent as a crisscross arrangement. In attempting to render the lines visible, they are forced as well to think through the pun on "son" and "sun." Another benefit of the exercise is that it emphasizes the auditory and removes words from the tyranny of the printed page, thus allowing those words the freedom of play. We ask students, quite literally, to stretch themselves and find the limits of their bodies in outlining these antitheses in order to feel as strongly as possible their oppositional force. The antitheses become imprinted in the students' motor memories as well as their conscious memories. Student actors physically become the verse. They become imbued with a deep sense of a play's arguments and the contradictory complexities of its characters.

Conclusion

One book especially has strongly influenced the development of our work in The Classical Studio: *How To Do Things With Words* (1962) by the British philosopher J. L. Austin, who coined the term "performative utterances." Performative utterances enact what they describe. For example, in saying that "I accept your apology," I am actually doing what I am saying. Or in declaring, "This meeting is now adjourned," the meeting is actually adjourned. Words, in these performative instances, are deeds. Echoing the performative nature of the text is the fact that Austin's book originated as the William James Lectures, delivered at Harvard University in 1955.

It is of particular interest for drama teachers that Austin deliberately excludes speech acts originating on stage. He writes: "a performative utterance will, for example, be *in a peculiar way* hollow or void if said by an actor on the stage, or if introduced in a poem, or spoken in soliloquy. ... Our performative utterances, felicitous or not, are to be understood as issued in ordinary circumstances" (p. 22). Austin, perhaps unknowingly, has touched a nerve of drama teachers in that he is describing the essence of acting: doing convincingly – doing to and with others in ways that embody the essence of argument, in the process persuading your scene partners (or the characters they play) to come around to your way of thinking. We lead students to enact performative utterances. In short, everything they say or do is placed in the context of performance. Rather than view the performative utterance as "hollow" or "void," we seek to imbue the utterance – whether in poem, scene, or soliloquy – with persuasive action even if that action is fictive rather than actual. Despite Austin's caveat, we strive to make the lines delivered on stage or screen as much as possible like word-deeds that occur in real life.

And we do that, at The Classical Studio, by directing students to identify the argument behind a character's words and deeds. This process allows student actors not only to better realize Austin's notion of the performative utterance, but also to better understand the intellectual and conceptual stakes of dramatic works. For us, reading takes place off the page as well as on, nonverbally as well as verbally, as our students engage in exercises that ask them to focus on the rhythm of language, and to sense and feel the argument implied in this rhythm through their own physical action. As in so much else, Shakespeare is our tutor and example in this, creating the illusion of spontaneous thought through his unparalleled use of the iambic pentameter line. Attending to the iambic pattern of his verse, and recognizing the lines of argument embedded in his language and the structure of his soliloquys, cultivates actors able to bring the language of theater to vivid and persuasive life.

References

Austin, J. L. (1962). *How to do things with words*. Cambridge, MA: Harvard University Press.

Bentley, E. (1946). *The playwright as thinker*. New York: Mariner Books.

Graham, M. (1991). *Blood memory: An autobiography*. New York: Doubleday.

Kazan, E. (2009). *Kazan on directing*. New York: Alfred E. Knopf.

Rice, R. (1957). Actors studio: Article V. *New York Post* (May 17).

Shakespeare, W. (1969). *The complete works*. Ed. A. Harbage. New York: Viking.

Shapiro, J. (2015). Modernizing the bard? *New York Times* (October 7), p. A27.

13

Approaches to Reading and Teaching Pop Songs

Thomas M. Kitts

Popular Music and Its Contexts

Studies in popular culture and popular music have emerged as an academic discipline, recognized by most scholars as a meaningful course of academic inquiry. With the lines between high art and low art blurred if not indistinguishable, it seems we have reached agreement with Duke Ellington, who once said, "There are simply two kinds of music, good music and the other kind" (1995, p. 326). As a result, in recent years academic journals have emerged dedicated to popular music: *Popular Music, Journal of Popular Music Studies*, and *Journal of World Popular Music*, as well as journals focused on genres like *Metal Music Studies* and *Punk & Post Punk*, along with two journals that I co-edit with Gary Burns of Northern Illinois University, *Popular Music and Society* and *Rock Music Studies*. As in other disciplines, scholars in journals like these take various critical perspectives, including biographical, historical, sociological, psychological, Marxist, gender studies, and more, when discussing pop music. They may focus on a specific song, album, artist, music scene, fandom, or type of recording technique. Consider some titles of recently published articles in *Rock Music Studies* and in *Popular Music and Society*: "'I sing out to the youth of the slums': Morrissey and Class Disgust"; "Discursive Construction of African-American Identities and Spirituality: A Comparison of Muslim Hip Hop and 1960s Jazz Avant-Garde"; "Patti Smith and Modernism: The Problem with Dandies"; and "Deconstructing the 'Bodies': Reading the Feminine Approach to the Sex Pistols."

Critical Reading Across the Curriculum, Volume 1: Humanities, First Edition.
Edited by Robert DiYanni and Anton Borst.

My own research has led to two critical biographies, on the songwriters Ray Davies of the Kinks (*Not Like Everybody Else*, 2008) and John Fogerty of Creedence Clearwater Revival (*An American Son*, 2016); they help me model for my students the complex intellectual process of reading music critically. A critical biography focuses more on the works than the life, considering the life only as it affects the work. Therefore, I write about Ray Davies' working-class youth and its influence on his songs, and John Fogerty's second marriage and its impact on his music. I take different approaches depending on the album or song under discussion. For example, I take a formalist literary approach to songs like Davies' "I Go to Sleep," emphasizing the internal drama implied by the song's use of *I* and *me* (eight of the fourteen lines begin with *I* and all lines but one end with *me*), or the river imagery in Fogerty's "Proud Mary" and other songs.

I take a more sociological approach to Davies' crafting of *Arthur* (a Kinks' album rooted in World War II) and an historical approach to Fogerty's "Fortunate Son" and "Effigy" (inspired by Vietnam and Richard Nixon), and I am always on the alert for influences on the development of pop music genres. There is, for example, a direct line from the humor of the English music hall to the satire of Davies' "Well Respected Man," to the wit of Damon Albarn in his work with Blur and the Gorrilaz. Rockabilly and echo effects of Sam Phillips and Sun Studios recur in Fogerty's production and rhythms on "Bad Moon Rising" and again in the alternative country fusions of Uncle Tupelo and Band of Horses – two bands that later performed Fogerty's "Effigy." Students are challenged to form similar continuums of development with their favorite artists. This pushes them to look beyond single songs, albums, and artists. It encourages them to take a longer view, to discover historical lineages, influences, and continuities.

However, before students can develop such a broad and rich understanding of pop music, or of a particular song or genre, they need strategies on how to "read" the music critically. They need to listen to it attentively, analyze both its lyrics and its music, and think about their relationship and implications.

Reading a Pop Song

Part of the pleasure we derive from music and other forms of pop culture is talking about it. However, these often casual conversations tend to be based on subjective responses and personal taste. The arguments made in such discussions are frequently vague and express overly enthusiastic judgments. As Simon Frith writes, "To be engaged with popular culture is to be discriminating, whether judging the merits of a football team's backs or an afternoon soap's plots. 'Good' and 'bad' or their vernacular ('brilliant,' 'crap') are the most frequent terms in everyday cultural conversation" (1996, p. 4). He concludes that "the exercise of taste and aesthetic discrimination is as important in popular as in high culture but is more difficult to talk about" (p. 11). By providing critical strategies for reading a pop song, I try to disrupt students' conversational habits and elevate their discourse, making them more perceptive, informed, and discerning listeners of pop music, and more thoughtful commentators on it.

Before approaching a pop musical work from any critical perspective, a critic, whether professional or student, needs to read it closely. Most students have no clue what that means. I tell them it is similar to interpreting a poem or literary work. It requires repeated and attentive reading or listening, something most students have not done even after hearing a song many times. I encourage them to be active listeners, jotting notes as they listen. I break the process into four parts: impressions after initial listening, lyrical analysis, musical analysis, and conclusions/evaluations, which should lead to a cohesive statement about the song. I emphasize that reading a song or poem is not like cooking, where, once you complete a step, you move on. The process is more recursive than linear, as we constantly go backward and forward among steps in our reexaminations and reconsiderations.

Initial Impressions

We start our analysis by considering initial impressions. But even in this early stage, students need to think critically, which means asking themselves the right questions: Did I like the song? Why? Did I respond physically to the beat – feet tapping, head nodding? Did a particular instrument stand out? What about the vocals and the lyrics? What additional thoughts do I have after second and third listenings? Do I find myself humming the song? Do I want to hear the song again? In short, what is my impulsive, visceral response to the song?

Analysis of Lyrics

After these initial reactions, we turn to an examination of the lyrics. What is the song about? Who is the "I" of the song? (More often than not, pop songs rely on the first person.) As with teaching poetry, I caution that the "I" of the song is not always the singer or composer. The singer can be a fictional presence. Mick Jagger, for example, is not the devil despite his use of the first person in "Sympathy for the Devil." After they identify the "I," they consider the main purpose of the song. Is it a love song? Is it intended to get the listener to dance? Is there a political theme? Does the song celebrate an event? Does it present a character portrait? Does it carry more than one purpose or theme?

The language of pop songs tends to be informal if not colloquial, while sometimes incorporating imagery, allusion, rhyme, alliteration, satire, irony, and other literary techniques. For a deeper understanding and appreciation of the song, students need to consider any such devices that the lyricist may have used.

Analysis of Music – The Singer's Delivery

Students are somewhat comfortable analyzing lyrics. Throughout their school years, they have been asked to analyze poems or other passages in literature. However, if they are inexperienced in writing about music, they too often focus only on the lyrics in their analyses. They need to be reminded that a song's words are only one part, albeit an extremely important part. They need to consider the lyrics in the context of the music and the delivery of the singer, which can bring urgency, irony, and depth to lines that at first might seem superficial. In "Can Madonna Justify Madonna," Barbara Grizzuti Harrison slams one of the pop star's hits, "Express Yourself." She describes the lyrics with disdain, as being "as profound as a greeting card," citing lines like "You deserve the best in life" (1991, p. 82). Is Harrison fair to Madonna and her lyrics? On their own, the lyrics certainly do not seem profound. However, in the context of the song, with its hammering backbeat and booming bass and Madonna's insistent delivery as she addresses women with low self-esteem, the lyrics are compelling, as compelling as similar lines can be in stage drama or film. After all, the meaning and effectiveness of a song result from the combination of lyrics and music.

Students need to reflect on the emotional quality of the song. Does the song elicit an emotional response? Does it evoke joy? Sadness? Sympathy? Anger? Do the singer's emotions shift over the course of the song, escalating or diminishing? We discuss how the song appeals to the senses and the emotions, to the intellect and the imagination.

Analysis of Music – Sounds

Students need to spend considerable time listening and re-listening to the song. I ask them to listen for, and then describe, the song's rhythm, tempo changes, tonal shifts, its hook, its lead and backing vocals, instrumental solos, and the sounds of various instruments. How do these musical elements contribute to the overall impact of the song? Are some of those elements more important to a particular song than others? Through multiple hearings, students listen to the "mix" of instruments and identify which instruments they hear more clearly or "higher" in the mix. They learn to listen not only for the voices and instruments that are highest in the mix, but also for secondary instruments and voices. In the process, students become more informed and appreciative listeners.

As part of the listening process, students should break the song into its structural parts, which will make the process of close listening less overwhelming. Many pop songs employ a typical and fairly simple structure. With allowance for variation, a song usually begins with an introduction followed by one or more verses and choruses, a bridge, additional verses and choruses, and lastly a movement to the song's end or fadeout. The bridge marks a shift in tone or a variation in the rhythm before reconnecting to a verse or chorus.

Conclusions/Evaluations

After (and during) the listening process, students draw inferences, conclusions, and evaluations about the song that will be more informed and more detailed than the usually non-specific language of most pop music discussions. They can be precise about what they liked about the song, about what made it so appealing, about nuances not grasped by casual listening, and about how the lyrics and music come together to forge a whole and make a statement.

Exercise 1 – Listening Actively

To guide students in the close listening process and to help them develop this set of skills, I lead them through an exercise based on John Coltrane's "Alabama," an instrumental from *Coltrane Live at Birdland*, which I have them listen to several times without telling them the title. They are asked to describe the rhythm and the role of the four instruments (Coltrane's tenor sax, McCoy Tyner's piano, Jimmy Garrison's bass, and Elvin Jones' drums). Students note the slow, mournful rhythm; the long, gloomy notes of the sax suggesting weariness, frustration, and sorrow; the quivering tremolos of the piano; the rattling, rising, and falling of Jones' drums and cymbal washings. These sounds create a frightening, ominous effect, while the bass, which rumbles in the introduction, becomes precise and controlled, anchoring the song and relieving some of the gloom. After we discuss these observations,

I inform students of the title and that Coltrane wrote and recorded the song in November 1963 in response to the 16th Street Baptist Church bombing in Birmingham, Alabama, that September. Students feel the emotional depth and richness of the song and usually request that I play it again. I also tell them that some critics have noted that Coltrane's sax resembles the cadence of the eulogy delivered by Martin Luther King, Jr. (Excerpts from King's eulogy superimposed on part of the song can be found on YouTube: see Rowland, 2010.)

Writing about Music

Songs, like literature, can be read in several ways: with a biographical emphasis, from a particular historical or social context, or in a context unrelated to the song's composer or historical time, as recommended by Roland Barthes in "The Death of the Author" (1977). There, Barthes argues that the interpretation and context of works depend upon the individual reader and his or her impressions.

Close reading is intertwined with writing. Writing focuses our attention. Writing prompts thinking, stimulating thought in ways that can surprise us with ideas we didn't know would be coming to us. I want my students to surprise themselves with discovering ideas through their writing – but only after they have done the repeated, careful, attentive work of critically reading and listening to the words and music of the pop songs they write about.

Exercise 2 – Writing an Essay

For their first assignment in my course, Writing about Music, students listen closely to and analyze a song of their choice and then write a cohesive 500-word essay in which they state and support a claim with textual evidence that includes the music and sounds of the song. They are asked to respond to the song's appeal to their senses, emotions, imagination, and intellect, and to consider all of its elements, including structure, lyrics, and rhythm.

I demonstrate how this can be done by playing for them "Lost and Found," a song written by Ray Davies and performed by the Kinks, and then showing them a portion of what I have written about it:

> "Lost and Found," as the title suggests, is about recovery. … On the surface the song tells of a ship barely surviving a hurricane to pull into port, now ready to face a "new frontier." Of course, ship and storm

serve as a trope, but for what? … That "Lost and Found" can be said to be about the recovery and revitalization of the Kinks is reinforced by the bridge, when Ray [Davies] seems to address brother Dave … and indicate[s] … [his own] renewed sense of vigor and urgency as he rallies his brother to the cause … Reflective and intensely emotional, "Lost and Found" represents Ray's most optimistic moment on *Think Visual*, as it demonstrates that despite industry demands and inequities, artistic renewal is possible. … Bob Henrit's pounding beat and Jim Rodford's sturdy bass line, both high in the mix, propel the song or ship forward while steel drums (probably via synthesizer) and Ray's acoustic guitar runs convey drama and struggle. More than halfway through the song, Dave Davies launches his first guitar break, a trademark Dave solo in its upward sweep, which supports the notion that "Lost and Found" is really about the Kinks fighting their way to triumph through the "dead of winter." (2013, pp. 48–52)

Students can see from this excerpt how they can write about both lyrics and music without using musical jargon. To do so, however, they have to listen carefully and struggle with finding the right words. They also have to make choices about what to omit. Above, for example, I did not write about the intro to "Lost and Found," believing it not significant for my discussion.

Before they submit this first essay, I review the characteristics of good writing: clarity, brevity, specificity, variety in sentence structure and language (with an emphasis on verb choices), and integrity. My students struggle especially with being brief and specific. To emphasize the importance of each word and of being concise, I quote from Strunk and White's *The Elements of Style*: "Vigorous writing is concise. A sentence should contain no unnecessary words, a paragraph no unnecessary sentences, for the same reason that a drawing should have no unnecessary lines and a machine no unnecessary parts" (2009, p. 23). To emphasize specificity and precision, I require that they dig deeply into songs and search for precise descriptives and word choices – no "brilliant" or "crap," to re-quote Frith, and no vague superlatives like *great* or *perfect*, or their approximate opposites, *terrible* or *awful*.

Students are encouraged to slow down and listen closely to the music about which they are writing. They need to learn to return to a song for a second and third and fourth hearing. And the same deliberation they give to close and repeated reading and listening to a song's words and music, they need to give to their prose. This is something they are not used to doing, and so to move them productively in this direction, I discuss the writing process and the importance of multiple revisions and of letting their works breathe and percolate, that is, letting them sit between revisions. Many students resist the revision process, trying to get an assignment over with or believing the assignment "good enough." But for them to improve and say something meaningful they have to learn the value and rewards of revision.

Writing about music is challenging. It's hard to translate sounds into words. It's not easy to describe the shape of a song's melody, the texture of a song's harmony, or the tone and spirit of its performance. But students need to attempt to capture in words the sounds and rhythms of guitar solos and bass beats. They need to work at describing the music rather than writing around it, hiding behind biographical details or chart success. Whatever extra-musical details they include must be relevant to the essay. For example, in a 500-word analysis of "Shake It Off," does it matter where Taylor Swift was born? If so, the student must explain why.

Exercise 3 – Comparing Songs

On the day the first paper is due, I have a few students read their work aloud after we have played the song they analyzed. I let other students comment on the readings of the songs. I try not to say too much, reserving my comments for when I grade the papers. Following this discussion, I explain the second assignment: Compare two songs on similar themes or two versions of the same song. Comparison is a powerful reading tool and analytical strategy. By comparing two songs, with each serving the other as a foil, students will develop new insights into each. They will notice artistic techniques and strategies in each song they might not have otherwise considered.

I demonstrate the assignment by playing Billie Holiday's "Strange Fruit" followed by Nina Simone's "Mississippi Goddam," with lyrics projected in front of the room. After listening to each song, I conduct a brainstorming session by asking for comments and writing them on the board. We do a Google search for some background information and begin to develop interpretive strategies that could be useful for their essays. During our discussion, students see immediately that both songs deal with racism in the South, but in different ways. We discuss the more poetic lyrics of "Strange Fruit," which was written initially as a poem by Abel Meeropol (also known as Lewis Allan). We note the rhyme scheme, the carefully arranged words (in contrast to the more colloquial, at times seemingly improvised, "Mississippi Goddam"), and the powerful use of contrast between images of the antebellum, "gallant" South, such as the sweet "scent of magnolias," on the one hand, and on the other the "strange fruit" of "black bodies swinging" with "bulging eyes" and "the sudden smell of burning flesh." We discuss how

Holiday's mournful, weary voice, combined with the piercing trumpet and tingling piano, create a sorrowful drama.

In "Mississippi Goddam," students note that the lyrics are direct and easily accessible, though some of them may not understand the references to "hound dogs," which were used to break up civil rights protest marches and sit-ins. Students concentrate on the vocal delivery, which they describe as angry, authoritative, and bitter. In describing the music, they note the rollicking piano, driving bass line, and the almost cheerful, up-tempo rhythm, which could be the backdrop for a Broadway show tune. We discuss the appropriateness of the rhythm of "Mississippi Goddam." Did they expect such a rhythm in a protest song? Most find the music ironic and agree that the irony adds force and urgency to the message. As our discussion winds down, I show images of lynchings, Emmett Till's open casket, and the police breaking up protests with dogs and fire hoses. (A video on YouTube, *Strange Fruit – Lynching in the 1930s*, presents images of segregation and lynchings to Holiday's song: see Surdyk, 2013.)

Critical Reading: Theodor Adorno's Criticism of Pop Music

Students' notions of popular music can be challenged through reading Theodor Adorno's "On Popular Music" (1941). Adorno thought that popular music was standardized to the point of making individual expression virtually impossible. He writes, "Every detail is substitutable; it serves its function only as a cog in a machine." Parts of songs are interchangeable with one another: a chorus in one song can be substituted for a chorus in many others. Adorno states further that for a song to be a hit, it needs to be "plugged," via the radio, for example, and it "must have at least one feature by which it can be distinguished from any other, and yet possess the complete conventionality and triviality of all others." Paradoxically, the new hit needs to be "fundamentally the same as all the other current hits and simultaneously fundamentally different from them." Adorno argues that such standardization makes audiences comfortable, so that "the listener always feels on safe ground" and will therefore buy or buy into the song.

After a brief review of Adorno's biography, I ask students to respond to his criticism of popular music. Usually, the majority vehemently disagree with him. Part of their argument is that Adorno was writing over seventy-five years ago, that he played classical piano, and that he was an aficionado of classical music. This, in their eyes, disqualifies him as a persuasive critic of pop music. They concede that hits do need to be "plugged," and admit to unconsciously humming a song they do not even like. However, they argue that many of the songs most meaningful to them have never been huge mainstream hits, and were, instead, songs recommended to them by friends. They also take especial exception to Adorno's statement that parts of songs are interchangeable. Even disregarding lyrics, they argue, how could the chorus of one pop song be inserted into another? The song wouldn't "flow." Adorno is not a careful listener, they argue. He is predisposed to dislike pop as it has displaced his music of choice.

After their comments, I work to give Adorno a fair hearing. I play De La Soul's "Transmitting Life from Mars" and then part of "You Showed Me," the Turtles record that De La Soul sampled. Opinions are reconsidered as we play other hip-hop tracks that make use of sampling, like "Can I Kick It?" by a Tribe Called Quest, which samples, among other songs, Lou Reed's "Walk on the Wild Side."

Then I play a mash-up or two. A mash-up blends two songs seamlessly to create a new work. Perhaps the most famous mash-up is Danger Mouse's *Grey Album*, a mashing of the Beatles *White Album* with Jay Z's *Black Album*, which because of copyright restrictions is now unavailable. However, a number of mash-ups are available on YouTube, like DJ Earworm's merging of the Sex Pistols' "God Save the Queen" and Madonna's "Ray of Light." Suddenly, Adorno gains credibility with the students, forcing them toward a more thoughtful consideration of his attack on their music.

If needed, I give them some help by noting that although Adorno is right about pop songs being generally limited in structure and form, talented artists can breathe new life into defined and strict structures. And though Adorno is also correct that much pop music is produced top-down by the recording industry, the history of pop music suggests many examples of potent new genres emerging organically from local scenes. Consider the development of hip-hop in the South Bronx in the early 1970s, and of grunge in Seattle in the mid- to late 1980s.

Socially Conscious Music

As the course proceeds, students become more probing and discriminating listeners of pop music and consumers of pop culture. Initially, they are often unaware of pop music's richness, its profound cultural influence, and its capacity to illuminate social issues and to change minds. To begin our discussion on the impact of pop music, I have students read "Antiestablishment Themes in American Songs," which serves as a starting point to draw comparisons between folk singer Woody Guthrie and gangsta rapper TuPac Shakur, both of whom celebrate the outlaw hero in songs like

"Pretty Boy Floyd" and "Changes," respectively (Kitts, 2013). We then discuss "This Land Is Your Land," the one Guthrie song just about all the students know, but which they are surprised to learn Guthrie wrote as a protest song in response to the celebratory "God Bless America" by Irving Berlin. We look at Guthrie's lyrics and note the lines that were likely omitted from their grade school sing-alongs. I then ask students to talk about an anti-establishment or socially conscious song of their choice, one that perhaps shaped their thinking about an issue or event.

We also discuss other means for an artist to express protest. We consider a performer's gestures (Elvis Presley's gyrations), appearance and dress (long hair in the 1960s), and the music itself (the volume of heavy metal). We discuss the appeal of the outlaw hero, or antihero, who is often at the center of emerging genres or movements: the Rolling Stones, Willie Nelson, Johnny Rotten, and others. (Sometimes I play them Kris Kristofferson's ironic "Blame It on the Stones.") I also read them statements by Langston Hughes, who described jazz as "one of the inherent expressions of Negro life in America; the eternal tom-tom beating in the Negro soul – the tom-tom of revolt against weariness in a white world" (2002, p. 35). Hans Joachim-Irmler of Faust, a German Krautrock band, provides yet another useful provocation: "The revolution would have succeeded if people had listened more to the sounds than to the lyrics" (Koch and Harris, 2009, p. 590). Students are required to respond to these and other anti-establishment comments, to read them critically, and to consider their implications.

New pop music trends have long threatened the established culture. Students are often surprised to see that artists and genres now considered safe and iconic, and which are played in public spaces like supermarkets, were once perceived as dangerous. We read articles written in the late 1950s condemning the day's pop music: "R&B: A Danger to the Music Business" by Abel Green (1955), "Elvis Presley and 'The Craze'" by John Crosby (1956), and "Beatlemania Frightens Child Expert" by Bernard Saibel (1964). Green calls on record labels to "forget the filthy fast buck" and to stop artists from singing "leer-ics" with references to sex before the government resorts to censorship. Crosby calls Elvis an "unspeakably untalented and vulgar young entertainer" (p. 13), while Saibel describes a Beatles concert as "an orgy for teen-agers," with the girls "possessed by some demonic urge" (pp. 53–54). Sometimes we review excerpts from *Raising PG Kids in an X-Rated Society* (1987) by Tipper Gore, who condemned the "new phenomenon" of heavy metal for promoting "barbarism" (p. 230) and for extolling "the virtues of torture, rape, and murder of women" (p. 53). During discussion of these readings, students will bring up how their parents banned the music of certain hip-hop or rock artists from their homes.

Such texts help us address several questions: Why are mainstream critics consistently threatened by new and innovative styles of music? Why do parents feel threatened? What makes new music such a social danger? And does the music lose relevance when it is co-opted and commodified? Lively discussions ensue as students recognize how hip hop, punk, heavy metal, and other new musics initially perceived as dangerous by the mainstream are ultimately co-opted. I mention my own disappointment when I first heard the Clash, one of my favorite punk bands, played over the loudspeakers in my bank.

Willa Cather's short story "Paul's Case," written in 1905, about adolescent dysfunction, provides an opportunity to consolidate and extend our discussions concerning the value of popular music. At first, students are confused as to why I assign this story at the end of the semester. They guess: "Because the main character worked in a concert hall as an usher?" "Because he never got beyond a superficial appreciation of music?" I lead a discussion of Paul's character focusing on his poor relationship with his father, his alienation from his community, his lack of a mentor, his resistance to conformity, his sexual confusion, his visceral appreciation of art, and his quest to live a life of beauty.

Paul longs to escape what he sees as the dreariness of working-class Pittsburgh. He yearns for a world of "starry apple orchards that bloomed perennially" and "Mediterranean shore[s] bathed in perpetual sunshine" (p. 200). Paul is a dreamer with no productive outlet for his dreams. His teachers dismiss him, concluding wrongly that his imagination "had been perverted by garish fiction" (p. 200). I ask students if they know of any songs about dreamers like Paul, about individuals anxious to escape and who proclaim their differentness. I mention two songs from my youth that capture these themes: Bob Dylan's "Mr. Tambourine Man" and the Kinks' "I'm Not Like Everybody Else."

I then turn to Steven L. Hamelman's *But Is It Garbage? On Rock and Trash*, an insightful study of rock music that reveals my reason for assigning "Paul's Case": to consider whether pop music, or a pop music scene, can rescue an individual from despair by confirming and nurturing self-worth. Hamelman believes that had Paul been born a baby boomer or later he "would have been an ideal candidate for salvation via the glories of rock music" (2004, p. 195). Paul, like many disenfranchised youths, tries to escape what Hamelman characterizes as "boring schools, and unhappy homes … or perhaps terra firma in general" (p. 199). The character's intense loneliness, which ultimately leads to his suicide, might have been alleviated had he access to a community of the alienated, such as those centered in the punk or grunge scenes. Pop music, argues Hamelman, may be disposable, but it is still capable of providing guidance and solace, and even salvation. Students also read Michael Azerrad's "Punk's Earnest New Mission," which examines how pop punk songs and videos from Blink-182 ("Adam's Song") and Good Charlotte ("Hold On") have served as "therapy rock" for teens in the early 2000s (2004, p. 1). Our discussion of Hamelman and Azerrad usually takes twists and turns: students respond with stories of how popular music helped them or friends through difficult times, but also acknowledge how "scenes" can be destructive as well as beneficial to self-worth.

Additional Writing Assignments

Following a sequence of exercises in single song analysis and comparative song analysis, I ask students to review an album or other collection of music. This assignment requires that they listen closely to individual songs, compare songs for thematic or musical similarities, and identify the "highlights" and "low points" of their chosen collection. To clarify the process of writing the review, I explain that it involves four phases:

1 *Description*: focusing on form, sound, setting, and other musical elements.
2 *Interpretation*: analyzing the content – textual, structural, and musical.
3 *Evaluation*: providing an overall assessment and possible recommendation.
4 *Contextualization*: explaining how the music relates to the artist's other works, to its genre, to the works of other artists, and to other relevant cultural touchstones.

Students are urged to include only the most necessary background information and, if possible, to include that information in the context of more substantive analysis.

Part of this assignment requires students to bring to class reviews they consider well written and informative. We discuss their selections and look at other music criticism from a range of sources, including the *New York Times*, the *Village Voice*, *Pitchfork*, *Popular Music and Society*, and *Rock Music Studies*. In comparing these very different publications, they learn about levels of formality in writing, how the intended audience of a publication shapes its form and content, and how best to consider audience when writing their own reviews.

During the semester students write in a variety of other genres associated with popular music, including an artist or band profile. Although not a very long assignment (I usually require 750–1,000 words), the form itself poses interesting and fruitful challenges for students. These profiles are not history or biography alone – the way Wikipedia pages are often written – but rather, depending on the artist, part history, part biography, part psychological portrait, and part musical analysis. Since profiles are about the present, students must develop an angle to make them relevant. Why profile the artist now? Is the artist on tour? Is the artist releasing a new album? Is the artist overrated or neglected? I also require students to use quotations from the artist, which they can acquire from other articles, websites, or social media. By reading a variety of profiles and articles about their subject, students develop a critical eye for identifying different levels of formality, credibility, and objectivity in the journalism they read. Critical reading and writing are thus experienced as interdependent and mutually beneficial processes.

Conclusion

Many students enter my classroom believing that Writing about Music will be a relatively easy course. They often think they can pass with weak writing full of generalities and that readings will be unchallenging. They believe the writing assignments will require them merely to repeat the informal observations and evaluations of casual conversations. Some think we will spend class time sitting around listening to music, watching videos, and then commenting. While they may not realize it, their attitude reflects that of Frank Zappa's famous 1977 statement: "Most rock journalism is by people who can't write, interviewing people who can't talk [for] people who can't read" (Lowe, 2007, p. xxii).

The first sessions of the class are, therefore, critical in changing these expectations. The close listening students do in class and in early assignments not only lays a foundation for future readings of songs, but also sets a tone of challenge and academic rigor. Similarly, the close readings of reviews and profiles establish the importance of critical reading while shaping students' approaches to writing assignments. I push them hard at the beginning of the semester. My marginal comments on their papers question their listening: "What expectations of the listener are established by the intro?" "What effect does the bass line have?" "Does the music in the bridge reflect the emotional shift of the lyrics?" I challenge them to find textual support for their inferences and evaluations – evidence from lyrics, their delivery, and from the music itself. They are surprised by the challenges imposed by the course, but their skills in writing, reading, and thinking improve as they develop a more critical perspective on pop music and its influence on culture.

References

Adorno, T. W., with Simpson, G. (1941). On popular music. In *Studies in philosophy and social science* (pp. 17–48). New York: Institute of Social Research.

Azerrad, M. (2004). Punk's earnest new mission. *New York Times* (January 4), sect. 2, pp. 1, 32.

Barthes, R. (1977). The death of the author. In *Image – music – text*. Trans. S. Heath (pp. 142–148). New York: Hill & Wang.

Cather, W. (1905/2002). "Paul's case." In *Great American short stories*. Ed. P. Negri (pp. 192–208). Mineola, NY: Dover.

Crosby, J. (2013). Elvis Presley and "the craze." In T. Cateforis (ed.), *The rock history reader* (pp. 13–14). New York: Routledge. Reprinted from *New York Herald Tribune* (June 18, 1956), sect. 2, p. 1.

Ellington, D. (1995). Where is jazz going? In *The Duke Ellington reader*. Ed. M. Tucker (pp. 324–326). Oxford: Oxford University Press.

Frith, S. (1996). *Performing rites: On the value of popular music rites*. Cambridge, MA: Harvard University Press.

Gore, T. (1987). *Raising PG kids in an X-rated society*. Nashville, TN: Abingdon Press.

Green, A. (2013). R&B: A danger to the music business. In T. Cateforis (ed.), *The rock history reader* (pp. 9–10). New York: Routledge. Reprinted from *Variety* (February 23, 1955), p. 2.

Hamelman, S. L. (2004). *But is it garbage? On rock and trash*. Athens: University of Georgia Press.

Harrison, B. G. (1991). Can Madonna justify Madonna? *Mademoiselle* (June), 80–82.

Hughes, L. (2002). The Negro artist and the racial mountain. In C. C. De Santis (ed.), *Essays on art, race, politics, and world affairs: The collected works of Langston Hughes* (vol. 9, pp. 31–36). Columbia: University of Missouri Press. Reprinted from *Nation*, 122 (June 23, 1926), pp. 692–694.

Kitts, T. (2008). *Ray Davies: Not like everybody else*. New York: Routledge.

Kitts, T. (2013). Antiestablishment themes in American songs. In J. Edmondson (ed.), *Music in American life: An encyclopedia of the songs, styles, stars, and stories that shaped our culture* (vol. 1, pp. 48–52). Santa Barbara, CA: ABC-CLIO.

Kitts, T. (2016). *John Fogerty: An American son*. New York: Routledge.

Koch, A., and Harris, S. (2009). The sound of yourself listening: Faust and the politics of the unpolitical. *Popular Music and Society*, 32(5), 579–594.

Lowe, K. F. (2007). *The words and music of Frank Zappa*. Lincoln: University of Nebraska Press.

Rowland, S. (2010). *Alabama John Coltrane and Martin Luther King*. Video file. https://www.youtube.com/watch?v = aiJ_0gp-T9A (accessed October 3, 2016).

Saibel, B. (2013). Beatlemania frightens child expert. In T. Cateforis (ed.), *The rock history reader* (pp. 53–54). New York: Routledge. Reprinted from *Seattle Daily Times* (August 22, 1964), p. 1.

Strunk, Jr., W., and White, E. B. (2009). *The elements of style* (50th anniversary ed.). New York: Pearson/Longman.

Surdyk, C. (2013). *Strange fruit – lynching in the 1930s.* Video file. https://www.youtube.com/watch?v = 98CxkS0vzB8 (accessed October 3, 2016).

Index

Page numbers in italics denote illustrations, tables, or figures.

Critical Reading Across the Curriculum, Volume 1: Humanities, First Edition.
Edited by Robert DiYanni and Anton Borst.
© 2017 John Wiley & Sons, Inc. Published 2017 by John Wiley & Sons, Inc.